# Carl Menger and the Evolution of Payments Systems

# Carl Menger and the Evolution of Payments Systems

## From Barter to Electronic Money

*Edited by*

Michael Latzer

*Deputy Director, Research Unit for Institutional Change and European Integration, Austrian Academy of Sciences, Vienna*

Stefan W. Schmitz

*Research Fellow, Research Unit for Institutional Change and European Integration, Austrian Academy of Sciences, Vienna*

**Edward Elgar**

Cheltenham, UK • Northampton, MA, USA

Published by
Edward Elgar Publishing Limited
Glensanda House
Montpellier Parade
Cheltenham
Glos GL50 1UA
UK

Edward Elgar Publishing, Inc.
136 West Street
Suite 202
Northampton
Massachusetts 01060
USA

A catalogue record for this book
is available from the British Library

**Library of Congress Cataloguing in Publication Data**
Carl Menger and the evolution of payments systems : from barter to electronic money / edited by Michael Latzer, Stefan W. Schmitz.
        p. cm.
Includes bibliographical references and index.
1. Money. 2. Menger, Carl, 1840–1921. 3. Payment. 4. Electronic funds transfers. I. Latzer, Michael. II. Schmitz, Stefan W., 1970–

HG221 .C355 2002
332.4–dc21

2002020236

ISBN 978 1 84064 9185

Printed and bound by CPI Group (UK) Ltd, Croydon, CR0 4YY

# Contents

# List of Contributors

*David F. Good*, Professor of History, Chair of the Department of History, University of Minnesota, Minneapolis

*Michael Latzer*, Deputy Director, Research Unit for Institutional Change and European Integration, Austrian Academy of Sciences, Vienna

*Stefan W. Schmitz*, Research Fellow, Research Unit for Institutional Change and European Integration, Austrian Academy of Sciences, Vienna

*George A. Selgin*, Professor of Economics, University of Georgia, Auburn

*Erich W. Streissler*, Professor of Economics, Department of Economics, Vienna University

*Monika Streissler*, Translator in Vienna

*Lawrence H. White*, Friedrich August v. Hayek Professor of Economic History, University of Missouri, St. Louis

*Leland B. Yeager*, Ludwig von Mises Professor Emeritus, University of Georgia, Auburn

# List of Tables

# Introduction

## Michael Latzer
## Stefan W. Schmitz

Carl Menger's article 'Geld' ('Money') – first published in German in the *Handwörterbuch der Staatswissenschaften* (1892) – is one of the most influential papers on the origin of money. A vast number of articles on the subject have been published since the 1970s, inspired by Menger's much shorter version, 'On the Origin of Money', which appeared in the *Economic Journal* in 1892.[1] Charles Goodhart (1998) even calls neoclassical theorists of the origin of money 'Mengerians'. Furthermore, Menger's method exerted strong influence on the New Institutionalists[2] who frequently cite his *Grundsätze der Volkswirthschaftslehre* (1871) and his *Untersuchungen über die Methoden der Socialwissenschaften und der Politischen Oekonomie insbesondere* (1883)[3]. Despite the continuing attention, the full version of Menger's 'Geld' has not yet been translated into English. One major intention of this book is to provide the English-speaking world with a full translation of Menger's article in order to facilitate and stimulate a broader and, at the same time, an in-depth discussion of his method, theory and findings. The translation is complemented by positioning Menger's 'Money' within the history of economic thought.

The current evolution of new payments systems, in particular of electronic money, is of importance for the development of the so-called Digital Economy in general and for the diffusion of e-commerce in particular.[4] Menger's institutional approach is promising for the analysis of this evolution. This provides further strong incentives to revisit his contribution to the theory of money.

We define electronic money as 'monetary value as represented by a claim on the issuer which is: (*i*) stored on an electronic device; (*ii*) issued on receipt of funds of an amount not less in value than the monetary value issued; (*iii*) accepted as means of payment by undertakings other than the issuer'.[5] Electronic money products are further subcategorized into electronic purses (embedded in smart cards) and digital cash (prepaid software products that are stored on computer hard-drives in the consumer's possession). Electronic money does not refer to instruments that allow consumers access to otherwise traditional payments systems (for example electronic banking, debit cards).

*1*

The diffusion of electronic money is combined with basic questions and uncertainties. What are the effects of electronic money on monetary policy? What regulatory developments are to be expected in retail and wholesale payments systems? What are the implications of the emergence of privately issued electronic money for currency competition and the unit of account? Obviously, there is the need for useful theoretical and analytical tools. Menger's method, as argued in this book, will contribute to a better understanding of the evolution of electronic money and its implications for the structure of the payments system, of its regulation and of monetary policy. Hence, the second major goal of this book is to apply and extend Menger's institutional approach to the analysis of electronic money. The twofold incentives and goals of our research project led to the following structure and content of this volume.

## CARL MENGER'S ARTICLE 'MONEY': FROM BARTER TO MONEY

In Chapter 1 *Erich Streissler* assesses Menger's article 'Money' within the context of economic thought in the second half of the 19th century. He argues that Menger should be seen as an economist in the tradition of the Older German Historical School of Economics. This is not to deny that he deviated from the mainstream of that school with respect to methodology and in his value judgements on certain issues. Apart from Wilhelm Roscher, Menger's approach in 'Money' was inspired mainly by Adam Smith.

Streissler describes Menger's contribution as a theory of the macroinstitutional development of society from economic motives and with very little role for government intervention. He briefly reviews the main themes of Menger's exposition in order to show the essential point of the analysis – the origin and development of monetary exchange is the unintended result of purposeful human action, and not the consequence of centralized decision making. The second part of the chapter is devoted to a discussion of Menger's treatment of the different functions of money and their interrelation, its effects on price formation, and the value of money in Menger's treatment.

Menger's analysis of the demand for money represents, according to Streissler, his most original contribution to monetary theory. Streissler critically evaluates the rejection of the quantity theory of money and the attempt to replace it with a subjective inventory theory of money demand. He concludes his contribution by emphasizing the influence of Menger's article on neoclassical monetary theory and on recent contributions to economic history.

Chapter 2 contains the translation of Carl Menger's 'Geld' by *Leland B. Yeager* with *Monika Streissler,* based on the third edition of the

*Handwörterbuch der Staatswissenschaften*, Vol. IV, Jena 1909, as reprinted in *Carl Menger Gesammelte Werke*, edited by Friedrich August Hayek (second edition, Tübingen 1970). In his paper Menger presents an account of the origin of money as the good with the highest marketability. He reconstructs the evolution of the social institution 'money' out of barter without recourse to government intervention. He argues that the emergence of money has positive real effects on the economy. Furthermore, Menger discusses various instances of institutional change in the monetary system and the role of government intervention. He emphasizes that the medium of exchange function is the fundamental function of money and that all other functions are only incidental to it. Menger concludes his paper by a discussion of the demand for money. The analysis in the article 'Money' covers the evolution from barter to 'conventional' money. His approach, however, can be extended to the evolution of electronic money.

## PERSPECTIVES ON THE EVOLUTION OF ELECTRONIC MONEY

In Chapter 3, *Stefan W. Schmitz* contrasts Menger's 'Money' with three neoclassical models of money – of Kiyotaki and Wright (1992), Samuelson (1958), and Townsend (1980). All the models attempt to reconcile Walrasian value theory with monetary theory. Schmitz argues that the Walrasian neoclassical approach does not prove successful since the models take the social institution of money as exogenously given. This social institution, however, does not have a role in general equilibrium theory. The models address questions of (*i*) whether it is individually rational to accept intrinsically worthless objects in exchange for goods, and (*ii*) whether the resulting allocation in a monetary economy Pareto-dominates the allocation in the same setting without money. However, the emergence of the social institution of money in a Walrasian environment is not addressed. Furthermore, all the models named are static in the sense that the institutional environment and expectations are given exogenously. There is no intrinsic uncertainty. Some of the authors quote Menger affirmatively and seem to be inspired by his article 'On the Origin of Money'. Their examination of Menger's contribution was based on this very short excerpt from his seminal paper 'Money', translated in the *Economic Journal* in 1892. Menger, however, provides an analysis of the emergence of the social institution of money from barter to monetary exchange. He takes into account the heterogeneity of agents and goods and discusses the role of asymmetries in the adoption of indirect barter, as well as that of imitation and learning in the process of the evolution of money. He emphasizes the importance of institutional change in the 'perfection' of the payments systems. An English translation of the entire article will thus shed more light on the understanding of both Menger's contribution and the social institution of money, its emergence and development.

Schmitz argues that the neoclassical models with essentially static equilibrium concepts are of limited use for the analysis of institutional change in the payments system, such as the evolution of electronic money. He concludes that Menger's approach to institutional change in the payments system is more promising in this respect.

In Chapter 4, *George A. Selgin* and *Lawrence H. White* apply and expand Menger's 'rational reconstruction of the development of money out of barter' to the analysis of current and future institutional change in the payments system and its implications for monetary policy. They provide a brief overview of the nationalization of money since the end of the 19th century and the first signs of its reversal in recent history. They argue that those currencies that have gained a reputation will increase their global market share. Furthermore, they expect governments to roll back regulation in the areas of money, banking and finance, and discuss the consequences of this for the future development of payment systems. As a departure point for their discussion of the future of money, Selgin and White provide a detailed account of the structure, functioning and prospects of electronic money systems. As the costs associated with electronic money shrink, the demand for government currency (coins and bank notes) might vanish almost entirely – which would affect the seigniorage revenues of central banks. However, base money would consist of settlement balances at the central bank, which would still serve as a medium of final settlement between issuers of electronic money.

Selgin and White analyse the evolution of multilateral clearing and settlement and net payments systems. They conclude that the processing of retail payments will be privatized in the future, enhancing the efficiency of the retail payments system. In discussing wholesale payments systems the authors emphasize that the shift towards real-time gross settlement systems was the result of government intervention rather than the outcome of a market process. However, as a result of implicit subsidies the private costs of real-time settlement are modest, so government intervention in the wholesale payments system is not expected to disappear in the near future.

Furthermore, the authors discuss the monetary policy implications of electronic money and the recent literature on the issue. They dismiss the pessimistic view that a shrinking monetary base will render monetary policy less effective. In general, the authors expect innovations in the payments system that foster privatization and globalization even to reduce the instability of aggregate demand. Nevertheless, Selgin and White do not believe that the demand for base money will be reduced to zero. They consider this a remote possibility and conclude that it would make the price level indeterminate.

In the final chapter of this volume *Stefan W. Schmitz* critically evaluates two interdependent claims: first, that privately issued electronic money will be denominated in new units of account; second, that the parallel use of multiple units of account would enhance the efficiency of the payments system and increase the stability of the price level. Based on a survey of the literature, he argues that the parallel use of multiple units of account is not considered desirable and, owing to a time inconsistency problem, is indeed not possible among privately issued fiat-type currencies. Furthermore, he assesses the potential emergence of new units of account based on an approach to institutional change in the payments system inspired by Menger. Issuers of electronic money will increase their demand by making their medium of payments economically compatible (that is, thus reducing switching costs for users) with the dominant medium of exchange. Schmitz shows that either free riding on price information established in the markets involving the standard unit of account is essential for trading in new units of account or, alternatively, that price discovery in multiple units of account will have negative implications for the information content of prices. He concludes that the institutional structure of electronic money schemes will build on both redeemability on demand and denomination in the prevailing unit of account in the relevant market.

This book is the product of a research project supported by the Austrian National Bank and carried out at the Research Unit for Institutional Change and European Integration (ICE) of the Austrian Academy of Sciences, of which Carl Menger was a prominent member. This book project is part of our research programme on the analysis of the emerging Information Society and complements our research efforts on the analysis of the Digital Economy in general and on e-commerce in particular. The institutionalist perspective of our research provided an incentive to focus on Menger's work. We hope our results will contribute to a better understanding of the evolution of electronic money and stimulate discussion and further research incorporating the method, theory and findings of Carl Menger.

# NOTES

1. See among others: Jones (1976), Kiyotaki and Wright (1989, 1991 and 1992), Selgin and Klein (2000) and the literature cited in Streissler's contribution to this volume.
2. See e.g. Furubotn and Richter (1997).
3. English translations were published as Menger (1950) and as Menger (1985).
4. See Latzer and Schmitz (2000, 2002).
5. EC Directive 2000/46/EC on the taking-up, pursuit of and prudential supervision of the business of electronic money institutions.

## REFERENCES

Furubotn, E. G. and R. Richter (1997), *Institutions and Economic Theory: An Introduction to and Assessment of the New Institutional Economics*, Ann Arbor: University of Michigan Press.

Goodhart, C. A. E. (1998), 'The Two Concepts of Money: Implications for the Analysis of Optimal Currency Areas', *European Journal of Political Economy*, **14**, pp. 407-32.

Jones, R. A. (1976), 'The Origin and Development of Media of Exchange', *Journal of Political Economy*, **84**, pp. 757-75.

Kiyotaki, N. and R. Wright (1989), 'On Money as a Medium of Exchange', *Journal of Political Economy*, **97**, pp. 927-54.

Kiyotaki, N. and R. Wright (1991), 'A Contribution to the Pure Theory of Money', *Journal of Economic Theory*, **53**, pp. 215-35.

Kiyotaki, N. and R. Wright (1992), 'Acceptability, Means of Payment, and Media of Exchange', *Federal Reserve Bank of Minneapolis Quarterly Review*, **16**, pp. 2-10.

Latzer, M. and S. W. Schmitz (2000), 'Business-to-Consumer eCommerce in Österreich: Eine empirische Untersuchung', in: M. Latzer (ed.), *Mediamatikpolitik für die Digitale Ökonomie. eCommerce, Qualifikation und Marktmacht in der Informationsgesellschaft*. Innsbruck-Vienna: Studien Verlag, pp. 286-306.

Latzer, M. and S. W. Schmitz (2002), *Die Ökonomie des eCommerce*, Marburg: Metropolis (forthcoming).

Menger, C. (1871), *Grundsätze der Volkswirthschaftslehre*, Vienna: Wilhelm Braumüller.

Menger, C. (1883), *Untersuchungen über die Methoden der Socialwissenschaften und der Politischen Oekonomie insbesondere*, Leipzig: Duncker & Humblot.

Menger, C. (1892), 'On the Origin of Money', *Economic Journal*, **2**, pp. 238-55, translated by C. A. Foley.

Menger, C. (1909), 'Geld', *Handwörterbuch der Staatswissenschaften* (3rd edn), J. Conrad et al. (eds), Volume IV., Fischer, Jena, pp. 555-610; reprinted in: F. A. Hayek (ed.) (1970), *Carl Menger Gesammelte Werke*, Volume IV Schriften über Geld und Währungspolitik, Tübingen: J. C. B. Mohr (Siebeck), pp. 1-116.

Menger, C. (1950), *Principles of Economics*, Glencoe, Illinois, translated by J. Dingwall and B. F. Hoselitz.

Menger, C. (1985), *Investigations into the Method of the Social Sciences with Special Reference to Economics*, with a new introd. by Lawrence H. White, ed. by Louis Schneider, New York: New York University Press.

Samuelson, P. A. (1958), 'An Exact Consumption-Loan Model of Interest with or without the Social Contrivance of Money', *Journal of Political Economy*, **66**, pp. 467-82.

Selgin, G. A. and P. G. Klein (2000), 'Menger's Theory of Money: Some Experimental Evidence', in: J. Smithin (ed.), *What is Money?* London, New York and Routledge: pp. 217-34.

Townsend, R. M. (1980), 'Models of Money with Spatially Separated Agents', in: J. H. Kareken and N. Wallace (eds), *Models of Monetary Economics*, Minneapolis: Federal Reserve Bank of Minneapolis, pp. 265-313.

PART I


Carl Menger's Article 'Money': From Barter to
Money

# 1. Carl Menger's article 'Money' in the history of economic thought

## Erich W. Streissler

### 1. MENGER'S MAIN THEMES

Carl Menger is perhaps best thought of as a late follower of the Older German Historical School of Economics; and nowhere more so than in his monumental encyclopedia article 'Money' for the first three editions of the *Handwörterbuch der Staatswissenschaften* from 1892 onwards. He may have been a somewhat more theoretical follower of that Historical School than the run of the mill of its members, but a follower nevertheless, in spite of his own pronouncements. Or, if this characterization of Menger sounds too shocking: Menger is an economist who tries to refashion the type of investigation pioneered by Adam Smith. He is an economist very much in the mould of Smith. A creative renaissance of Smith's thought had been achieved in Germany already a quarter century before Menger by Wilhelm Roscher, once more, as with Menger, without explicitly stating that aim. And it is on Smith and Roscher that Menger's article rests almost exclusively.

This is astonishing. Menger's article on money owes nothing to many of the giants of monetary theory: nothing to Cantillon, nothing to Hume, nothing to Thornton. All mention of notions of either the Currency or the Banking School are missing. If Menger is philosophically a (vulgar type of) Aristotelian, as some think, it certainly does not show in his monetary thought: Aristotle is quoted only to be refuted. More astonishing, the grandmaster of German monetary thought in the generation before Menger, with whom both Boehm-Bawerk and Wieser had studied and with whom Boehm kept permanently in touch, Karl Knies, is mentioned again and again, but always only to be contradicted. W. S. Jevons' *Money and the Mechanism of Exchange* (1875), a book immediately (1876) translated into German by an author congenial to Menger, is not even mentioned. Authors on whom Menger heavily depends are legal historians in the fields of Roman and Germanic Law; in this he once more follows Roscher, though as a lawyer he studied the legal pronouncements perhaps more thoroughly than Roscher had done. On the whole, however, the article is Menger at his most original, developing and reshaping themes initiated by Smith and Roscher. Even more so than these authors, Menger shows interest only in the very longest run.

*11*

The article is highly idiosyncratic. As so few monetary topics are touched upon – surprisingly there is even nothing on banking – one might even criticize the title of the article, 'Money', as confusing and slightly inappropriate.

In this article Menger certainly does not prove himself a marginalist, and, of course, not at all a 'neoclassical' author in the sense of showing a central interest in static allocative efficiency. The article demonstrates, if need be, the complete unimportance of marginal utility to Menger, which in the original edition is mentioned once in passing[1] and later dropped altogether. The article is much more macroinstitutional than the usual type of study in microeconomics. It is, on the other hand, exactly his ideas about money, and these alone, which Menger wanted to communicate to an international audience by an article in the *Economic Journal*.[2] This article follows nearly verbatim the first chapter of Menger's encyclopedia article, published in the same year. The *EJ* article is basically Historical School, to boot; and it contains what was most important to Menger, as it is the only part of the longer encyclopedia article that he published both in German and English.

In what sense is Menger's treatment at one with the Older Historical School? That tradition tried to show the consequences in historical development of theoretically explainable economic motives and actions: In this it might be called applied theory. Furthermore it illustrates theoretical economic concepts by historical examples and frequently copious statistics and thus comes close to econometric verification. Above all it is a theory of the development of society and its legal and economic framework. And this is what Menger achieves in his article 'Money': He provides a vision of historical development. It would be too narrow to call his approach merely institutional, although, in his view, money is an institution, of course. Much rather Menger provides an altogether more comprehensive theory of development.

In order to understand what Menger tries to argue we have to go back to the first four chapters of the first book of Adam Smith's *Wealth of Nations*. Studying Smith we can see that Menger tries to show the same effects as Smith but with a line of causation opposite to that of Smith. As everyone knows, the first chapter of *WN* is called 'Of the Division of Labour' and is the basis for a production-oriented theory of economic and social development. The second chapter is on *exchange*, more precisely on barter which, to Smith, is a 'propensity of human nature', in fact a distinguishing characteristic of man relative to animals. But why then, Menger evidently thought, should exchange merely be a 'principle which gives occasion to the Division of Labour', as the chapter heading says, why only a subsidiary principle and not much rather a *basic principle* of equal importance with the production aspects in the division of labour for explaining human development?

Adam Smith has made the progressive division of labor the central factor in the economic progress of mankind – in harmony with the overwhelming importance he attributes to labor as an element in human economy. I believe, however, that the distinguished author ... has cast light, in his chapter on the division of labor, on but a single cause [!] of progress [!] in human welfare while other, no less efficient [!], causes have escaped his attention.[3]

The next chapter in Smith is on the fact 'That the Division of Labour is limited by the extent of the Market'. Markets are of eminent importance to someone as interested in exchange as Menger is. But why, as with Smith, should the extent of markets only depend on the amount of capital accumulated, thus once more only on the production side? Finally, the fourth chapter in Smith is 'Of the Origin and Use of Money'. But again, after saying relatively little on money, Smith veers off and immediately lands, already in the same chapter, in his theory of value, which is determined by the cost of production. At every turn, Smith lets slip the opportunity of a more exchange-oriented explanation of the development of society.

In his basic intention Menger is fully in conformity with Smith: to explain a free society by the effect of economic forces, to explain an autonomous development of society through economic propensities and with minimal recourse to the power of government (the 'state' in German) and to explain in economic terms the development of the 'obvious and simple system of natural liberty', that is, competition in its widest sense. A governmental system of preferences in the 'mercantile system' will only hinder that development. Menger's intention is to explain all this not from the production side, but by recourse to exchange, centred on the development of money. Money to Menger, in a sense, replaces Smith's pivotal concept of (material) capital and its accumulation. (Replacing production and capital accumulation by exchange and money is one of those transformations in argument in the sense of Michel Foucault, that were so dear to 19th century economists, according to Klaus Hamberger.)

Wilhelm Roscher to whom, as everyone knows, Menger's *Principles* are dedicated, had very creatively further developed Smith's production-oriented system, which is based on the accumulation of capital. Roscher argued, for example, that if labour is too cheap it is not in the interest of producers to substitute capital for labour and therefore society does not proceed to a liberal social framework; and this is exactly the bane of a slave-owning society. In contrast to Smith, with Roscher rational modes of production shape the distribution of income by the marginal productivity reward of factors of production. And perhaps most tellingly Roscher shows in his book on agricultural [!] policy[4] how agricultural development demonstrates three extremely important 'natural laws', the first one being 'the development of personal freedom and of private property to free competition'.[5]

But it is not only a Smithian production-oriented argument for the development of a free and rich society – of 'progress' as these authors would have said – that Menger could learn from Roscher; it is also an exchange-based one as well. Roscher always tries to be catholic, to be comprehensive, even at the cost of – a perhaps too simple – logical consistency. In contrast, it is Smith and then again Menger who tried to argue monistically.

In book 2, chapter 1 of Roscher's theory treatise[6] we are introduced to 'circulation in general'. 'Social economic man has primarily to think in terms of *markets*, i.e. the margin of exchange of all goods against each other'. 'With economic growth an ever greater rapidity of circulation is usually associated, both as effect and as cause'. 'In particular higher culture leads to greater freedom of circulation ... *Free competition*, freedom of commerce and industry (all technical terms for freedom in economic affairs as such) is the natural consequence of the principles of personal independence and private property.'[7] Already in this first chapter Roscher makes much of the concept of the 'ability to circulate' of commodities, a concept close to Menger's central notion of 'marketability' or 'saleability' of commodities. The third chapter of Roscher's book is on money. And there we find a creative misquotation of Adam Smith by Roscher, a misquotation soon to become central for Menger's thought: 'In any case we can call the introduction of a money economy (*where every man becomes a merchant and the society itself a commercial society*: Adam Smith I, Ch. 4) instead of a barter economy on the whole one of the greatest and most beneficent causes of progress.'[8] Smith, however, in his production-oriented view had said in the first paragraph of his chapter IV on money:

> When the division of labour has been once thoroughly established, it is but a very small part of a man's wants which the produce of his own labour can supply ... Every man thus lives by exchanging, or becomes in some measure a merchant, and the society itself grows to be what is properly a commercial society.

Not monetary exchange, but the division of labour in production creates a 'commercial' society, which is, more than we may be aware of today, the technical 18th century British expression for a free society geared to serve economic needs.[9]

We can now proceed to the main ideas Menger expounds in his encyclopedia article 'Money':

> The direct provision of their requirements is the ultimate purpose of all economic endeavors of men. The *final end* of their exchange operations is therefore to exchange their commodities for such goods as have use value to them. The endeavor to attain this final end has been equally characteristic of all stages of culture and is entirely correct economically. But economizing individuals would obviously be behaving uneconomically if, in all instances in which this final end cannot be reached *immediately and directly*, they were to foresake it altogether.

Seeking monetary exchange is thus a roundabout means of production, as Boehm-Bawerk would have said. But Boehm-Bawerk essentially belongs to the production line of argument, which Menger considered 'back-sliding' and never forgave him: With Menger it is, of course, a roundabout means of *exchange*!

> As *each* economizing individual becomes increasingly more aware of his economic interest, he is led by this *interest, without any agreement, without legislative compulsion, and even without regard to the public interest*, to give his commodities in exchange for other, more saleable, commodities, even if he does not need them for any immediate consumption purpose. With economic progress, therefore, we can everywhere observe the phenomenon of a certain number of goods, especially those that are most easily saleable at a given time and place, becoming, under the powerful influence of *custom*, acceptable to everyone in trade, and thus capable of being given in exchange for any other commodity.

Note the *cognitive* explanation, cognition becoming generalized by custom.

> Money is not the product of an agreement on the part of economizing men nor the product of legislative acts. No one invented it. As economizing individuals in social situations became increasingly aware of their economic interest, they everywhere attained the simple knowledge that surrendering less saleable commodities for others of greater saleability brings them substantially closer to the attainment of their specific economic purposes.

Today, we would perhaps speak of a network effect of information. Thus money demonstrates most clearly that the economy can work perfectly well without any need for the 'state', and even without conscious agreements and compacts of men. Unconscious actions within a free and competitive society serve men best, a very Smithian theme.

But all these quotations were already taken from Menger's *Principles*![10] And that, of course, on purpose: all the key sentences, at least of the first third of the encyclopedia article, are already there in the *Principles* and reproduced verbatim by Menger; moreover, he republished them a third time in the *Economic Journal* article (1892). They are the quintessential Menger from the start, his most important message, the proof of the pudding in eating of his subjective value framework.

Menger proudly quotes Roscher 'since the tenth edition, 1873', that is, the very edition in which Roscher first liberally quotes Menger's then very new *Principles*, inserting the Mengerian sentence in his text: 'The cleverer economic agents gradually arrange on their own [!] to have themselves paid in whatever are the most marketable goods at the time.'[11] Thus the essential point of Roscher's analysis for Menger is that in order to create money there is no need whatsoever for any action of the government, no need for 'the state'. Arguing by example it is suggested that the 'state' is unnecessary in many other economic affairs as well. Absolute anathema to Menger is the idea that money might be the creature of the 'state' or even Georg Fr. Knapp's dictum that money is the creature of the legal system. Much rather money has increased competition in the economies because it makes it easier to compare values and to calculate in money terms. Price consciousness has been increased by it. And thus, in a sense, one might add that it is money which has changed and developed the legal system, not the other way round: Menger, as a historically trained legal scholar, knows, of course, that Roman law introduced the idea that all obligations which cannot otherwise be fulfilled can be compensated for in terms of a money payment:

> Performance in money as a rule offers not only the greatly increased chance of performing obligations, but also of performing them with the relatively smallest economic sacrifices. It is only a natural consequence of the progressive division of labor and [!] of market trading, both of which are brought about by the emergence of money [!], that compulsory transfers (taxes, damages [!] or fines, etc.) are most suitably requested in money.

While in the method of argument Menger shows himself as a belated member of the Older German Historical School, he differs from that School in his value judgements. According to methodological individualism, the 'state' is no holistic concept, but rather merely the sum of the wills of the people. Moreover, in economic affairs government action is largely superfluous (one relies on the judiciary and on common law). German economists in contrast had tended to see a much more active role for the state.

But actually, Menger is not so far away, even on this point, from the head of the Older Historical School, Wilhelm Roscher. According to him the 'state' is explicitly seen as an entity in itself; but in actual argument Roscher always takes an individualist viewpoint, not least in his monumental refutation of the economic viability of socialism. Roscher explicitly speaks of the need for government action in economic life but then argues that government is weak and ineffective, and, furthermore, that the need for state action withers away with the development of competition and a mature economic society.[12] (I use the term to 'wither away' on purpose, as this is one of the many ideas which Karl Marx took over from Roscher – though with a different value connotation – just as he took over so much of Roscher's arguments on the production-based side of economic development; both Smith and Roscher have, of course, a basically 'materialist' notion of historical development.)

Thus the difference between Menger and Roscher and the fundamental social message Menger tries to impart in his article on money is: Roscher thinks the state is dwindling away in economic affairs and is becoming more and more liberal by the 'ripening' of the economy, while to Menger it is superfluous in the first place. At most, 'government interference in the monetary system ... proves to be a necessity or seems justified precisely in the interest of free, unhampered trade (see chapter V)'. This concession has to do with governmental guarantees that improve information and reduce search costs.

## 2. THE FUNCTIONS OF MONEY AND THE CONCEPTS OF ITS VALUE

Originally about one third of the encyclopedia article 'Money' was taken up by material already presented by Menger in his *Principles* and republished simultaneously with the encyclopedia article in the *Economic Journal*. The remainder of the article contains, first, a long and rather discursive treatment of the functions of money and the different kinds of concepts of its value (the flabby middle part of the article, as one might say); and, second, a short but very original treatment of the demand for money. The first of these additional parts is a totally predictable application of the subjective value propositions of Menger's *Principles*; the second is also based on subjective notions but not quite so evidently. It is Menger's main contribution to the theory of money in the narrower sense. While, as I have shown, in what Schumpeter would have called the 'magnificent' theory of the first part of the article, Menger follows one strain in Roscher's argument closely and composes a counterpoint argument to Smith, he now, in the details of the second part, opposes both Roscher and Knies in a rather nitpicking way.

In order to understand what Menger opposes, one has to know what Roscher and Knies had written – the main authors on the topic in the eyes of Menger. In fact, especially in the first (1892) edition of his article, Menger not infrequently quotes verbatim in inverted commas, without, however, giving the author of the quotation: this is in full conformity with the usage then current; the student was supposed to know all the main scientific sources on a given topic of the last thirty years or so and thus to recognize key quotations. The difficulty arises only for the present-day reader.

Roscher concludes §116 of his theory treatise, which is so often quoted by Menger (in the *Principles* once wrongly as §16), as follows:

> Such a commonly esteemed commodity, which for that very reason [i.e.: common estimation; E.S.] is used for the intermediation of all the different exchange operations and to measure exchange values in general, we call money. (*Produit préféré* according to Ganilh; *marchandise intermédiaire* according to Bastiat.) If state sanction is added that the same commodity should be used as the tacitly understood means of payment for all contracts the concept of money is perfected.[13]

The first half of the first sentence is to Menger's liking; especially so as Roscher inserts between the first and second sentence quoted here the Mengerian clause quoted above. But in the 'measure of exchange values in general' he suspects an objective value notion, which probably overinterprets what Roscher wishes to say in his very short statement. The second sentence is Roscher quoting (explicitly) Knies. It is anathema to Menger: The 'state' perfecting anything in economic affairs, what a horrible notion! Actually, he is again over-reacting. In the footnote to this sentence Roscher says: 'Knies shows nicely how the designation by the state of money as legal tender is only of secondary [!] importance, but not at all irrelevant.'

There is a further statement by Roscher against which Menger polemicizes at length. Roscher commences his vast – and vastly erudite – footnote on all that has been said before him about the nature of money by the unexplained and somewhat mysterious sentence: 'The wrong *definitions of money* can be divided into two main groups: those which take it to be more and those which take it to be less than a commodity'.

What Menger most dislikes in Knies is that by the caption of his fourth chapter he states as the very *first* function of money:[14] 'The function of money as a common measure of value' (Menger prefers to speak of a 'measure of price'). Knies says that 'only a valuable commodity, only a commodity with value of its own' can serve as a measuring rod of value; and this measuring rod is determined by 'the quantum [!] of value of the pieces of money of fixed weight'. He then polemicizes at length against Marx – whom Menger does not even mention – and concludes that in order to set two 'values in use' equal to each other one has 'to reduce these to a common value in use'.[15] All these are much too objective value notions to Menger.

I have pointed out that Menger likes to base his case partly on Roman Law of the classical period with its liberal notion of freedom of contract and on the Germanic Law investigations of his time which thought of the ancient Germans as free men freely associating (that is, *Die Genossenschaft* – the cooperative – of Otto von Gierke). Later Roman Law, however, was much more statist: in a decree, Diocletian had introduced the notion of a 'true' price, which is also called – already *before* the introduction of Christianity as the state religion – a 'just' price and is to be legally enforced by the 'state'. This decree entered the *Corpus juris*. This notion, then as now part of Austrian law, is, of course, anathema to a liberal and subjective value economist. Menger says: 'The fallacious doctrine that money represents an "abstract quantity of value" which government can regulate at will by mere declaratory act is indeed supported by a few passages of the *corpus juris*, but not by the requisite particular regulation of rights concerning money.' What is called 'fallacious' here is doubly reprehensible to Menger: first because of the objective value notion of a value embodied in a commodity and, of course, second because of the idea of state regulation.

Menger's own ideas on the nature of money are quickly stated. In fact, as pointed out already, they are predictable from the *Principles* as only exchange is a subjective value notion: money is above all the general medium of exchange. All its other functions are derived from this one. Price formation is purely subjective and the price will be found between the wide margins of the two parties' reservation prices. There is no need to compare these relative prices to anything else (note that there is no equalization between price and marginal utilities whatsoever in the whole article; it is all in terms of consumer and producer rent, as Marshall would say). However:

The influence of the gradually emerging new situation on price formation is clear ... Formerly, when the supply of the good by an individual market participant ... was met by the demand of a single participant ..., haphazard prices ... were easily the rule, but now all those who offer a commodity on the market in question and at the same time all those who seek to acquire this commodity will participate more and more in price formation.

In one word: the general medium of exchange creates an *information network* between all the participants in the market. Likewise in *asset* markets money assists in the 'widening and deepening of the money economy'.

As to the *value* of money, Menger distinguishes *two* types of value. There is an 'inner exchange value', which is the effect of money on the (change of) prices of other goods and an 'outer exchange value', which is the effect of the (change of) prices of other goods on the value of money, that is, the purchasing power of money. 'Under different conditions of place and time money value (the "exchange value" expressed in money) of goods is no appropriate standard of the inputs and results of economic activities'. Of course, in subjective value terms this has to be so: we cannot know how individuals will value a given situation. Menger dismisses the Ricardian problem: the search for a 'universal and invariable standard' of value is following a 'chimera'. (How can it be otherwise if you think in subjective value terms; it is already extremely difficult to find an invariable measure in terms of inputs into production.) Menger concedes, however, that index numbers form a rough measurement of changes of the 'outer exchange value' of money and might be useful in practice. And as for the 'inner exchange value': 'The question whether particular price movements (or interlocal price differences) are to be traced to causes on the side of money or of the goods traded' is to Menger an important topic for research.

## 3. THE DEMAND FOR MONEY

In this chapter Menger completely rejects the quantity theory of money: in effect, his velocity of circulation (a concept that he ridicules) would be totally unstable. As I have written on this topic already,[16] I shall be very brief. First, it is somewhat astonishing to quote as main authors for the quantity theory Smith, Ricardo and J. S. Mill! (Much rather he should have given Hume, of course.) Menger seems to suggest that the quantity theory is part of the – to him so very objectionable – objective value notion of the classical authors. Even worse, Menger in fact says that the 'formulation is an error which classical economics took over from late mercantilism'! Thus Menger does not seem to understand that at least the quantity equation is none other than the budget constraint under another name, true by definition in bilateral exchange. (Of course, this says nothing about the stability of velocity!)

Menger's key sentence, unchanged from the first to third edition, reads: the classical authors

> ignore the fact that the quantity of money used for payments at any time forms only a part, indeed only a relatively small [!] part, of the stock of money required by a people, while another part must be held in the form of reserves of various kinds, providing for uncertain payments that in fact in many cases never take place at all.

This is a highly subjective *inventory theory* of money holdings. While I am very much in favour of this approach, thinking that monetarists greatly overdo the stability of the velocity of circulation in the short run (especially with regard to the likely amount of yearly percentage *changes* in velocity), I have to point out that in the medium run Menger is empirically wrong. He speaks of the *real* demand for money here, and with a large proportion of reserves presumably not depending on real income, the real income elasticity of money should in his case be in the medium run substantially below one, while actually it is close to one, as the quantity theory would imply. Nevertheless, Menger's doubts on the quantity theory are very original and memorable.

There is probably no great economist who is entirely free of the most glaring characteristic of the profession, namely to contradict himself. Menger apparently does not notice that in the last paragraph of this chapter he actually endorses the quantity theory in its most important conclusions:

> The distinctive character of money ... has the effect that with every change in the outer exchange value of money (be it in consequence of influences on the side of money or of the goods traded) the demand for money of the individual economic units (and so, too, of the economy) changes, that every increase in the outer exchange value of money tends to reduce and its every decline to increase the demand for money.

If we remember what 'outer exchange value of money' means, this is nothing other than a statement of the invariance of real money demand with changes in the price level! Actually, the whole statement would be even clearer to us if Menger had kept to the terminology of the original version of the article, where we read – to our surprise – of the 'nominal need (*Bedarf*) for money' and the 'real need for money', which must have been one of the very first usages of that modern terminology, 'nominal' and 'real'. Menger goes on to say:

> Growing prosperity tends to increase a nation's demand for money for a twofold reason: on the one hand through increased turnover of goods, increased payments, increased capital accumulation in money, and the expansion of the 'money market'; on the other hand through the individual economic units gradually becoming accustomed to holding larger amounts of money (be it directly or

indirectly, in the form of bank accounts), to satisfy their economic need for cash more completely, for the sake of convenience and safe management.

So the quantity theory holds after all, and in real terms as well; in the long run even embodying M. Friedman's idea of relatively increasing real balances with an increase in real incomes as 'money is a luxury'. (Needless to say Friedman, to whom it had even to be pointed out that he was using substantially the same arguments as Hume, has completely ignored Menger, the monetary economist.) But in contrast to Friedman, Menger adds that 'in a developed credit economy this tendency [that is, of a long-run income elasticity of money above unity; E.S.] is counteracted by all sorts of compensating procedures, credit in general, and the emergence of institutions whose function of economizing on coined money or cash in general has been explained above'.

## 4. THE INFLUENCE OF MENGER'S MONETARY THOUGHT ON LATER THEORY

Menger's monetary ideas, which were so dear to him, had astonishingly little immediate effect. In a large part this is due to the fact that historical argument was running out of fashion with the mainstream economists; possibly also because of his prolix style, ever more difficult to digest; and perhaps also because of the antipathy against him of a younger generation of German economists of the Younger Historical School. The influence is, of course, strongest within his own Austrian School. There, however, the opinionated Wieser stood against him; he rewrote the article 'Money' completely for the fourth edition of the *Handwörterbuch der Staatswissenschaften*. Ludwig von Mises' *Theorie des Geldes und der Umlaufsmittel* (1912) follows Menger closely in some of the basic aspects. But that book, again, was of little impact. The intensive interwar discussion on the *neutrality of money* (then a political desideratum), which was largely instigated by the Austrians, may have owed more to Menger: Hayek at least points out that it derived from the (Mengerian) notion of the 'inner exchange value' of money.[17]

That the inventory-theoretic approach to the holding of money, taken up once again by Baumol in 1952, has serious problems, was shown by Hellwig in his presidential address:[18] if one individual wishes to hold a certain time pattern of reserves, what is the consequence then on other individuals and can they do anything about the (change in) money holdings they suffer? Menger's reserve-holding problem, which is partial equilibrium, still awaits a general equilibrium solution.

Menger's historical and institutional perspective had a delayed reception; but from at least the 1980s onwards such analysis has once more come into fashion. Menger's quest to explain the 'mystery of money' was taken up by

Jones,[19] quoting the *Economic Journal* (1892). He is followed by White, who saw in Menger's treatment of 1892 the 'classic invisible hand explanation of the emergence of money from an initial state of barter' (White, 1984, p. 703)[20]. The question of the most marketable commodity progressively turning into 'money' received a thorough treatment by Kiyotaki and Wright.[21] These authors name Menger as one of their important sources, citing the *Economic Journal* (1892) article for his ideas on money. They use the typical Mengerian idea of 'marketability' as one of their two key notions (the other is the cost of storage of goods). Actually, they have a footnote which demonstrates the difficulties of translation: 'Marketability is closely related to Menger's notion of saleability' (p. 935). Menger's terms *'Absatzfähigkeit auf Märkten'* or *'Marktgängigkeit'* are probably more correctly translated as 'marketability'. Anyhow, Kiyotaki and Wright started an avalanche of articles.[22]

Menger's 'magnificent' theory of the development of a free enterprise system through the use of money has a distinguished modern progeny as well, but by authors who never knew about him. E. L. Jones, *The European Miracle: Environment, Economics, and Geopolitics in the History of Europe and Asia,* Cambridge (1981), has to be mentioned prominently and, perhaps also, most recently Richard Pipes, *Property and Freedom*, New York (2000).

## NOTES

1. 'Die Gesetze des subjektiven Güterwertes und des sogen. Grenznutzens insbesondere finden auch auf das obige Problem ihre Anwendung.' (Wieser 1884, p. 126).
2. See Menger (1892), pp. 238-55.
3. See Menger (1950), p. 72.
4. See Roscher (1859).
5. My translation, p. V in the seventh edition, 1873.
6. See Roscher (1864). Note that Roscher, in contrast to his footnotes, changes his text only slowly and practically never the number of paragraphs. The translations are my own.
7. Roscher (1864), §95, p. 177, §96, p. 179, §97, p. 180.
8. Ibid. §117, p. 222. The quotation from Smith is in the original English of that age.
9. See Langford (1992).
10. See Menger (1950), pp. 259, 260, 262.
11. 'Money', 3rd edition (1909), footnote 12.
12. See Streissler (forthcoming).
13. See Roscher (1864), §116, p. 216 f.
14. See Knies (1885), p. 146.
15. See Knies (1885), pp. 148, 150, 160.
16. See Streissler (1973), pp. 164–89.
17. See Hayek (1933), p. 659.
18. See Hellwig (1993), pp. 215–42.

19. See Jones (1976), pp. 759–75.
20. See also Selgin and White (1987), pp. 439–57.
21. See Kiyotaki and Wright (1989), pp. 927–54.
22. See especially: Aiyagari and Wallace (1991), pp. 901–16; Kiyotaki and Wright (1993), pp. 62–77; Trejos and Wright (1995), pp. 118–41; Cavalcanti, Erosa and Temzelides (1999), pp. 929–45.

# REFERENCES

Aiyagari S. R. and N. Wallace (1991), 'Existence of Steady States with Positive Consumption in the Kyotaki–Wright Model', *Review of Economic Studies,* **58**, pp. 901–16.

Baumol, W. J. (1952), 'The Transactions Demand for Cash: An Inventory Theoretic Approach', *Quarterly Journal of Economics*, **66**, pp. 545-56.

Cavalcanti, R. de O., A. Erosa and T. Temzelides (1999), 'Private Money and Reserve Management in a Random-Matching Model', *Journal of Political Economy,* **107**, pp. 929–45.

Hamberger, K. (2001), *Structural Patterns in Early Capital Theory – A Study by the Methods of Transformations*, Dissertation, University of Vienna, small part of a privately circulated, comprehensive manuskript intended for habilitation.

Hayek, F. A. von (1933), 'Über neutrales Geld', *Zeitschrift für Nationalökonomie,* **4**, pp. 659–61.

Hellwig, M. F. (1993), 'The Challenge of Monetary Theory', *European Economic Review,* **37**, pp. 215–42.

Jevons, W. S. (1875), *Money and the Mechanism of Exchange*, London: Paul Kegan, Trench, authorized translation published as *Geld und Geldverkehr* (1876), Leipzig: Brockhaus.

Jones, E. L. (1981), *The European Miracle: Environment, Economics, and Geopolitics in the History of Europe and Asia,* Cambridge: Cambridge University Press.

Jones, R. A. (1976), 'The Origin and Development of Media of Exchange', *Journal of Political Economy,* **84**, pp. 759–75.

Kiyotaki, N. and R. Wright (1989), 'On Money as a Medium of Exchange', *Journal of Political Economy,* **97**, pp. 927–54.

Kiyotaki, N. and R. Wright (1993), 'A Search Theoretic Approach to Monetary Economics', *American Economic Review,* **83**, pp. 62–77.

Knies, K. (1885), *Das Geld. Darlegung der Grundlehren von dem Gelde*, 2nd edn, Berlin: Weidmannsche Buchhandlung.

Langford, P. (1992), *A Polite and Commercial People, England 1727–1783*, Oxford: Clarendon Press.

Menger, C. (1892), 'On the Origin of Money', *Economic Journal,* **2**, pp. 238–55.

Menger, C. (1909), 'Geld', *Handwörterbuch der Staatswissenschaften (3rd edn)*, J. Conrad et al. (eds), Volume IV., Fischer, Jena, pp. 555–610; reprinted in: F. A. Hayek (ed.) (1970), *Carl Menger Gesammelte Werke*, Volume IV Schriften über Geld und Währungspolitik, Tübingen: J. C. B. Mohr (Siebeck), pp. 1–116.

Menger, C. (1950), *Principles of Economics*, Glencoe, Illinois, translated by Dingwall/Hoselitz.

Mises, L. von (1912), *Theorie des Geldes und der Umlaufsmittel*, Munich: Duncker & Humblot.

Pipes, R. (2000), *Property and Freedom*, New York: Vintage Books.

Roscher, W. (1859), *Nationalökonomik des Ackerbaus und der verwandten Urproductionen*, Stuttgart: J.G. Cotta.

Roscher, W. (1864), *Die Grundlagen der Nationalökonomie*, Stuttgart: J.G. Cotta.

Smith, A. (1776), *An Inquiry into the Nature and Causes of the Wealth of Nations*, London: Strahan and Cadell, quoted after Glasgow edition: Oxford Clarendon Press, 1976.

Selgin, G. A. and L. H. White (1987), 'The Evolution of a Free Banking System', *Economic Inquiry,* **25**, pp. 439–57.

Streissler, E. W. (1973), 'Menger's Theories of Money and Uncertainty – a Modern Interpretation'; in: J. R. Hicks and W. Weber, *Carl Menger and the Austrian School of Economics*, Oxford, pp. 164–89.

Streissler, E. W. (forthcoming), 'Nationalökonomik als Naturlehre – Roscher als Wirtschaftspolitiker verglichen mit dem "liberalen" Rau'.

Trejos, A. and R. Wright (1995), 'Search, Bargaining, Money, and Prices', *Journal of Political Economy,* **103**, pp. 118–41.

White, L. H. (1984), 'Competitive Payments Systems and the Unit of Account', *American Economic Review,* **74**, pp. 699–712.

Wieser, F. v. (1884), *Über den Ursprung und die Hauptgesetze des wirtschaftlichen Wertes*, Vienna: Alfred Hölder.

# 2.   Money

### Carl Menger[*], translated by
### Leland B. Yeager with Monika Streissler
### Consultant to the Translator David F. Good

[1]

## MONEY

I. The Origin of Generally Used Media of Exchange. – 1. Introduction. 2. The difficulties of barter. 3. The different degrees of marketability (saleability) of goods. 4. The emergence of media of exchange. 5. The effect of the emergence of generally used media of exchange on commodity markets and on price formation. II. The Controversy among Economists and Jurists over the Nature of Money and Its Distinctive Character as Compared with Other Goods. 1. The controversy among economists. 2. The distinction between 'money' and 'commodity' in jurisprudence. III. The Emergence of Precious-Metal Money. IV. The Perfecting of Metallic Money through Coinage of the Metals. V. The Perfecting of the Monetary and Coinage System by Government. VI. Money as Medium of Unilateral and Substitute Transfers of Wealth. VII. Money as Medium of Payment (or Settlement). VIII. Money as a Medium of Hoarding, Capital Accumulation, and Transfers of Wealth in Time and Space. IX. Money as Intermediary in Capital Transactions. X. Money as Measure of Price (Indicator of Price). XI. Money as Standard of the Exchange Value of Goods. 1. Introduction. 2. Should the valuation of goods in money be regarded as measurement of their exchange values? 3. The practical significance of the valuation of goods in money. 4. Under different conditions of place and time the exchange value of goods expressed in money is no appropriate standard of the inputs and results of economic activities. 5. The desire for a good of universal and invariable outer exchange value. 6. Attempts at measurement of interlocal differences and of variations in the outer exchange value of money. 7. On interlocal differences in and on movements of the so-called inner exchange value of money. 8. The popular conception of the constancy of the inner exchange value of money. 9. The scientific conception of the inner exchange value of money [2] and its movements. 10. The idea of a universal and invariable standard of the 'inner exchange value' of goods. 11. The question whether particular price movements (or interlocal price differences) trace to causes on the side of money or of traded goods. 12. Whether the inner exchange value of money and its movements can be measured. XII. The Concept of Money Derived from its Development and Functions. XIII. Is Legal Tender of Payment Part of the Concept of Money or Is the Latter Merely Perfected Thereby? (A) The juridical point of view. (B) The economic point of view. XIV. The Demand for Money. (A) The demand for money of individual economic units. (B) The demand for money of the national economy.

[3]

# I. THE ORIGIN OF GENERALLY USED INTERMEDIARIES OF EXCHANGE[1]

1. Introduction. The phenomenon that certain goods, which in advanced civilizations are coined gold and silver and subsequently documents representing these, become media of exchange has always attracted the special attention of social philosophers and people active in economic life. That a good may be given up by its possessor in exchange for another one more useful to him is obvious even to the most ordinary intelligence. But that among all somewhat civilized peoples every economic agent should be willing, indeed eager, to trade away goods intended for exchange for small metal discs that seem useless in themselves or for documents representing these: this is so contrary to the ordinary course of things that we must not be surprised if it seems downright 'mysterious' even to so eminent a thinker as Savigny.[2]

One should not think that the puzzling aspect of the above phenomenon is the coin or document form of the media of exchange used nowadays among all civilized peoples. Even if we disregard that and go back to those stages of economic development when, as among not a few peoples still today, precious metals in uncoined form and even [4] other commodities (cattle, animal skins, bricks of tea, slabs of salt, cowrie shells etc.) function as media of exchange, we are confronted with the same phenomenon requiring explanation: the phenomenon that economizing persons are willing to accept certain goods, even when they do not need them or when their needs for them have already been satisfied, in exchange for the goods that they have brought to market, whereas they tend to consult their needs first when it is a matter of other goods that they acquire by way of exchange or by any kind of economic sacrifice.

Thus, from the first beginnings of reflective observation of social phenomena down to our own days there stretches an uninterrupted line of inquiries into the nature of money and its distinctiveness as compared with the other objects of trade. What is the nature of those small metal discs and documents which, in themselves, seem to serve no useful purpose and yet, contrary to all other experience, pass from hand to hand in exchange for the most useful goods and for which, indeed, everyone tries so eagerly to give up commodities? How did money come about? Is it an organic part of the world of goods or an anomaly of the economy?

2. The difficulties of barter. Theoretical analysis of the origin of media of exchange must begin with that stage of development of human societies when 'the no-exchange economy' has already made the transition to 'the economy with barter'.[3] Before this had taken place, people had probably tried to satisfy their wants, over immeasurable periods of time, essentially in tribal and family no-exchange economies until, aided by the emergence of private property, especially personal property, there gradually appeared multifarious forms of trade in preparation for the exchange proper of goods[4] and finally [5] exchange itself: as products of the general process of civilization. Only then, and hardly before the extent of barter and its importance for the population or for certain segments of the population had made it a necessity, was the objective basis and precondition for the emergence of money established.[5]

On barter markets, however, some obstacles inherent in the nature of barter must have hindered the further development of trade and thereby also the development of the occupational division of labour – obstacles which, with such forms of trade, could be overcome only with difficulty, if at all. To be sure, the difficulty often emphasized, namely, that with the prevalence of barter the person offering a commodity is unlikely to find those persons whose commodity he needs and to be found by the persons who need his commodity, had already been overcome by the emergence of markets wherever trade had reached a considerable extent and importance and could count on the requisite legal security. As a rule, the commodities offered on barter markets, which we find with quite similar institutions in the Sudan as well as in the steppes of Asia, on the islands of the Indian Ocean, and in ancient Mexico, tend to be arranged so expediently that every market participant will just as easily find those who are offering the commodities that he wants as he can easily be sought out and found by those who want the commodities he is offering: therefore, the essential difficulty of barter is [6] not the meeting of the contracting parties. Likewise, the difficulty entailed in the quantitative adjustment of supply and demand of each of the contracting parties on barter markets because of the indivisibility of certain goods seems to me to be greatly exaggerated in theory, since on those markets large goods (for example, slaves, cattle, elephant tusks, etc.) tend not to be exchanged at all against small goods, as experience shows; indeed, in most cases small goods, occasionally even cowrie shells, are not at all accepted in payment for large goods; and whoever wants to obtain a dish of millet or a handful of bananas or dates does not come to market with slaves or cattle. The difficulties hindering the development of barter really lie elsewhere. They lie in the fact that on barter markets pairs of contracting parties who need each other's commodities are actually present only in a relatively small number of cases, and it is therefore anything but easy for a person offering a commodity to find another market participant who is offering the commodity he is looking for and at the same time wants the commodity he is offering. But this is a difficulty that only keeps increasing with the progress in the division of labour and with the multiplication of the kinds of goods brought to market.

The famous travellers V. L. Cameron and H. Barth give us a vivid description of these difficulties in their travel reports. 'To obtain boats to proceed on my Tanganyika cruise', writes Cameron, 'was my first consideration; but the owners of two promised me ... were away ... I discovered a good one, however, belonging to Syde ibn Habib ... and managed to hire it from his agent ... Syde's agent wished to be paid in ivory, of which I had none; but I found that Mohammed ibn Salib had ivory, and wanted cloth. Still, as I had no cloth, this did not assist me greatly until I heard that Mohammed ibn Gharib had cloth and wanted wire. This I fortunately possessed. So I gave Mohammed ibn Gharib the requisite amount in wire, upon which he handed over cloth to Mohammed ibn Salib, who in his turn gave Syde ibn Habib's agent the wished-for ivory. Then he allowed me to have the boat.'[6]

[7] Barth reports as follows:

'A small farmer who brings his grain to the Monday market in Kukaua (in the Sudan) refuses outright to be paid in shells and is seldom content with the taler coin. Accordingly, the buyer who wants to have grain must, if he has only talers, first exchange these for shells, or rather he buys shells and with these buys a shirt – "Kúlgu" –; and only after multiple exchanges is he in a position to acquire ... his grain. The trouble that the market participant must take is actually so great that I have often seen my servants return in a state of utter exhaustion.'[7]

If one bears in mind that success achieved with such great trouble and loss of time, and undoubtedly also with economic sacrifices demanded by the activity of market assistants, is to be regarded as an exception and that under these circumstances the exchange of goods as a rule does not take place at all, then one can easily appreciate that on barter markets the development of trade and indirectly of the occupational division of labour is seriously impeded and to no small degree made downright impossible. One can see why on such markets it is not enough for someone offering a good that one or more fellow market participants should want to obtain it nor for someone wanting to acquire a good that one or more market participants should actually offer it, and why instead the direct exchange of goods is basically restricted to those relatively rare cases when each of the contracting parties actually needs the very goods offered by the other.

3. The different degrees of marketability (acceptability) of goods. Despite various arrangements for facilitating trade that are already characteristic of the barter stage, these difficulties would have posed downright insurmountable obstacles to progress in trading goods and in the occupational

division of labour, but especially to progress in the production of goods for uncertain sale, had not the seed of a remedy that was gradually to overcome one of these obstacles already lain in the very nature of things: differences in the marketability of goods.

[8] On barter markets (where, because of the above-mentioned difficulties of barter, even someone going to market abundantly provided with goods is still not at all sure of being able to trade for goods meeting his special need, not even when there is a demand for the goods he is offering and when the goods he wants are in fact to be found on the market!) everyone must make the observation, which at this very stage of development of trade is of practical significance, that for certain goods there is only a slight or occasional demand, while for other goods there is a more general and constant demand, so that someone who brings goods of the first kind to market to trade for goods that he particularly needs is as a rule less likely to achieve this goal or must at least make greater efforts and greater economic sacrifices than someone who goes to market with goods of the latter type.

We need not look far for examples to illustrate this fact. Every explorer who visits countries where barter still exists proceeds from the same considerations when he puts into his trading supplies not just any goods, but those goods whose especially easy marketability in the territories to be passed through is known to him from his own experience or has been tested by those who went before.

4. The emergence of media of exchange. In this situation it will occur to everyone bringing goods to market to exchange them for goods meeting his special need that if his goal is not directly attainable because of the limited marketability of his goods, he could exchange them for goods that are considerably more marketable than his own even if he has no direct need for them. To be sure, he does not thus attain the ultimate goal of his intended exchange (acquisition of the goods he especially needs!) immediately and directly. But he comes closer to this goal. In the roundabout way of an intermediary exchange (by giving up his less marketable goods for more marketable ones), he gets the chance of reaching his ultimate goal in a surer and [9] more economical way than by restricting himself to direct exchange. Surely nowhere was this discovered by all members of a society at the same time; rather, as with all cultural advances, at first only some economic agents will have recognized the advantage for their economic activities arising from the procedure just described – an advantage actually independent of the general recognition of a good as medium of exchange; for always and under all circumstances such an exchange brings an economizing individual considerably closer to his ultimate goal, the acquisition of the consumption goods that he needs, and thus improves his supply of goods. As is well known, however, there is no better way to enlighten someone about his economic interests than for him to perceive the economic success of those who have both insight and energy to use the right means to attain theirs; it is therefore also clear that nothing may have promoted the spread and general

acknowledgment of this insight as much as the fact that the most reasonable and efficient economic agents, in their own economic interest, have long accepted eminently marketable goods in exchange for all others. Such progress in economic knowledge did indeed occur as a result of general cultural progress wherever external conditions did not hinder it. The interest of individual economic agents in their supply of goods and the increasing recognition of this interest led them to pursue their individual economic ends more and more by means of intermediary acts of exchange, without mutual agreements, without the force of law, indeed without any regard for the common interest, and eventually to regard these as a normal form of exchanging goods; that is, they exchanged the goods that they brought to market and that are exchangeable only with difficulty or occasionally not at all for the objects they need, first for market goods they did not actually need but whose possession, on account of their high marketability, offered them the prospect of easily acquiring the goods they actually wanted on the market.

As experience has shown everywhere, such goods have turned out to be commodities of eminent marketability as are generally needed and desired, but are available only in limited quantities, and for which there tends to be a constant, [10] relatively large open (unmet) demand on the part of market participants able to pay for them. These include:

1. Goods available in limited quantities the abundant possession of which testifies to the prestige and power (especially the social status) of their owners: goods for which, consequently, there is a constant and practically almost unlimited demand on the part of the market participants best able to pay (a constant unmet demand for them); depending on the diversity of circumstances and of ideas dominating the population of a territory, for example, livestock, or livestock of a particular kind, slaves, distinctive ornaments (rings, clasps, shells and shell ornaments), precious metals, among which copper and copper alloys, tin, etc. are often counted.

2. Domestic products destined for home consumption, inasmuch as they are objects of the most general desire and need, but are produced either not at all or not in sufficient quantity in the households of numerous market participants able to pay for them, so that there is an extensive and constant or recurring unmet demand for them, particularly for highly popular products (for example, in many countries even today weapons, ornaments, cotton fabrics, mats, blankets, furs, grain, rice, cocoa beans).

3. Goods of extensive and constant need and use, insofar as they are either not produced in a territory or not in sufficient quantity, and consequently are articles of import trade for which an extensive and constant demand exists on the markets of the territory in question, for example, in many countries slabs of salt, tea bricks, precious metals, the most common useful metals (copper, brass, lead, and especially

bars and wires of these metals), woollen blankets, shells and shell ornaments, dyestuffs for tattooing purposes, and occasionally grain, rice, dried fish, cotton fabrics, and the like.[8]

[11]

4. Goods in which, because of social customs or prevailing power structures, certain frequently repeated unilateral performances are effected or have to be effected (for example, gifts and dues to be paid by custom or because of obligations in specific goods to chieftains, priests, medicine men, etc., compensation for damages specified in particular goods, fines for having killed someone, certain goods customarily paid in bride purchases, etc.); for precisely for these goods, which are mostly eagerly desired anyway by those members of society who are best able to pay for them, there is the added special, ever-renewed demand for the above-mentioned purposes.

5. Export articles (furs, cod, benzoin cakes, and other staples) which, on the barter markets in the trading posts of the export merchants, may be exchanged at any time for goods that are generally needed or wanted by the home population and are therefore already stocked by these merchants and which acquire, from the viewpoint of the latter population, almost unlimited (artificially created!) saleability, as a rule at fixed prices.

In an era of barter, goods of these and similar kinds offer advantages to the person who brings them to market to exchange for goods he especially needs, in that he is far more likely to achieve his purpose with them than if he goes to market with goods that are not or only to a lesser degree distinguished by their marketability; in addition, he also stands a greater chance of trading them away at a relatively more favourable barter price because the demand for them is more extensive, constant, and effective than the demand for other kinds of goods.

With growing recognition of the above-mentioned economic interest, especially because of insights passed down and the habit of economizing, those commodities which – under the prevailing conditions of place and time – are the most marketable [12] on all markets have thus become the ones that everyone has an economic interest in accepting for his own less marketable goods and the ones which in fact everyone readily accepts; and they are the most marketable ones because only they sell better than all other commodities, so only they could become generally used media of exchange.

The history of media of exchange of all times and peoples and the trade phenomena still observable today in countries of primitive culture confirm the above law of development, which is grounded in the economic nature of human beings and their respective situations. Everywhere we see that the goods most marketable under the prevailing conditions of place and time, besides being put to actual use, also acquire the function of generally used media of exchange.[9]

It is obvious how important custom must have been for the emergence of generally used media of exchange. In the cases considered here, exchanging less easily saleable goods for goods of higher saleability certainly is in the economic interest of every single economizing individual; the general willingness to accept a medium of exchange presupposes, however, not only that economic agents recognize this interest but also that they become accustomed to an action whereby they trade away their commodities for goods which as such are possibly quite useless to them.

Surely in this case, too, practice, imitation, and custom, with their effect of making people's actions more mechanical, contributed a lot to turning the commodities that were most marketable under the prevailing conditions of place and time [13] into generally used media of exchange, that is, into commodities accepted not only by many but eventually by all economizing individuals in exchange for the (less easily saleable!) goods that they brought to market, and accepted right from the outset with the intention of trading them away again. Only in this way did the phenomenon of money come into existence[10] (money in the sense of a generally used intermediary of exchange).

The further development of money and its functions, too, at first took place along essentially organic lines. With the spatial extension of trade in goods and with provision of goods for meeting needs extending over ever longer time periods, everyone's economic interest made him pay attention, among other things, to trading his less acceptable goods especially for those media of exchange which (besides the merit of high local marketability) also had wide boundaries of saleability in space and time, in other words, commodities whose value, easy transportability, and durability gave their possessor purchasing power over all other market goods that was not only local and temporary, but as far as possible unlimited in space and time.

[14] The great importance that the divisibility of trade-mediating goods, especially of the more valuable ones among them, has for their possessor because the range of persons to whom these goods can be sold is thereby greatly expanded, was bound also to create a special preference precisely for those media of exchange which, besides having the distinctive properties already emphasized, could also be cut into pieces as the individual case demanded without loss of value.

Finally, the fungibility of commodities tends to be of major importance for their easy transfer and receipt in exchange and thus for their acceptability and to be one of the main reasons why highly fungible goods in particular become generally used media of exchange. If one keeps in mind that in every act of exchange both parties must check the quantity and quality of the goods exchanged, which is troublesome and time-consuming and in addition requires a certain expertise, one will easily recognize the importance of fungibility, which greatly facilitates receipt of those commodities that are to become intermediaries of exchange, since their transfer from hand to hand is an essential part of that function. Indeed, we see mainly fungible goods becoming generally used media of exchange everywhere; all those that by their very nature come in countable units (cattle, sheep, cowrie shells, cocoa beans, etc.) or goods that come in countable units because of their manner of production (tea bricks, salt slabs, etc.). In the progressive development of trade in goods, the still imperfect fungibility of precisely the most important of the above goods (domestic animals, furs, slaves, etc.) was one of the main reasons why, above all, commodities that are of comparable quality and traded by measure and weight became generally used intermediaries of exchange, with a tendency apparent everywhere to turn these goods as completely as possible into countable units (thus avoiding the troublesome tasks of portioning, measuring and weighing, which would sometimes involve economic sacrifices) and adapt them to the needs of trade.

Commodities that have become generally used intermediaries of exchange, if only within certain geographical boundaries and possibly even only within certain segments of the population of a territory, **[15]** are called money (livestock money, shell money, salt money, etc.) in scientific usage (not necessarily in everyday life!).[11]

Like other social institutions, the institution of intermediaries of exchange, which serves the common good in the fullest sense of the term, may, as I shall explain later, **[16]** emerge or be promoted, but also impeded, in its automatic development** by the influence of authority (for example, public or religious) and especially by legislation. This manner of emergence of media of exchange, however, is neither the only nor the earliest one. Here, a relation exists similar to that between statute law and common law: media of exchange originally emerged and eventually, through progressive imitation, became generally used not by way of law or agreement but by way of 'custom', that is, through similar actions, corresponding to similar subjective impulses and similar intellectual progress, of individuals living together in society (as the unreflective result of specific individual strivings of the members of society)[12] – a circumstance which subsequently, as with **[17]** other institutions that arose in like manner, does not rule out, of course, their being established or influenced by government.

**[18]** 5. The effect of the emergence of generally used media of exchange on commodity markets and on price formation. As soon as one or more goods have become generally used media of exchange on a country's markets, a profound and striking transformation of market relations occurs. Above all, the fact that one good becomes the generally used medium of exchange **[19]** substantially increases its marketability, already quite high from the outset, both absolutely and in relation to other market goods. Now whoever goes to market with a commodity that has become money is not only (as before) quite likely but certain of being able to acquire at any time and as he likes and chooses such quantities of all other goods on the market as are in proportion to the amounts he possesses. *Pecuniam habens habet omnem rem quam vult habere.* On the contrary, whoever brings other commodities to market now finds himself, as a rule, in a more unfavourable position than before if he wants to exchange these directly for the goods that he especially wants. On the markets he already finds the use of a medium of exchange being practised, in consequence of which a direct exchange of goods – already uncertain and difficult on barter markets! – becomes even more difficult and eventually, as a rule, well-nigh impossible,[13] especially since many arrangements characteristic of the barter stage for facilitating barter also tend more and more to disappear with the emergence of a generally used medium of exchange. Thus the fact that one commodity becomes the generally used medium of exchange substantially increases its marketability, which had been high from the outset, while the emergence and generalization of the use of media of exchange progressively reduce the marketability of the remaining goods characteristic of the barter stage – the possibility of their being exchanged directly – and eventually (with the progressive development of the money economy!) bring it to an end almost completely.

Thus, the fact that one good becomes the generally used medium of exchange causes its acceptability to differ increasingly from that of all other commodities – a difference that can no longer be called merely one of degree but in a certain sense already a difference in kind. In a community where certain goods have become intermediaries of exchange and have been established as such by general use, he who goes to market in order to trade goods for other goods and wants to achieve this goal not only must have the economic interest to sell them first for money but in all probability will actually have to do so; [20] and he who wants to acquire goods on the market mostly finds himself actually compelled to obtain in advance 'money' for this purpose. It is this distinctive function of mediating all trade in goods – the fact that every other commodity on the way from its original producer to the consumer again and again passes through the stage of trading at a money price – that establishes the exceptional position of money in the universe of goods; it is this property that distinguishes it so markedly from all other objects of trade.

But the emergence of generally used media of exchange has still another, incomparably more important effect on the exchange of goods and on market relations. As long as barter prevails on a market, he who offers a good for sale may meet many market participants who need his good, yet it will not be easy for him to find among them just those persons who are at the same time offering to sell the very good he needs and therefore are effective demanders of his good. In any case there will be relatively few of them. But as soon as generally used media of exchange come into operation, this situation is strikingly changed: from now on, all those who need a commodity offered for sale for money by a market participant and so obtainable for money become, for practical purposes, demanders of this commodity. Formerly, he who brought his commodity to market ran the risk of not being able to sell his commodity, although numerous market participants needed it; but now he can choose from among all of them and thus can sell it to whoever offers him the most advantageous recompense (the highest money price). To be sure, this situation, which turns out so much more favourable for the seller of a commodity, also has its drawback. Until the emergence of generally used media of exchange, all those who offered the same commodity on the market as the above-mentioned economic agent were in a situation similar to his (the effective demanders of their good were likewise few in number, and – unless they intended to acquire the same goods – in a situation quite different from his); but from now on all of them appear as his competitors in supplying the same commodity, since all of them try to sell their commodity for money. It would be going too far **[21]** to assert that only through the emergence of money does competition emerge in the demand for and supply of commodities traded. Yet it is certain that it is thereby greatly increased, in fact multiplied.

The influence of the gradually emerging new situation on price formation is clear from what has been said. Formerly, when the supply of the good by an individual market participant or a limited number of them was met by the demand of a single participant or likewise a small group of participants, haphazard prices and other kinds of uneconomic price formations were easily the rule; but now all those who offer a commodity on the market in question and at the same time all those who seek to acquire this commodity will participate more and more in price formation. Price formation will become more concentrated and be adapted to the general market situation or, at least, will correspond to it far better than it could on barter markets. Current market prices are formed, and from now on the valuation of goods in money terms is incomparably more exact and economic than on barter markets, with their fragmented trading in goods and with price formation influenced by all kinds of chance occurrences or by rigid customary exchange ratios and statutory prices.

[22]

## II. THE CONTROVERSY AMONG ECONOMISTS AND JURISTS OVER THE NATURE OF MONEY AND ITS DISTINCTIVENESS AS COMPARED WITH OTHER GOODS

1. The controversy among economists. The distinctiveness of money, its strikingly exceptional position among all other objects of trade, has always drawn the special attention of monetary theorists. The fact that money is sought and accepted in trade not because of its direct utility for us due to its technical properties but ordinarily (at least primarily and directly!) because of its exchange value – or rather the difficulty of a satisfactory explanation of this fact, which seems to run counter to the ordinary course of things – has frequently misled monetary theorists into regarding money as an anomaly of

the economy. The possibility, observable precisely with money, of an arbitrary regulation of its (nominal) value by government, and also the often misunderstood phenomenon of document money, whose substance is valueless, have considerably fostered the above error and induced many students of monetary theory to regard money as a mere token of value, as a mere (immaterial) pledge of an expected return performance, as something valueless in itself (like a trading ticket!) whose actual exchange value derives only from an agreement among the people, from custom, or from a government order.

The opposition to this doctrine, which is widespread especially among those monetary theorists who proceed from the basic idea that money or the monetary unit contains abstract quantities of exchange value and which has also become pernicious for the coinage policies of many states, was expressed in the proposition that money is a commodity. Originally, then, this proposition [23] had a quite different meaning from the one that was later, and often still is, attached to it in economic theory. With this proposition the knowledgeable opponents of the above fallacious doctrine did not want to express anything like the shallow notion that money is 'a good meant for trading' (in this sense a commodity!). Nor did they mean to deny that money, as compared to all other objects of trade, has significant exceptional features, nor to assert that money is only 'a commodity like any other, nothing more and nothing less than a commodity'. That proposition, which has become so important for monetary theory, was meant only to combat the above fallacious doctrine. With all due recognition of the distinctiveness of money as compared with other objects of trade, especially its distinctive function of mediating the exchange of commodities and capital, money is still an object of trade that derives its exchange value primarily and directly from the same causes as the other objects of trade: metal money from the value of its material and from its being minted; document money (as one might add to the older doctrine), like other bearer securities found in circulation, from the value of the legal claims connected with its possession. 'Money is no anomaly of the economy, no trading ticket, no mere token of value.' The proposition 'that money is a commodity' originally had only this meaning among monetary theorists and in this sense is still true today, apart from particular cases requiring special treatment (see chapter V). Even today, the refutation of the above fallacious doctrine is not a matter of 'quibbling over words'.

The fact that money shows special characteristics as compared with other goods contradicts the above proposition just as little as, for example, the fact that roads and paths differ strikingly in many respects from other pieces of land (fields, meadows, woods, building sites, etc.) should mean that they are not pieces of land.

What individual theorists are accustomed to citing as the fundamentally significant distinction between money and other objects of exchange refers only to the distinctiveness of money as compared with other commodities and accordingly proves nothing against the general character of money as a commodity in the above sense, the only sense significant for economic theory. It is true that in the stage of the money economy everyone **[24]** tries to sell his commodities for money, not in order to hold it, as a rule, but to acquire the goods that he needs in exchange for it; it is likewise true that, as a rule, we seek to acquire money for the goods we bring to market not on account of the useful properties of the money material but rather, at least primarily and directly, for the sake of its exchange value. All this, however, only points to the medium-of-exchange function of money, that is, to the distinctiveness of the 'commodity' that has become money; it is not evidence against the character of money as a commodity as such. It is without fundamental significance for the question under discussion: whether money is a commodity at all in the sense that is relevant here. Indeed, it does not even touch upon the essential feature that distinguishes money from other commodities; for the merchant also, but especially the speculator, acquires commodities not in order to hold them nor with direct regard to their useful properties but rather in order to sell the commodities again, and only for the sake of their exchange values.

Furthermore, the feature of money, cited by some respected recent monetary theorists, that essentially distinguishes it from all other objects of trade – 'that a commodity, to fulfil its purpose of being used or consumed', must disappear from the market, while 'money' provides its services by being spent and remaining on the market – refers only to the already emphasized distinctiveness of money as compared with other commodities, that is, to its function of mediating trade in commodities, and is without fundamental significance for the question treated here. It goes without saying that money, the commodity that mediates trade in commodities, especially when it has become a medium of circulation (see footnote 10), in contrast to those commodities whose turnover it effects, ordinarily remains in the market, while the latter move into consumption. But it is a mistake to infer from this that money is not a commodity in the sense relevant here. It would be much more natural (from the economic point of view!) to conclude that money is vested with the character of a commodity permanently, the other goods only temporarily; and that money already performs an important economic function as the commodity mediating the trade in goods (already in the market!) whereas the other commodities tend to provide the utility inherent in their respective natures only **[25]** when they move into consumption and thus cease to be 'commodities'.

Moreover, even precious metals functioning as money may be and are nevertheless consumed and actually do disappear from the market. This is true even for our developed money economies. Now think of the market conditions of peoples where less developed forms of media of exchange still persist, where those portions of a commodity that are to serve as media of exchange are not yet sharply distinguished (even outwardly!) from those that are to be devoted to consumption, and where the goods intended for exchange are actually being used in the meantime or the goods that only yesterday were media of exchange in the hands of one market participant are consumption goods today in the hands of another or even the same market participant! The above interpretation is ahistorical, by the way.

What distinguishes money from all other objects of trade is its function as an intermediary of exchange and the functions derived therefrom.

Here, in this – for practical purposes – eminently important fact (and not in the fact that money supposedly is no 'commodity') we have not only the essence of but also the explanation of the distinction between money and all other objects of trade, the explanation of the distinctiveness of money as compared with other goods. In treating the question 'whether money is a commodity', those who do not pay attention to the nature of money and its position among other objects of trade but instead start from some particular definition or other of the controversial concept of money and from a similarly ambiguous concept of commodity and proceed to investigate whether the former may be subsumed under the latter without inconsistency fail to recognize the true nature of the above-mentioned problem and its significance for the theory of money. In fact, their controversies may in large part be described as mere quibbling over words. For advancing our theoretical insights, we shall have to thank those whose conception of the nature of money and its position among other objects of trade eventually proves correct.

2. The distinction between 'money' and 'commodity' in jurisprudence. The property distinguishing money from other objects of exchange is quite evident in everyday business and, accordingly, also in civil law, [26] namely, that money is that object of trade which mediates the exchange of all other objects of trade (especially also the fungibility of money, which is already extraordinarily high in itself and is further considerably increased by minting of the monetary metals and subsequently by legal fictions that serve to facilitate transactions,[14] as well as its purpose of serving as medium of exchange and changing hands, or circulating, with as little hindrance to trade as possible). The acquisition and transfer of possession, of ownership, and of the economic use of sums of money over time, the establishment and cancellation of money claims, and so forth, are in many cases different from those involving other kinds of goods: for example, the legal regulation of purchase and sale (*emptio – venditio*) differs in part from that of barter trade (*permutatio*), that of a loan of money or credit (*mutuum*) differs from that of the loan of a specific object (*commodatum*), and so forth. It is not through discretion of the legislator but because of the distinctiveness of money as compared with other objects of trade that, with respect to purchases and sales, jurisprudence distinguishes between a money price (*pretium*) and a return performance in other kinds of goods (*merx*), between a loan of money or credit and the loan of an object[15] and partly attaches different legal consequences to legal transactions, depending upon whether they concern a sum of money or other kinds of traded object.[16]

[27] The different treatment of rights and obligations when they concern money and when they concern other goods, for which numerous analogies are found in private law (think, for example, of the different legal treatment of acquisition of ownership, of protection of possession, etc. for movable and for immovable goods!), should not, however, be lumped together with the economists' controversy over whether money is a commodity. Jurisprudence is correct when in those cases in which the distinctiveness of money as compared with other goods requires special regulation of the legal relationships in question it actually effects this. But evidently it can in no way be inferred from this that money is an asset whose exchange value is not governed by the economic laws of the exchange of goods, that it is a mere token of value, a trade ticket, an anomaly of the economy.[17] The fallacious doctrine that money represents an 'abstract quantity of value' which government can regulate at will by mere declaratory acts is indeed supported by a few passages of the *Corpus juris*, but not by any requisite particular regulation of rights concerning money.

[28]

# III. THE EMERGENCE OF PRECIOUS-METAL MONEY

Depending on prevailing conditions of place and time, the goods that were most acceptable acquired the function of generally used media of exchange (in addition to their previous uses!) among the same peoples at different times and among different peoples at the same time; these were goods of very different kinds.

That it was metals, especially the precious metals, that were pre-eminently used as intermediaries of trade, by some peoples even before they appeared in history, and in historical times by all peoples with advanced economic culture, finds its explanation in their great marketability, which exceeded that of all other goods, especially in developed economies.

Because of their usefulness and particular beauty, precious metals (among which copper is also to be counted in earlier stages of economic development) are ornaments among peoples of lower culture, and, as a result, the preferred materials for sculptural and architectural decoration and especially for ornaments and utensils of all kinds. Everywhere they are thus objects keenly desired from early on by all classes of the population, especially in cultural stages and in climates where clothing and even weapons served primarily decorative purposes. Although they (especially gold!) are widely available in nature and may be extracted by relatively simple processes (particularly gold and copper), the available quantity of the precious metals in relation to the demand for them is nevertheless so small, because of the scantiness of their production, that both the number of people who have an unmet or not fully met demand for these goods and the volume of the open (unmet) demand for them is always relatively great, incomparably greater than with other more important [29] but more abundantly available goods. The demand for them (both open and latent) is as extensive as it is constant. Also, because of the nature of the needs satisfied by the precious metals, the range of people who wish to acquire precious metals quite particularly includes the members of the population with the greatest purchasing power; the wide and constant (open!) demand for the precious metals is, as a rule, also an effective demand. But the easy divisibility of the precious metals and the fact that even very small quantities of them can be enjoyed in private households (as ornaments and as decoration!) extend the boundaries of the effective demand for the precious metals to include those strata of the population with lesser purchasing power. Add to that the wide spatial and temporal boundaries of the saleability of the precious metals, which is a consequence of the nearly unlimited extent of the demand for them in a spatial sense, their low transport costs in relation to their value, and their essentially unlimited durability.

In a market economy that has gone beyond the first steps of its development, there are no goods with even remotely as wide personal, quantitative, spatial, and temporal limits to their saleability as the precious metals. Long before the precious metals had attained the function of intermediaries of exchange among all economically advanced peoples, they were goods that met an open and, as a rule, effective demand: nearly everywhere, at all times, and in any practically considerable amount that came to market.[18]

That meant that the precious metals had become eminently qualified, in the way I mentioned in the previous section, to become generally used media of exchange: to function as goods for which (in all cases in which a [30] direct exchange of goods proved impossible or especially difficult) everyone seeks first and directly to sell his own tradable goods. All this happened as a rule not so that the precious metals thus acquired could be used to satisfy one's own needs directly but rather with a view to their special marketability and with the intention of subsequently exchanging them, as opportunity and need occurred, for other goods immediately required by the possessor. It was neither an accident nor the consequence of legal compulsion or voluntary agreement but rather the proper recognition of individual interests which caused the precious metals, as soon as a sufficient quantity of them had been accumulated and put into circulation, gradually to drive out the older media of exchange and to become the generally used media of exchange among economically advanced peoples. The switch from the less valuable to the more valuable metals also has analogous causes.

This development was substantially promoted by those properties of precious metals which have already been pointed out: they can be stored conveniently and at hardly any cost, and as a consequence of their distinctive production, consumption, and market conditions, and of their durability, the exchange ratio between them and the other goods shows far smaller fluctuations than the exchange ratio between most other goods, which is one more reason for everyone to hold his available stock of tradable goods first (that is, until using it to exchange for goods he directly requires) in precious metals, which are relatively stable in value and may be stored easily, or to shift into them. In addition, the important fact should be stressed that, because of their properties, precious metals are particularly well suited for hoarding and have always been employed for this purpose (long before the emergence of precious-metal money). Finally, the significant fact [31] that the precious metals, because of the distinctiveness of their colour, their sound, and partly also their specific gravity, may be recognized without difficulty by any fairly knowledgeable person and, because of their sufficient durability and malleability, especially in alloys, once struck, tend to retain their features and can thereby be made easily testable for quality and weight even by nonexperts, helped to increase their acceptability and quite significantly advanced the process through which they became generally preferred media of exchange of economies in an advanced stage.[19]

[32]

## IV. THE PERFECTING OF METALLIC MONEY THROUGH COINAGE OF THE METALS

Various arguments suggest that even before scales came into general use, precious metals were in circulation not only in the form of utensils (weapons, axes, ornaments, etc.) but also as unprocessed or as semifinished products (as bars, rods, wires, etc., with their shapes and dimensions adapted to the needs of consumption). As is true of some goods even today, at a time when the weighing of goods in trade was unknown or had not yet become common, a variety of such products (the variety being due to the different kinds of metals and their places of extraction) and customary sub-units of them may have substituted, as it were, for scales; and in this form metals may also have functioned as media of exchange on some markets.

As scales became more common in trading goods (at first probably for the most valuable goods and goods requiring special accuracy in use, for example, precious metals, spices, medicines), the less exact types of units and measures were for many goods displaced by scales, and the monetary metals especially were meted out by weight. Even in our century, and even now, we can still observe this manner of trading goods on numerous markets, with the monetary metals being received not by tale but by weight.

The weighing of monetary metals, however, involved disadvantages that severely impeded trade in goods. Reliable assaying of the genuineness and fineness of the metals has to be left to experts, who must be compensated for their trouble; and dividing hard metals into such portions as happen to be required in trade is a task that, because of the accuracy with which it must be undertaken, especially with the precious metals, [33] requires precision instruments and involves a not inconsiderable loss of material (from fragmenting and repeated melting!). Both operations, moreover, cause both a loss of time, extremely irksome in trade, and inconveniences of various kinds (think of the inconvenience that arises simply because market participants usually must bring scales and weights with them!).

Removing these obstacles to general trade must have seemed more urgent the more their constant recurrence sensitized market participants to them.[20] On various markets this will first have happened automatically as metal pieces whose weight had been determined by means of scales (if they were easy to carry and corresponded to the weights most common in trade) came into and were kept in circulation. Occasionally, metal pieces of this sort must have had to be reweighed or assayed for fineness; but the trouble and loss of material caused by cutting up the bars was avoided.

Furthermore, quite early on, the fineness of the bars or of the pieces of bar metal in circulation must have been made recognizable by small marks struck onto them. At first, as even today frequently in East Asia, this was done probably by private persons, especially merchants, for their own purposes and understood only by fellow traders, who were reminded by the stamps that the bars and metal pieces had passed through their hands already and had been assayed and [34] found to be of good content. Subsequently, this was often done in a more general and trustworthy manner by assayers working on the market, who were liable both for their assaying and for the quality of the money to the contracting parties who used and paid for their services.

But experiences on the markets of those peoples who, up to most recent times, had not yet achieved an orderly system of coins show us how inadequately the disadvantages inherent in the circulation of uncoined metals were overcome by the above automatic development. The tests of weight and especially of fineness by the assayers active on these markets prove unreliable and, seeing how easily the stamps of these functionaries may be counterfeited, have to be repeated, as a rule, with every transaction, a circumstance that makes payments highly time-consuming and costly. (Commission charges in Rangoon, for example, are reported to be between 1 and 1.5 percent of the value, to which is added the loss in weight due to frequent assaying and stamping.)

Basically, the disadvantages arising from the circulation of uncoined metals, which were felt especially in retail trade, could be overcome only when a quantity of the monetary metals sufficient for trade was divided up in advance into uniform pieces intended for circulation (and adapted to the requirements of trade) and a stamp guaranteeing their weight and fineness (and also protecting them against counterfeiting and fraud as far as possible) was struck onto them.

Metal pieces of this kind that are intended for or actually serve in intermediating trade are coins.[21] [35] Now, compared to the circulation of unminted metals, this form of media of exchange has the advantage that it saves the trouble and economically costly operation of dividing and weighing metals that function as intermediaries of trade. Coins spare us from or facilitate the task of assaying fineness and weight when we accept precious metals and the proof thereof when we pay them out.

But this is not the entire importance of coining monetary metals. The reliable establishment of gross weight and fineness is [36] far from being its sole essential purpose. Let us imagine the monetary system of a country where coins circulate with each one having a different weight, a different shape, and a different fineness; even if the gross weight and the fineness of the individual pieces were determined and certified most precisely and reliably, they could satisfy the needs of trade only in a very incomplete way. It is only because in the process of coinage the monetary metals are divided from the start into pieces that are identical within the limits of technical feasibility in the respects essential for the monetary purpose (that is, primarily with regard to fineness and also with regard to gross weight, alloy, and shape) that we are in a position to present, pay, and receive specified quantities of precious metals merely by tale, not only, as a rule, without checking gross weight and fineness of the individual pieces but also without troublesome and time-consuming calculations. Only in this way do the monetary metals qualify for being transferred from hand to hand (for being paid and accepted) without trouble or cost; only thereby do they acquire the great capacity for circulation characteristic of coined monetary metals.

Coining the monetary metals into identical pieces has yet another important result, however. It becomes possible thereby to specify quantities of coined (therefore easily transferred and circulated) monetary metal in a simple and exact manner (by merely naming the kind of coin and the number of pieces!), a fact whose significance for trade can hardly be overestimated, especially for fixed-term obligations concerning monetary metals. It is not because simply, by being coined, individual metal pieces are certified in a trustworthy manner as to weight and fineness but only because they are also divided into identical pieces (fungible with regard to weight, shape, and fineness!) that they qualify as objects of obligations as easily entered into as fulfilled, whose substance is the payment of certain quantities of monetary metal fit for circulation. Only coins of this kind (not just any single piece of monetary metal, be it ever so precisely specified as to weight and fineness) [37] are truly coin-money: fungible pieces of monetary metal serving to facilitate and perfect both the circulation of metallic money, originally received by weight, and the payment of certain quantities in certain grades of fineness simply by tale.

Probably the most striking proof of the great importance that coining monetary metals has for trade is the fact that in nearly all places where coin-money comes into use, it eventually deprives weighed monetary metal of its function as medium of exchange and becomes the exclusive and generally used medium of exchange, while uncoined monetary metal is largely turned into a commodity.

To be sure, coining monetary metals for trade purposes also entails the disadvantage of making precise adjustment of money prices to things given in return more difficult in all those cases in which prices cannot be represented precisely by the circulating coins, as these are inherently indivisible.[22]

The most obvious suggestion for dealing with this disadvantage inherent in the coined form of the monetary metals is to cut the monetary metals up right at the time of minting into pieces having the values most often met with in trade. It is not improbable that even before monetary metals were coined, those kinds of metal pieces that were adapted to the requirements of trade already circulated among some peoples as their preferred medium of exchange. Actual coinages, however, especially those by the state, have in the nature of the case been governed mainly by a concern to render feasible the easy and most exact possible representation in coined metal of all prices occurring in trade by means of a graduated system of types of coin. In this way, the above-mentioned disadvantage was indeed effectively overcome. Nearly all systems of coin types developed in reference to existing commercial weights or metal weights and their usual subdivisions. In the course of historical evolution, many kinds of influence (fiscal exploitation of the coinage prerogative, variations in the value ratio of the monetary metals, the requirements of foreign trade, necessary regard for the valuation practices of the population, etc.) have led [38] to present-day coinage systems, which essentially combine the advantages of a system of coin types easily and (within the limits of technical feasibility) exactly representing all price grades with those of a coinage unit and coin denominations that have been adapted as far as possible to the requirements of trade and the valuation practices of the population.[23]

When such a system of coin denominations comes about, it is of the greatest consequence for trade and private law. It means (especially in connection with government measures that I deal with in the next section) that definite quantities of the coinage unit can be easily and simply represented and paid with coins of different denominations. It becomes possible to contract not only debts whose amount is a specified number of coins of a specified kind but also debts whose amount is a specified quantity (representable in coins of different kinds) of coinage units or units of account (with sums of money owed!), debts that are most important in everyday life.[24, 25]

To sum up what I have said: it turns out that coining the monetary metals, especially the precious metals, has far greater significance for economic life and for the legal system [39] than is commonly ascribed to it. Coins not only save us the troublesome and (in terms of economic sacrifices) costly assaying and weighing of the monetary metals in trade. Their significance goes far beyond this. When that part of the precious metals that is to be used as money is coined, so that uniform systems of coin types develop within the boundaries of a state, these monetary metals acquire the capacity to be specified, transferred, and received easily, exactly, and almost costlessly in any quantity suitable to the requirements of trade. They lend themselves to being circulated to a degree equalled by very few other types of goods, especially not even remotely by bullion.[26] At the same time, however, coined precious metals in the shape of coins of the same denomination (and, taking account of alloy and weight relations, as a rule also of different denominations) attain an extraordinary degree of economic fungibility; this means that the objects of monetary obligations, which essentially consist of quantities of metal of specified weight and fineness, may be specified in a manner as simple as it is precise: through mere specification of the denomination and the number of coins, indeed through mere specification of a number of coinage units. By being coined, the monetary metals become suitable, like hardly any other good, as objects of generic debts (including sums of money), whose substance is exactly specified and whose settlement (by coined metal!) may be accomplished by tale in a manner as exact as it is simple and effortless.[27]

[40] To be sure, even the most rational system of coins and the technically most advanced coinage of the monetary metals cannot fully eliminate some deficiencies in fungibility due to technical aspects of coinage, varying relations among the monetary metals, etc. To achieve this, government will have to exercise its influence on the system of money and coins in various ways.

[41]

# V. THE PERFECTING OF THE MONETARY AND COINAGE SYSTEM BY GOVERNMENT

An advanced economy's demands on the monetary system are not to be met by a system such as develops automatically. Money was not created by law; in its origin it is not a governmental but a social phenomenon. Government sanction is foreign to the general concept of money. Certainly, though, the institution of money (its function as intermediary of exchange and the functions following from this) has been perfected and adapted to the diverse and changing needs of developing trade by government recognition and regulation, just as the common law has been affected by legislation and as all aspects of social life, especially trade, have been affected by government intervention.

Above all, wide experience has shown that coining the monetary metals, as soon as and insofar as[28] this proves necessary for the economy, makes government intervention more and more inevitable. The costly supplying of the markets with coined metals appropriate (in kind and quantity) to the requirements of the economy is certainly in the interest of both individuals and the economy as a whole; but, as experience shows, it cannot be expected from a country's individual economic units, which are under the pressure of competition and are dependent on and oriented toward profit. Accordingly, even in recent times, private coinages have met the general requirements of trade only imperfectly.[29]

[42] It is clear that, as a rule, only government has an interest in, and will even bear the cost of, continually supplying the economy with coin-money according to the requirements of trade; for only government also has the instruments of power at its disposal for effectively protecting the coinage against counterfeiting and the media of exchange in circulation against fraudulent reductions in weight and other kinds of violation harmful to trade. History offers us any number of examples of cases in which governments (to a considerable extent relying on mistaken monetary theories) have misused the coinage prerogative naturally theirs in a way that was as selfish as it was detrimental to the community. But ever since governments have abandoned the essentially fiscal interpretation of the coinage prerogative that had led to such abuses and have properly realized the great economic importance of a coinage system whose intrinsic value shields it from any arbitrary interference (as foundation of the entire monetary system!), all civilized countries recognize that supplying the economy with reliably minted coins is properly a task of government concern; and, in fact, this task has regularly been performed in a manner fully conforming to the requirements of trade only by government or under government supervision.

The state exercises a far more important influence on the monetary system by uniformly regulating this system within its boundaries and subsequently even beyond them, through international agreements. Naturally, the automatic development of the monetary system easily leads to a multiformity of money, with respect to monetary metals, their alloys, and the units of weight and their fractions used in calculations, which is highly harmful to and troublesome for trade. As soon as coining the monetary metals becomes common, the fragmentation of the coinage prerogative tends to have similar effects [43] and to lead to a multiformity – no less harmful to trade – of coined moneys with respect to metals coined, alloys, standard weight and its fractions, especially of the coinage unit, precision of minting, shape of coins, and even naming of the types of coin. Government performs one of the most important tasks of economic policy when it does not confine itself to the trustworthy certification of gross weight and fineness of the coins (when it is not content with being the trustworthy mintmaster of the population by forgoing excessive or even dishonest profit), but instead, by establishing uniformity of the coinage system (as to currency metals and their alloys, unit weight, coinage unit, coinage standard, denominations, shapes of coin, names of coins, etc.), uniformly regulates the monetary system of the state or of larger territories in a way appropriate to the needs of the population, and when it creates a uniform national money (or national currency) in the fullest sense of the word by putting this sort of coin in circulation and withdrawing from or driving out of circulation coins that do not meet these requirements.

When government thus meets the needs of trade for uniform weights and measures just as in all other areas and especially in the highly important and distinctive one of coined money (through establishing a national currency), it provides the foundation and prerequisite for a highly simplified and secure system of calculation and payments, a medium of exchange that, in contrast to the multiform money that developed automatically, is largely perfected and fungible within the limits of technical feasibility and especially prevents, in various ways, doubts and controversies over the legal object of money debts.

Still, even after the introduction of a uniform system of national coins and even with the most efficient minting, there will remain a number of deficiencies of the monetary system to which trade is sensitive and which cannot be remedied by measures merely having to do with coinage technique and coinage policy as mentioned above. Such disadvantages are: the fact that coins (capable of circulation!) which represent all the different quantities of the monetary metal (all money prices) that occur in trade [44] cannot be minted from one and the same metal (especially when it is a precious metal), and particularly that the types of coin to be used in retail trade must be minted from monetary metals other than those of the full-bodied coins; that in many countries even the full-bodied coins are usually minted from different monetary metals (gold and silver); that gross and fractional coins, even when they are minted from the same metal and even more so when they are minted from different metals, do not require the same expense in mintage so that amounts of the same nominal value have different production costs; that even with advanced technique and careful minting, individual pieces of the same type of coin differ in fineness and weight (are not completely fungible, economically speaking!) even as they leave the mint, a deficiency which is only increased through wear in circulation; that frequently, aside from the national coins, generally used means of payments of other kinds (bank notes, state treasury notes, foreign coins) come into circulation; etc.

The common element in these disadvantages, which cannot be fully remedied by measures of coinage technique nor even by the most efficient coinage system, is that they reduce the strict economic fungibility of coins of the same type and still more the mutual fungibility of corresponding quantities of coins of different types; because of this, the advantages of a uniform system of national coins, and especially those of a uniform system of calculation, would not be fully achieved if the effects of these disadvantages could not be remedied. Imagine the state of the monetary system of a country where coins of the same type are valued differently because of inevitable inaccuracies in their minting and regularly occurring losses from wear in circulation, or a situation in which coins produced from different money materials (particularly token coins) function like parallel currencies because of fluctuations in the relative prices of the monetary metals concerned, etc. In this way, obviously, the essential advantages of a uniform national money and of a however efficiently graduated and implemented coinage system would partly be cancelled out. A fully reliable system of calculation and payments suited to all the requirements of trade **[45]** is not attainable by mere measures of coinage technique and of coinage policy as mentioned above.

The above difficulties (which in part arise not only with the minting of the monetary metals, as hardly needs saying) and their effects can be overcome only by a system of government measures, some of which pertain to regulating the settlement of money debts and therefore belong not only to the sphere of coinage policy but also to that of private law and consist in part of government's assuming certain obligations concerning property law.

Measures of this kind are: that for settlement of money debts, government confers the same legal paying power to the individual pieces of the same type of coin despite certain deviations in gross weight and fineness (so-called remedy and abrasion allowances); that government establishes the paying power of coins minted from different precious metals by law (by fixing the value ratio at the time of minting and by setting the values of the types of coin); that it brings the paying powers of the fractional coins minted below value into a fixed relation with those of the coinage unit by promising to redeem them or by declaring them legal tender at their face values; etc.

Only through this combination of government measures pertaining to coinage technique, administrative law, and private law does a country's system of types of coin become a system of legally strictly fungible units of account, a circumstance that contributes greatly to simplifying the calculation and payments system and enables even a person inexperienced in the complexities of the monetary and coinage system, when he uses the national coins in his transactions in goods and credit, to specify any quantity of coined monetary metal occurring in trade with attainable exactness, merely by naming the number of units of the national currency, and to make and receive payments in a legally secure manner, simply by tale.

When in a country with a well-ordered coinage system everyone, every day labourer, indeed every child, is able to share in the advantages of a uniform monetary system that can indicate all possible price schedules easily and exactly and functions normally even in times of severe crisis, **[46]** mostly without the great majority of the population even being aware of these benefits and their causes, this result, hardly to be overestimated, is to be attributed not least to the system of government measures described above, through which all avoidable and thus unnecessary economic costs, dangers, and inconveniences of the monetary and payments system are effectively circumvented as far as possible.

Only thereby do uniform national currencies fashioned for the requirements of advanced commercial and legal activities truly come into being.

**[47]**

## VI. MONEY AS A MEDIUM OF UNILATERAL AND SUBSTITUTE TRANSFERS OF WEALTH

Voluntary as well as compulsory unilateral transfers of assets (that is, transfers arising neither from a 'reciprocal contract' in general nor from an exchange transaction in particular, although occasionally based on tacitly recognized reciprocity), are among the oldest forms of human relationships as far as we can go back in the history of man's economizing. Long before the exchange of goods appears in history or becomes of more than negligible importance for the supply of goods, we already find a variety of unilateral transfers: voluntary gifts and gifts made more or less under compulsion, compulsory contributions, damages or fines, compensations for killing someone, unilateral transfers within families, etc.

As long as trading in goods is of no more than negligible importance for the supply of goods to individual households, transfers of this sort are, as a matter of course, offered or embodied in goods having use value for the recipient. In the case of compulsory transfers in the barter economy, there is the additional consideration that they must be specified in goods that the obligated party actually has at his disposal or (for transfers at a set time and periodically recurring transfers) is likely to have at his disposal. The disadvantages inherent in such obligations, which are highly important in the barter stage, basically have to do with the fact that in many cases they force the obligated parties into lines of production that are either unsuited to their household economies or become troublesome and uneconomical for them in the course of time, while actually they often are or come to be of little value to the entitled party and are not at all proportionate to the sacrifices to be made by the obligated party. **[48]** Besides, with unambiguously specified transfers in kind it is always doubtful whether the obligated party will be able to satisfy the lawful claims of the entitled party under all circumstances, especially when it is a matter of fixed-time or recurring transfers.

In the era of barter, with its overly harsh law of obligations, which is only partially mitigated by patriarchal relationships, the disadvantage just mentioned tends to promote the specification of substitute performances that in many cases, which can be found in great numbers in the oldest documents and statute books, make it easier and in others possible at all for the obligated party to perform and for the entitled party effectively to obtain performance.[30]

But as soon as trade in goods gains in extent and importance among a people, as generally used media of exchange emerge, and as, with the progressive division of labour and the expansion of market trading, an ever growing number of market goods may be bought and sold for money, there also arises from this changed situation a new and much more perfect means of overcoming the difficulty that prevents the assured fulfilment of unequivocally specified economic obligations in the barter economy and that sometimes necessitates the arrangement of substitute economic performances: the specification of unilateral transfers in money. By their very nature, substitute performances have no precisely specified form; the recipient is not at all sure of receiving exactly the goods he wants nor is the obligated party sure of being able, under all circumstances, to deliver the required goods, even in substitute form. In contrast, performance in money gives the former command over proportionate quantities of all goods found on the market, from which he may choose the ones he most desires; but to the obligated party, whose circulating capital always takes the form of money in the age of a money economy, performance in money as a rule offers not only the **[49]** greatly increased chance of meeting his obligations but also of meeting them with the relatively smallest economic sacrifices. It is only a natural consequence of the progressive division of labour and of market trading, both of which are brought about by the emergence of money, that, with the broadening and deepening money economy, compulsory transfers (taxes, damages or fines, etc.) are most suitably specified in money wherever it is not a matter of direct compulsory transfers of consumption goods (requisitions, dues paid in kind for the recipient's own use, etc.) but rather transfers of wealth; at the same time extant obligations in kind are progressively converted into obligations in money, so that with the progressive development of the economy, it is money that more and more becomes the preferred medium of unilateral compulsory performances.

What has just been said essentially holds for voluntary unilateral transfers also. Whoever wants to give another person something of value for free (as a gift, legacy, wedding present, etc.) will in certain circumstances do so in goods intended to serve the recipient's production or consumption purposes directly; in all other cases, however, in which it is a question of economic performance (and not of acts, for example, of personal attention or devotion, where the economic aspect is subordinate to the personal one), he will most appropriately employ that exchangeable good which gives the recipient command over all goods on the market, namely, money. Other kinds of exchangeable goods must first be sold for money by the recipient, which involves various inconveniences and economic sacrifices and, as far as the amount of the proceeds is concerned, also tends to involve more uncertainty the lower the marketability of the goods in question. With the development of the money economy, voluntary unilateral transfers of an economic nature, too, will be most appropriately offered in money, as a rule, in cases not involving gifts of goods intended to serve the recipient's production or consumption purposes directly.

The same holds true of substitute transfers of wealth. As soon as the money economy broadens and deepens among a people and every economic agent becomes more and more dependent on the market for the satisfaction of the greater **[50]** part of his needs, money is an asset that every economic agent requires, that everyone needs ever anew because of the nature of money as medium of exchange (see chapter XIV). If instead of an unsatisfied legal claim, a sum of money is awarded to the entitled party by way of a substitute or compensation, he receives an asset that puts at his disposal appropriate quantities of all goods offered on the market. Not only will he be able, under all circumstances, to make use of the amount of money paid to him as substitute fulfilment, but if he is awarded a sufficient quantity,[31] he may also acquire on the market, according to his own (subjective) valuation and choice, the goods withheld from him by his debtor's default, or at least goods of equal value to him. Thus, for the entitled party, the substitute performance in money is the relatively most complete and economical replacement for the material loss that he suffers by the nonfulfilment of his claim. At the same time, for the debtor who did not fulfil his obligation it is, as a rule, the least oppressive manner of substitute performance, since any other manner, leaving the choice of the goods to be delivered as substitutes to the creditor or to the discretion of the judge, would demand far greater economic sacrifices from the tardy debtor and would bring about his economic ruin in far more cases than with the settlement of substitute performances in money.[32]

**[51]** As soon as a commodity functions as a generally used medium of exchange, it also becomes the most suitable medium for unilateral (both voluntary and compulsory) and substitute transfers of wealth.

**[52]**

## VII. THE 'FUNCTION' OF MONEY AS MEDIUM OF PAYMENT (OR SETTLEMENT)

If one keeps in mind the function of money as the thing that mediates commodity and capital transactions, a function that already includes the payment of money prices and of borrowed sums,[33] and if one also recognizes (for those stages of economic development in which money already mediates practically all transactions on commodity and capital markets) that money is preferably used for unilateral and substitute performances, there is no need or reason for dealing separately with a preferred use or indeed a function of money as medium of payment. In this situation it would be redundant to ascribe to money a special function as medium of payment or even as general medium of payment, since the above functions and ways of employing money already embrace all money payments that actually occur in the economy.

Nor would the fact that money is in incomparably more cases than any other thing the object of obligations, and accordingly also of settlements, justify an assumption of the above sort. Other goods, especially those of everyday use, are in very many cases also objects of market trading and thus of settlement without having any special function as a medium of settlement ascribed to them.

What certainly distinguishes money, in the respect considered here, from other kinds of asset is the fact that with the broadening and deepening of the money economy – for reasons that essentially [53] are to be traced to the characteristic mediating position of money on the commodity and capital markets – money also tends to become a preferred medium of unilateral and substitute performances. While for this reason money may indeed be called a 'general intermediary of the commodity and the capital market and preferred medium of unilateral and substitute performances', it is clear, however, that the function of a general medium of payment (along with the above functions) must not also be ascribed to it.

The definition of money 'as generally used medium of exchange and payments' thus rests on a misunderstanding. It is too narrow because it does not contain a reference to the mediating function of money on capital markets, but at the same time it is redundant in that it refers to a particular form of the use of money, which is largely a part of its function as intermediary of the commodity and capital markets anyway, once more as a general function of money.

The above inaccuracy would be of little account had not the exaggerated significance ascribed by no small number of monetary theorists to the very 'function of money as general medium of payment' caused those authors to turn their attention mainly to the legal form and legal formalities of the act of paying money debts while largely losing interest in the genuine economic problems of monetary theory. The erroneous doctrine, so crucial for monetary theory, that legal tender is inherent in the concept of money; the distorted interpretation of substitute performances, which, after all, are undertaken essentially in the economic interest of the entitled party, as being forced acceptances of money in settlement; the conception of money as specifically a government institution; and a few other such aberrations of monetary theory, all essentially trace back to the misunderstanding that money, by the very concept, is a legal medium of payment[34] and to the exaggerated [54] significance attached by no small number of monetary theorists to the very 'function of money as medium of payment'.

[55]


## VIII. MONEY AS A MEDIUM OF HOARDING, CAPITAL ACCUMULATION, AND TRANSFERS OF WEALTH IN TIME AND SPACE

In ordinary life, hoarding is understood to be the accumulation and preservation of rare and valuable movable goods for occasional extraordinary use or for the mere joy of possession. For a good to be a suitable medium of hoarding, it must be durable, valuable, capable of being preserved (or hidden) with as little economic sacrifice and trouble as possible and, above all, be secure against any appreciable reduction in its use value and, with the growing importance of trade, especially also in its exchange value. In the self-contained households of the primitive economy, therefore, the goods used for hoarding, which by its nature is older than the phenomena of goods trading and money, are chiefly (apart from goods accumulated for the mere joy of possession) the above-mentioned kinds of rare and valuable goods that are suitable for one's (occasional) own use and for unilateral transfers and, with the progressive occupational division of labour and developing goods trade, increasingly also trade goods, though at first and immediately not necessarily those commodities that had become generally used media of exchange.

The properties required for a suitable medium of hoarding, that is to say, are not necessarily and everywhere found in sufficient degree in the usual media of exchange. Under certain circumstances, rather, a good may be the most suitable medium of exchange yet a more or less unsuitable medium of hoarding. Economic history offers us examples of situations in which certain goods (domestic animals, bricks of tea, slaves, etc.) function as media of exchange while **[56]** others (precious metals, precious stones, pearls, and other precious objects) are preferred media of hoarding. It is imprecise to speak of a preferred use of money, to say nothing of a function of money (quite simply money!) as a medium of hoarding.

Generally used media of exchange frequently become the preferred media of hoarding and in places where coined precious metals circulate tend to become almost exclusively used as media of hoarding, especially in advanced stages of civilization; but this is not completely explained by the fact that some of the most important properties that help turn certain commodities into generally used media of exchange are also of decisive influence in their being chosen as media of hoarding. In addition, there is also an inner connection between the function of certain commodities as money and their being chosen for the purpose of hoarding.

With the progressive occupational division of labour and the growing dependence of individual households on the market, trade goods in particular gain in importance for hoarding purposes, and among these most preferably the intermediaries of exchanges. Commonly, when a person who hoards trade goods of another kind wants to use the accumulated stock, he has to exchange them first for the general medium of exchange, while a person who has hoarded the latter avoids (or has already got past) the trouble, uncertainty, and economic sacrifices of such a transaction. Only those commodities that exhibit the properties of durability, high value, and relative stability of value and can be stored at little cost and trouble are suitable for hoarding, and among goods of this kind quite particularly the generally used medium of exchange. Conversely, the special suitability of a good for hoarding and its consequent widespread use for the above purpose is one of the most important causes of its increased marketability and thus of its suitability as medium of exchange. It is in the nature of this relation that with the development of trade precisely the generally used media of exchange and, as soon as the precious metals function as media of exchange, these latter regularly also become preferred media of hoarding.

The above holds true not only for hoarding, that is, for the accumulation and storage of valuable and rare movable assets [57] for uncertain or extraordinary consumption requirements, but also for the accumulation of movable productive assets, that is, for capital accumulation; as soon as chiefly money is hoarded, capital accumulation requires only one step beyond hoarding, that is, the additional intention of creating income.[35]

With an advanced division of labour, the producer depends on the market for the required means of production just as much as the consumer does for consumption goods. Even someone who accumulates assets for productive purposes will therefore make sure of the means of production that he will require in the future by having a stock of tradable goods, but most expediently and economically of all, a stock of money, and therefore, as a rule, will accomplish capital accumulation in money; all the more so, the more advanced the economy. In the latter, money will, as a rule, also be the most expedient means for accumulating movable productive assets.

For the same reasons and under the same limiting assumptions, money is also preferably employed when it is a question not of hoarding or of accumulating capital but only of exchanging less durable or less stable-valued goods for more durable or more stable-valued ones in order to save the wealth they represent from destruction (to maintain one's economic position) or to transfer it into future economic periods. Likewise, for the reasons set out above, money is especially suitable for the interlocal transfer of wealth so far as it can be transported easily and with relatively little cost, for example, precious-metal money; and in fact it is often employed for the above purposes, but that is no reason for speaking of a function of money for the above purposes.

   [58]


# IX. MONEY AS INTERMEDIARY IN CAPITAL TRANSACTIONS

As soon as developed media of exchange are functioning, it is usual in those cases in which it is not a question of a 'lease' (in the sense of BGB.f.d.D.R. [Bürgerliches Gesetzbuch für das Deutsche Reich] §§598 ff.) or the rental of an object (*ibid.* §§535 ff.) but rather of a loan (in the sense of ibid. §§607 ff.) that the delivery of movable assets for temporary use in the legal form of a loan tends to take place most advantageously in quantities of the generally used medium of exchange (for reasons arising from what has already been said), especially when the latter, as tends to be characteristic of the money of developed economies, exhibits a high degree of fungibility, which for metallic money is still considerably increased by coinage and various government measures (see chapter V). In the age of money economies, the recipient of a consumption loan granted in 'money form' regularly receives the quantity of assets transferred to him in the form most suitable for his use (apart from obtaining on credit the consumption articles he directly requires); the borrower of a sum of money for production purposes as a rule receives such a sum in the form of entrepreneurial assets most suitable for his business (apart, for example, from obtaining on credit the means of production he directly requires). Where precious metals or coins minted from them already circulate as generally used media of exchange, no form of a loan tends to be more desired by the borrower, and likewise no form of investment property more desired by those who seek to draw an income from the transfer of goods to other persons in the legal form of a loan, than that of money capital: on the one hand, for the reason given above, on the other hand, because of the definiteness of what is to be given and what is to be returned and the relatively great 'stability of value' of the precious metals, which is especially important for credit transactions. Essentially because of its function as intermediary in the economy's entire trade in goods, money also becomes **[59]** the chief intermediary in capital transactions, the most important medium in loan contracts. Indeed, apart from the function of money as medium of exchange (as intermediary on the commodity market!) and its use as preferred means of hoarding and capital accumulation, no other function of it in fact claims such considerable quantities of money and is of such great importance for the economy as the function of money as intermediary in capital transactions (on the 'money market'!).

**[60]**

## X. MONEY AS 'MEASURE OF PRICE' (INDICATOR OF PRICE)

If it is stipulated, as a demand of justice, that in an exchange of goods each of the two contracting parties receive and must receive goods of equal value (an equal 'quantity of value'), for otherwise one party loses as much as the other gains – *quidquid alicui adicitur alibi detrahitur* – there follows the necessity for normal trade, as has been repeated countless times since **[61]** Aristotle,[36] of measuring the values of the goods to be exchanged before concluding the deal and of equating them on the basis of this measurement. According to the above doctrine this happens in such a way that the values of the goods to be exchanged are measured by money, that is, the money unit, and on this basis goods of equal value (goods comprising equal quantities of value) are given up for one another. Money thus functions in goods trade as a measure of value – as an abstract quantum of value by which the 'quanta of value comprised' in the other market goods are measured and the equalization of their values in the exchange of goods becomes possible.[37]

This doctrine, which appears in the most varied forms and modifications among economic theorists, especially those concerned with monetary and price theory, and which **[62]** is supported by a popular prejudice to which it owes its origin and probably also its persistence, is founded on a twofold error: first, the popular error that in an exchange of goods both parties must receive equal amounts, for otherwise one party loses as much as the other gains; second, the error, no less widespread among economic theorists who ascribe to money a special function as measure of price, that the values of the goods to be exchanged can and must be measured beforehand (before the exchange!) for a normal exchange of goods to take place at all (for the required equality of values of the goods to be exchanged to be realized).

The first-mentioned view is above all contrary to the purposes that economizing persons pursue, as experience shows, when trading in goods. As a rule they perform acts of exchange only when each of the two contracting parties has the prospect of gaining an advantage for his economic position (for his supply of goods), and only within the limits set by this consideration. To establish an 'equality of value' of the traded goods, in whatever sense this may be understood, is no intention of the traders. Economizing persons do not strive to exchange goods that satisfy equal needs (Aristotle), equal 'utilities' (Condillac), equal 'quantities of labour' contained in the goods (Ricardo) or equal 'production costs' (J.B. Say), services of equal value for both traders (Bastiat), 'goods of the same overall economic usefulness' (Goldschmidt) nor indeed 'equal quantities of fungible use value contained in the goods' (Knies). Rather, both contracting parties normally trade to assure better and more complete satisfaction of their needs than would be the case without the exchange, in other words, to reap a gain.

Yet the striving of economic agents, that is, of both contracting parties, to gain an economic advantage from the exchange of goods, as from all other economic acts, is not only the true cause of the emergence of trade in goods but also the decisive consideration in price formation. In exchange for the other's goods, each of the two contracting parties offers the other only such a quantity of his own goods as gives him the prospect of reaching the above goal. **[63]** For the goods to be acquired he normally offers and delivers only such quantities of his own good as permit him to gain an economic advantage, with the haggling over price mainly referring only to the greater or lesser share of the advantage to be obtained by each of the two parties, or else causing the exchange in question not to take place at all. The effective prices of goods are the end result, not the precondition, of the above process of price formation. It is fanciful to suppose that even before the exchange, certain quantities of exchange value are contained in ('comprised by') the goods to be exchanged and that these quantities of exchange value are measured, before price is established, by the exchange value of the money unit (by the abstract quantity of exchange value represented by it) and that a 'value equivalence' of the goods to be exchanged is thus established.[38] Actually, the process of price formation [64] requires neither previous measurement of the quantities of exchange value supposedly existing in the goods nor any other measurement by abstract 'magnitudes of value'. Even if the contracting parties in exchange transactions did intend to measure the exchange values of the goods to be exchanged by the exchange value of money (perhaps the exchange value of the money unit) before entering into agreement, one still could not see how they could realize this intention, since a piece of money is as useless for this purpose as it is superfluous.

It is an untenable idea that before every exchange of goods the exchange values of the goods to be exchanged must be, or actually are, measured by the exchange value of money (of the money unit) and that in this sense money is a measure of price.[39]

If one may speak at all of a function of money as a measure of price in a way corresponding to actual circumstances, [65] one must do so only in a fundamentally different sense.

As soon as media of exchange are functioning on the markets of a country and the money economy increasingly penetrates all walks of life, trading in goods regularly takes place through the intermediary of money. On every market of a money economy and at every point in time there thus exist, as the result of economic interests concentrating and operating on the market, for all or at least for most of the commodities offered there, a large or small number of prices (though mostly not at all uniform!) expressed in money units; these prices provide at least a valuable reference point for judging the actual exchange relations of market goods and their variations on the same market, and likewise for comparing the exchange relations of goods on different markets – in other words, for a survey far simpler than that gained by the knowledge of barter prices and yet far more exact than the latter. In this sense neither money as such nor the money unit, both of which are useless for the above purpose, but rather the actual money prices of market goods are to be described as highly significant (for practical purposes) and as clear indicators of the exchange relations of market goods and their variations, while the money unit is to be described as a measure not of the quantities of exchange value contained in goods but rather of money prices, in the very sense in which the money unit (for example, the mark in Germany!) is the measure of all other monetary quantities.

**[66]**

# XI. MONEY AS STANDARD OF THE EXCHANGE VALUE OF GOODS

1. Introduction. Establishing a measure of the inputs and results of economic activities, one's own and those of persons with whom we are connected by business or have other social relations, is of the greatest practical importance in very many cases of private and public life (in the sharing of inheritances and other divisions of wealth, in marriage contracts, in credit transactions, in the assessment of taxes, in the fixing of property damages, etc.); indeed it is the foundation and prerequisite of purposive action. And establishing a measure of the striking differences in the importance of goods or combinations of goods for the economic activities of individuals or groups of persons who possess these goods or intend to acquire them is the indispensable prerequisite of appropriate economizing in numerous instances of economic life (in sales, mortgages, compensations, expropriations, insurance, calculations of profitability, etc.).

In an era of barter one could arrive at a precise estimate of the wealth or the periodic receipts of a person only by listing the components of his wealth in kind or the inflows to his household in kind. The oldest reports on the wealth and revenue of certain individuals or groups of persons are therefore of this kind. Figures are given for the flocks, landed estates, slaves, etc. making up their wealth, or lists of the kinds and quantities of goods (cattle, sheep, grain, butter, cheese, wine, honey, flax, etc.) available for consumption by the persons in question during specified periods of time. In the same way, the importance of individual goods and combinations of goods (especially also their relative importance) for the economic activities of the owner or user in that age can be assessed only through **[67]** knowledge of the natural qualities of the goods and their positions in the economies of the persons considered.

The clumsiness of this procedure, typical of the barter era, leads to restricting oneself, when ascertaining and describing someone's material circumstances, to listing the chief components of wealth or periodic receipts, but especially to listing those goods (such as, depending on place and time, cattle, reindeer, camels, and other herd animals, slaves, plots of land, etc.) that permit a conclusion about the general economic position of the persons in whose wealth and revenues one is interested. This is a deficiency of the above-mentioned practice, compounded by the still greater one that even the enumerated assets are mostly specified only by kind and quantity, while their quality is mostly disregarded or can be taken into account only in a manner as cumbersome as it is inaccurate.

This deficiency is remedied only slightly by the valuations already characteristic of the barter economy. When discussing the emergence of media of exchange (see footnote 18), I already pointed out that in those stages of a people's economic development in which there can yet be no question of exchange, let alone of mediation of exchanges by money, certain valuations of goods by means of other goods, or at least something like that, nevertheless do occur. Above all, rough valuations of goods by their use values, although of a subjective nature, basically depending on the personality and wealth of the possessor, may yet achieve a kind of objective significance (because of the uniformity of needs and economic circumstances of one's peers at low levels of civilization). I also mentioned the fact that even in the period of economic development that is essentially without trade, and still more so in the period of barter, relations of unilateral obligation and unilateral performance can be observed; but, in order to be able to be carried out, these are in many cases alternatively defined (are specified in different goods), for otherwise the obligated party might not at all be able to fulfil his obligation nor might the entitled party at all be able **[68]** to obtain what was due to him (cf. VI, pp. [47] ff.). But every alternatively specified delivery of goods presupposes a value relation between the goods, or at least something like that. Since these relations are naturally limited to a narrow range of goods and mostly are quite rough, however, both of these kinds of value relation are of very limited significance both for the emergence of money (see footnote 18) and also for estimating the wealth and periodic revenues of economic agents, and likewise for assessing the relative importance of individual goods for the economic activities of their owners.

Even when barter gains in extent and importance and numerous prices are actually formed, an estimate of a person's wealth and revenue and even the appraisal of individual goods on the basis of barter prices is as difficult as its results are uncertain; for the number of traded goods is naturally small, yet their possible combinations are numerous – and barter prices therefore offer a basis for valuations as inadequate as it is hard to assess. At the time of Homer, barter was already highly developed among the Greeks, and in the acquisition of substantial items of wealth, as even today on many barter markets, the larger of the domestic animals must have been preferably accepted in payment; that is why he could value their heroes' arms in cattle, even though his assessments could not claim meticulous exactness. But it would certainly not have been easy for him, had he tried, to estimate the wealth or the annual revenue of Ulysses or Priam in cattle with any degree of exactness – even being allowed the widest limits of poetic licence.

As soon as trade in goods becomes a routine matter and its development and that of the money economy cause more and more goods and eventually even plots of land and the rights bound up with them to be regularly both acquired for and sold for money, that is, as soon as essentially only money prices appear, but these to the widest extent, a new method arises, inordinately valuable for the needs of practical life, of forming a judgment about one's own and other people's wealth and about the relative importance [69] of certain goods and combinations of goods for the economy. Whoever wants to make a judgment of this sort can now do so in a greatly simplified and very clear-cut manner by ascertaining the amounts of money for which the goods in question are likely to be sold or bought on the market (their 'money values') or by having them reported to him. Now in many cases of economic life one no longer needs a list of the components of a fortune or an income to be informed of their sizes, nor does one need an exact description of an economic object to assess its relative economic importance. For the above purpose, it is enough now to know the 'money value', the monetary 'exchange equivalent', of the goods or combinations of goods in question, more exactly: the money prices for which these are likely to be acquired or sold, depending on place and time.[40]

If the rights and obligations of economic agents [Menger's 'Wirtschaftsobjekte' to be read as 'Wirtschaftssubjekte' in this sentence] estimated in money are also taken into account in this valuation, we can in fact, by determining the exchange value so defined of the 'goods and combinations of goods' considered (their 'money value'!), assess the wealth of the economic agents concerned and the relative importance for their economic activities of the goods in their possession, an assessment that is as straightforward as it is clear and also – despite the inherent defects of this procedure! – far more exact than the analogous results in the age of barter. Beyond that, the question could indeed arise whether the 'money value' of goods is not of still more general significance for the economic life of socially organized human beings, whether it is not also an expression of the significance that particular goods and combinations of goods have acquired for the population as a whole.

2. Should the valuation of goods in money be regarded as measurement of their exchange value by the monetary unit? The valuation of goods, especially in money, has a certain [70] superficial similarity to measurement, a procedure by which we determine the as yet unknown magnitude of an object by comparison with a known magnitude of the same kind taken as a unit.

If the 'trade equivalent' of a good in the above sense is called its 'exchange value' and the amount of money involved (the monetary 'trade equivalent' of a good) is called its 'exchange value' in the strict sense, then indeed the act of valuation – the procedure by which, in a specific case, the previously unknown 'money equivalent' of a good is determined and expressed in money units – represents a kind of 'measurement of the exchange value' of the good, at least superficially.

For example, if by an act of valuation the money value, at first unknown to us, of a good is established at 100 marks, that of another good at 30 marks, the money value of the assets, so far unknown to us, of one economic agent at 100 000 marks, and that of another at 40 000 marks, and if the monetary 'trade equivalents' so established, which permit a comparison, are called the 'exchange values' of the above goods and combinations of goods, then one may regard the above valuation procedures, which constantly recur in ordinary life and are highly important in practice, as measurement of the 'exchange value of the goods' and regard money or the monetary unit as a 'measure' of the latter, even if only figuratively.

One must not downright accuse of an unrealistic approach even those who interpret the 'exchange values of goods' (in a sense differing from the above!) as the economic power of disposal that the possession of goods affords us over the commodities available on the markets, in particular over the corresponding 'money equivalents' (that is, as the 'exchange power' of the goods in question!) and who call money the standard of 'exchange value' so interpreted. If no other sense is read into the words used above than that in the age of money economies the wealth of an economic agent and the importance of particular goods for him are mainly expressed, and in a way measured, by the 'trade equivalents' of the goods he owns, in particular by their 'money values' (in other words, that we 'measure' the economic power of disposal over market goods which an asset [71] affords us by its 'trade equivalent' expressed in money units), then this conception, too, although in many respects it needs to be specified in more detail and corrected, cannot simply be called unrealistic.

3. The practical significance of the valuation of goods in money. The great practical importance for all of economic life of ascertaining the 'exchange value' of goods expressed in money and the substantial advance that this valuation procedure signifies (despite its various theoretical and practical shortcomings) as compared with barter, discussed above, is already clear from what has been said. For most practical purposes, this renders possible an incomparably more clear-cut and exact measurement of inputs and results of economic activities than with barter.[41] One of the most advanced and meticulous younger representatives of our science characterizes it in the following way:

'Only the general adoption of the valuation of goods in money makes possible accurate calculations of production costs and revenues in individual enterprises and so their detailed comparison and the exact quantitative assessment of the success of production for the wealth of the entrepreneur. The valuation in money of all goods and services entering or leaving the enterprise is the necessary basis for every calculation of profitability and so for careful [72] management. Furthered by competition among the individual enterprises, it contributes substantially to making the principle of maximum efficiency prevail in their management. In particular, it provides for an accurate calculation of prices and a mathematically accurate estimate of the limits of profit and loss.'[42]

Obviously, the valuation of goods in money becomes more important for people's economic deliberations and actions the more generally money performs its mediating function in trade, the more – with the development of the division of labour and the money economy – individual economic units depend on the market, and, finally, the sounder and the more stable a country's monetary system is.

4. Under different conditions of place and time the money value (the 'exchange value' expressed in money) of goods is not an appropriate standard of the inputs and results of economic activities. Under the same conditions of place and time (on the same market and at the same point in time) the 'money value' of the wealth or income of a person is also a more or less appropriate expression of his real wealth and real income. If the money value and the market conditions are known to us, it is possible for us to form a judgment on this basis of the wealth of the person in question that is adequate for most purposes of practical life (although not impeccable theoretically!). In this way we can also compare the material circumstances of different persons living at the same time and in the same place. Under such conditions, the 'money value' of certain goods also offers us a sufficient basis for judging their relative importance for an economy. Thus, the 'money value' of the wealth and income of a person is in fact, under the same conditions of place and time and for most practical economic purposes, a sufficiently accurate measure of the means available to the person in question and the results of his economizing; and the 'money value' of certain goods is such a measure of their relative economic importance for their owner.

[73] The same does not hold for different markets or different points in time. On different markets and at different points in time, equal amounts of money and likewise equal nominal wealth or nominal income do not necessarily assure us of a command over equal stocks of goods or (even under the same subjective conditions) of the same economic position.

Even apart from the difference in subjective circumstances, a person with an income of 5000 francs will be able to satisfy most needs in quite different degree depending on whether he lives in a big city or in a small market town (for example, in Paris or in a little Romanian country town). Likewise, it would be wrong to conclude that two persons, one living in the fifteenth and the other in the nineteenth century but with the same nominal incomes, were thereby afforded equal economic command over market goods, let alone that they had the same standard of living.

The explanation of this phenomenon lies in the different exchange relations between money and goods observable on different markets and even on the same market at different points in time – in what has often been called the 'interlocally and intertemporally different purchasing powers of money' (its exchange value expressed in commodities) or also 'the interlocal differences and variations in the outer exchange value of money'.

5. The search for a good of universal and invariable outer exchange value. The obvious fact that equal quantities of money (for example, equal quantities of coined precious metal) on different markets and even on the same market at different points in time do not give us the same command over market goods, which makes for quite noticeable differences and

fluctuations in economic life, has led people to the obvious idea of searching among the objects of trade for another good (or sets and combinations of goods!) that might serve the above purpose outright or at least better than precious-metal money. This is the **[74]** problem of identifying a good of universal and invariable outer exchange value.[43]

The significance that a good with such 'constancy of value' would have for practical economic life cannot be overestimated. A definite income consisting of this good would assure us, for example, a definite style of life in all places and at all times; a definite quantity of the good in question would in general – regardless of local and temporal market conditions – assure us the means of realizing definite economic ends. A good of this kind would also be highly important for long-term credits, supposedly invariable perpetual payments, etc. If there were such a good, it would be possible to eliminate much of the uncertainty currently prevailing in economic life.

A good of this kind would be of great importance for the theory and practice of human economy for still another reason. It would offer us a standard equally applicable to all markets and the remotest points in time for assessing the relative wealth of economic agents.

The search for a solution to the above problem, which has often and indeed not without good reason been called the squaring of the circle in economics, turns out, however, to be hopeless.

Both from experience and from impartial analysis of market phenomena, it is clear **[75]** that there exists on present-day markets no object of trade whose exchange relation with all other goods (with each one of them or with any set of goods in whatever quantitative and qualitative combination) would be the same everywhere and would remain unchanged in the course of time; indeed, such a good is unthinkable in our present-day market conditions. A good of this kind would necessarily presuppose the stability of exchange relations among all goods, including those of market goods (or their being identical on all markets). Only with stable prices, perhaps with prices uniformly, strictly, and perpetually regulated by government for an administrative district, would goods of stable exchange value in the above sense be thinkable (or more exactly, could any item of trade – including money! – be used for the above purpose). But under present-day market conditions, trying to find a good of this kind is altogether hopeless.

The idea of choosing goods of relatively constant 'inner exchange value' for the above purpose is fundamentally flawed (on the particular factors determining their price movements, see section 7 below). That there are goods in the economy whose 'inner exchange value' is fairly constant is beyond doubt, as is the fact that the goods in question therefore also have more stable outer exchange value, of course, than do market goods not satisfying the above presupposition. No one doubts, for example, that the precious metals or the most commonly used cotton fabrics (because of their relatively constant inner exchange values!) also give us command over the other market goods in a way that is less dependent on conditions of the time than would be the case, say, with hops or items of fashion. But this procedure is deficient because even the choice of goods whose inner exchange value is relatively constant would not eliminate the influence of the factors determining price movements that operate on the side of all other goods.

The problem of identifying an absolutely stable measure of the outer exchange value of goods, which has occupied so many outstanding minds so deeply, may be regarded as having been clarified in theory by science, but as unsolvable. Yet the problem of identifying a relatively stable measure of outer exchange value essentially coincides with the problem of identifying a good of relatively stable inner exchange value and will be treated in the next section[s].

[76] 6. Attempts at measurement of interlocal differences and of variations in the outer exchange value of money. Ever since monetary theorists realized that precious-metal money has different and variable outer exchange values under different conditions of place and time and that it is hopeless to search for other goods or combinations of goods with an outer exchange value that is everywhere the same and invariable, their efforts have been directed to numerically identifying the interlocal differences and the variations in the outer exchange value of money, that is, to measuring it. The idea was obvious. If the differences and variations in the outer exchange value of money were acknowledged and if the uncertainty that they cause in economic life could not be overcome by a good with an outer exchange value that is always and everywhere the same, they should at least be measured so that in this way the above element of uncertainty in business life would be brought under control, instead of its controlling us.

Research on the above problem aims at numerically identifying the general purchasing power of money (the exchange relation between money and goods bought and sold in general, goods by and large, taking into account different markets and different points in time). It would be solved if we were able to ascertain, for example, that on one market the same sum of money can or could buy – even if only in general (by and large) – a quantity of goods that is larger by one third, say, than that on a particular other market, or that on the same market the same sum of money can or could buy in general one sixth less, say, or one fourth more of goods than at another point in time, perhaps a century earlier or later.

Likewise, the problem would essentially be solved if, for example, it could be ascertained that by and large (as an overall average) the same quantities of commodities can or could be acquired for money on one market at the same time dearer or cheaper by a definite percentage than on another market, or on the same market at a certain point in time dearer or cheaper by a definite percentage than at an earlier or later point in time.

[77] The measurement and comparison under discussion here of the intertemporally or interlocally different purchasing powers of money can be undertaken in quite different ways. If it is a question of assessing variations in the general purchasing power of money (the exchange value of the latter

expressed in commodities!) on one and the same market (for example, in Hamburg), then it is probably the simplest procedure first to add up the prices observed on the market in question at a certain point in time for the respective units of a set as large as possible of various commodities (the so-called unit prices) and to compare the result with the similarly obtained totals of prices at other points in time on the same market for the same set of commodities. The comparison of these so-called index numbers provides us with a basis – in many respects quite deficient, but for some practical purposes still useful – for considering the question whether the prices of goods on a certain market have in general (by and large) gone up or down between two points in time.

The above procedure is undoubtedly improved in certain respects if, instead of the prices of the moment, subject to many kinds of random influence, and instead of price averages calculated only for short time periods, such averages are ascertained for longer time periods, for example, for five- or ten-year periods, and used as the basis for the above calculations. The results of this procedure permit a comparison of the 'general' movement of prices from one period to another (for example, from one five- or ten-year period to another) that is in many respects more exact and reliable than is the case with the first-mentioned procedure.

The fact that the prices of various kinds of commodities are not equally important for the purpose of the above schematic summary of price movements (think, for example, of the prices of indigo and wheat, of pepper and potatoes, of silk, whose unit price is exceedingly high, and of cotton, whose unit price is relatively very low!) has led a number of authors to base their calculations not simply on the unit prices (the prices of unit quantities) but also to take account of the quantities consumed or imported of the goods in question in order thus to recognize the different degrees of importance [78] of different commodities for the economy and to take account of the above reservations about the accuracy and especially also about the practical value of the construction of index numbers on the basis of mere unit prices.

With appropriate modifications, the above methods may also be applied to calculations concerned not with the movements of prices of goods on the same market but rather with comparison of the general price levels of commodities on different markets at the same point in time or over the same period of time (for example, a comparison of the general price levels on the Hamburg and London markets).

The schematic results obtained by the above methods concerning the movement of prices on the same market at different points in time and periods of time or concerning differences in price levels on different markets at the same point in time or period of time belong first and immediately to the sphere of price theory. But they are also important for the problem, pointed out at the start, of measuring the differences (by time and/or place) in the purchasing powers of money; for they permit a certain conclusion, though not strictly to be vouched for, about the greater or lesser outer exchange value (the greater or lesser purchasing power) of money at different points in time or periods of time on the same market and at the same point in time or period of time on different markets. For it is clear that the higher the index numbers calculated for certain points in time and on certain markets, the lower, by and large, may the purchasing power of money be assumed to be at the points in time and on the markets concerned (in comparison with the purchasing power of money at other points in time and on other markets); and conversely the higher, the lower the corresponding index numbers.

It goes without saying that when ascertaining the outer exchange value (expressed in commodities) of money (the general 'purchasing power' of the latter), one has to keep in mind not only the differences among money units (especially, that is, changes in coins, a possible depreciation of paper money, etc.) existing on different markets or at different points in time but also the fact that changes in the metal content of coins and the depreciation of paper money do not find expression immediately and simply in the exchange relation between money [79] and goods. But the main difficulty of the above procedure, especially in calculations for modern times, is not the question of how to take account of mint parities and exchange rates. It lies rather in circumstances whose extraordinary complexity makes it most difficult to pay attention to them.

When it is to be undertaken for different markets or points in time, even the calculation of the exchange relation between money and a particular kind of good (for example, wheat) requires that the underlying prices refer not only to identical quantity units but also to identical qualities of the good in question, a requirement that leads to major difficulties with a considerable number of goods (think of dwellings, labour services, domestic animals, and especially also of quality changes in many goods because of technical and other kinds of economic progress, etc.) and with a few kinds of goods to nearly insuperable difficulties. This is the main reason why even in the simple calculation of index numbers (which are nonetheless supposed to make us aware of the price movements of market goods by and large), only the prices of a relatively small number of homogeneous (fungible!) market goods can be taken into account, while the countless prices of goods with statistically not ascertainable quality differences must be left out. While index numbers ought to present a schematic picture of the overall price movement (if they are to provide a basis for assessing changes in the outer exchange value of money), for the most part they actually provide only a survey of changes in the wholesale prices of a relatively small number of arbitrarily chosen fungible commodities on individual markets (in part taking account of the quantities imported and consumed of the commodities). Thus, even with regard to particular markets, they doubtlessly provide only a very insufficient basis for assessing the changes in the purchasing power of money, and most certainly no adequate basis for a universal survey of them.

In calculating index numbers, almost equally great difficulties of applying the statistical method make us neglect retail prices, which are highly important for a satisfactory solution of the above problem but statistically difficult to obtain, or make us include them quite inadequately.

[80] Finally, the requirement arising from the nature of the above problem, namely, that in the calculation of index numbers the quantities bought and sold of the individual goods be taken into account, is either overlooked altogether by most authors or else the quantities bought and sold of the goods, exceedingly hard to obtain statistically, are replaced by the quantities imported or by estimates of the quantities produced, although neither of these are in any way immediately connected with the problem of determining the price movements, which, after all, become manifest only in the trading of goods. In the first-mentioned connection, think of goods produced at home and still largely traded there and think of commodities imported but then re-exported, either unprocessed or processed, without being traded domestically; in the latter connection, think of the large quantities of goods consumed by their producers, especially farmers, without being traded, etc.

The great practical value of the surveys of price movements undertaken on a statistical basis, and the great progress made therein as compared with some earlier attempts of this kind, hardly need mentioning, despite the numerous deficiencies of the above procedure. As compared with attempts – still to be encountered in the classical school of economics – to draw conclusions about the value of money and its movements from deficient series of or from individual, often uncritically recorded, grain prices, wage rates, etc., they undoubtedly represent an advance as great and useful as it is commendable.[44]

7. <u>On interlocal differences in and movements of the so-called inner exchange value of money.</u> In the preceding sections I dealt with the outer exchange value of money (expressed in commodities), with its local differences and its movements, and finally with attempts to find a measure for it that takes account of different conditions of place and time. Basically different from the questions just dealt with (which chiefly concerned the power of disposal, associated with the possession of money, over [81] greater and lesser quantities of goods traded on different markets or at different points in time) is the problem of the so-called inner exchange value of money.

I shall first try to clarify the problem itself, which is often lumped together with that of the 'outer value of money'.

Exchange ratios among goods are the result of determining factors operating on both of the objects traded. It is unthinkable that the exchange ratio between two goods should be traced exclusively to determining factors operating on only one of the two objects traded. Yet, already existing exchange ratios among goods may certainly be modified by a change in determining factors operating on only one of the objects traded. In no case are the constituent factors of price formation as a whole active only on one side of the goods to be exchanged, although the merely modifying ones may be so occasionally.

What has been said holds also for market prices. The exchange ratios between goods traded and money are always the result of determining factors both on the side of the goods and on the side of money. In a particular case, though, the fluctuations in the money prices of commodities may be caused by a change in the determining factors of price formation that occurs with only the one or only the other of the objects in question here – either on the side of the goods traded or on the side of money.

The important question of the nature and extent of the influence that a change in the determining factors of price formation on the side of money exerts on the exchange ratios of money and the goods trade, that is, on market prices, is the problem of the so-called inner exchange value of money and its movements.

8. The popular conception of the constancy of the inner exchange value of money. It is an inaccuracy typical of popular economic thinking and continually found in many economic situations that the movements of the inner exchange value of money remain unnoticed. Businessmen are commonly inclined to trace every change in the market prices of goods (every shift in the exchange [82] ratio between money and the goods traded) to determining factors acting only on the goods, but to see in money an object of trade uninfluenced by the determining factors that modify the above exchange ratio, in this sense an 'unchangeable value quantity'.

That old error is still noticeable everywhere in practical economic life: in everyday language, in the economic calculation of the rentier, in the popular value judgment about perpetual money annuities, even in the balance sheets of the manufacturer and of the merchant.[45] The fact that all goods regularly tend to be valued in sums of money (by their 'money value') but that money is not valued in quantities of goods traded (by its 'commodity value'), in other words, the fact that in contrast to the eagerly watched changes in the 'money value of goods traded', changes in the 'commodity value of money' remain almost completely unnoticed in common life, is probably the main reason for the above phenomenon. In the economic thinking and behaviour of the masses, money, which indeed occupies a distinctive position in the economy in many respects, is regarded as an exceptional phenomenon in the above respect also, that is, as an anomaly of the economy.

9. The scientific conception of the inner exchange value of money and its movements. The above popular conception, shared almost without exception by the writers of antiquity[46] and the monetary theorists of the Middle Ages, was not able to hold its ground against the advances in economic research. Any impartial analysis of market phenomena makes us recognize the far-reaching influence exerted on the exchange ratio between money and the goods traded by the variations in the quantity of money in circulation, the variations in the economy's demand for circulating media, the increasing or decreasing production costs of the money metals, the more [83] or less

increasing use of document money, and many other changes in the determining factors of price formation occurring only on the side of money.

Science advanced only very gradually, however, to the above insight, which has since been confirmed by the widest experience. Even Aristotle knew about fluctuations in the value of money. But it was only Bodin (under the influence of the flow of precious metals from America to Western Europe and the price revolution that it caused, especially in the middle and the second half of the sixteenth century) who fought effectively and with great clarity against the popular prejudice which prevented proper understanding,[47] while the rigorous scientific formulation of the above doctrine was undertaken only in our time.[48]

10. The idea of a universal and invariable standard of the 'inner exchange value' of goods. Ever since precious-metal money was also recognized as an object of trade influenced by the factors determining price formation, monetary theorists have been striving to discover some other market good whose exchange ratio against other goods is not influenced by determining factors on the side of this good. They are looking for a good whose outer exchange value (whose exchange ratio against all other goods), though it could after all be exposed to local differences and change, would still be subject only to effects of causes on the side of the latter (the other goods, [84] not the good in question of stable inner exchange value); they are looking for a good of universal and invariable 'inner exchange value'.

The significance of the discovery or invention of a good of this kind for the theory and practice of human economy would be scarcely less than that of a good of universal and invariable outer exchange value (see above, chapter XI, section 5). With its help we would be able correctly to assess the interlocal differences and the variations in the exchange ratios of all goods from a point of view of great practical importance. For if the exchange ratio between the first (the good of stable inner exchange value!) and any other good should undergo a change, we would know right away and without any further investigation that this difference or change traces to determining factors of price formation on the side of the latter (the commodity in question). As to the question, so inordinately difficult to decide at present, whether the cause of an observed shift in the exchange ratio between money and a commodity inheres in the former or in the commodity, any doubt would then be eliminated. A good of the above kind would provide an unfailing point of reference in the movement of prices that nowhere affords us a firm base.

A good of this kind would be of quite inestimable practical importance in another respect also. Whoever had a certain quantity of it at his disposal (for example, an annual income or a claim expressed in it) would then still be dependent in his economic activities and in his command over the other objects of trade on interlocal differences and variations in the exchange ratios of goods, but only insofar as the factors determining them (for example, a change in supply and demand, changes in the conditions of production and consumption, technical progress in production, etc.) were active on the side of the goods to be exchanged for the good of constant value. But he would be safeguarded against a change in his economic position as a result of a change in the 'inner exchange value' of the goods (of constant value) that make up his income, of the substance of his claim, etc.

First of all, as far as the particular difficulty of the theoretical clarification of the above problem is concerned, this seems to me to be exaggerated in any case.

[85] Yet it is likewise beyond all doubt that no object of trade is to be found on our markets whose exchange ratio against all other goods remains invariant over time, nor is there one for which the price-modifying influences operating on the other objects of trade do not assert themselves at all (thus, on our markets there is no object of trade whose 'outer' nor one whose 'inner exchange value' is the same everywhere and at all times). Nevertheless, a fundamental difference exists between the problem of identifying a good of stable outer exchange value and that of identifying one of stable inner exchange value. The chief difficulty in solving the first problem is how to take account of price-changing influences on all other market goods (of variation in their inner exchange values), while in solving the latter problem this difficulty is excluded from the start – by the very definition of the problem! The problem of identifying a good of constant inner exchange value is incomparably simpler than the analogous one of outer exchange value.

In addition, there is a fact of the greatest importance, especially for the question of putting the above idea into practice. Price-changing influences affect the same commodities partly in a positive and partly in a negative direction. They could accordingly cancel out in determining the price of the commodity in question. The price-changing influences affecting a certain object of trade alter the exchange ratio between it and all other goods (the actual price movement) only if no such cancelling-out occurs. The price of wheat, for example, will neither fall nor rise if an increase in supply has its effect cancelled by an increase in demand. Such inner balancing of positive and negative price-determining factors, making stability of the 'inner exchange value' of a specific good possible, is not inconceivable theoretically; a good of stable inner exchange value is not utterly unthinkable.

But it seems to me that even in practice the search for a good of stable 'inner value' should not be ruled out from the start. The fact that the quantities of certain goods reaching the market [86] may be regulated at will offers us the possibility of neutralizing the influences that would otherwise come from their side and modify their exchange ratios with other goods. With free trade, there are no goods whose 'inner exchange value' is invariable; but there may be goods whose 'inner exchange value' could possibly be kept unchanged if the quantities reaching the market were regulated for this purpose. This holds in particular for that object of trade that is primarily to be considered in the present context, money; for it is within the power of states and associations of states to regulate the quantity circulating in internal trade (by restriction of coinage or by promoting or restricting the efficacy of money-substituting institutions!). Even with respect to international trade, the possibility of regulating the inner exchange value of money does not seem to me to be utterly ruled out. The idea of an object of trade whose 'inner value', to stick with the metaphor, would always be held 'at the same level' is in no way self-contradictory, no economic squaring of the circle, especially with regard to money, where to some extent this happens automatically even now. It is not unthinkable to try to counteract the effects of the price-modifying influences that money left to itself would have on the prices of goods by influencing the quantity of money in circulation, especially of document money, and thus to create circulating media of constant value in the sense explained here.

It goes without saying that implementing the above idea would presuppose not only sufficient knowledge of the pertinent statistics but also correct theoretical understanding of the interconnection of price phenomena and the factors determining their variations. The practical difficulties and pitfalls of realizing the above idea must not be overlooked either.[49] At present, fluctuations in the world-market prices of the precious metals seem **[87]** to me to involve still lesser dangers than regulation of the inner exchange value of money by governments or social and political parties. Quite especially, one cannot overlook the difficulties that would accompany an international regulation of such an important matter. At any rate, it seems to me that the search for a stable standard (in the above sense) of the inner exchange value of goods involves a problem whose solution in theory is but a question of progress in scientific knowledge and whose solution in practice, to which the world economy might possibly be forced, does not presuppose unattainable conditions (this would be a matter not of absolute exactness, but only of a degree of exactness sufficient for practical purposes).

11. <u>The question whether particular price movements (or interlocal price differences) trace to causes on the side of money or on the side of traded goods.</u> The great practical interest attaching to isolated observation of movements of the 'inner exchange value' of money and of the influence of these movements on the formation of goods prices brought up the above question, particularly since the problem of establishing a stable standard of the outer exchange value of goods has faded into the background of scientific interest. Its solution has been sought by way of probabilistic inferences from price movements (that is, on the basis of price statistics), but without fully satisfactory results. If the statistical phenomenon of a uniform rise or fall of the money prices of all goods traded on all markets were to be observed, it would permit a probabilistic conclusion approaching certainty that the shift in the exchange ratio between goods and money traced to causes that had operated on money **[88]** (to a decline or rise of the 'inner exchange value' of money!); but even in this case one could not completely exclude the

possibility that the price shift was due to causes that had operated uniformly on all goods and all markets. – A shift in the money prices of all goods on all markets in the same direction, even though not uniform, would permit the almost as reliable probabilistic inference that the price change of the goods traded was the result of a combined operation of causes partly affecting money and partly (not uniformly!) affecting the goods. But even in this case an explanation of the price movement by determining factors operating (not uniformly) only on the goods traded would in no way lie outside the realm of possibility. Conversely, the rise or fall of the money prices of a single good or a relatively small number of goods traded, with the money prices of the other goods remaining unchanged, permits the probabilistic inference that the factors determining the price changes were active on the side of the goods in question, although even in this case the possibility of a contrary explanation is not to be ruled out entirely.

The above and similar conclusions are based on the principle that, among the various possible kinds of explanation of a shift in market prices, the one claiming the relatively highest degree of probability is the one that assumes the simultaneous appearance of price-changing influences operating in the same direction for the smallest possible number of objects of trade. A general rise of market prices, for example, could be explained in a far more probable way by a 'decline of the value of money' than by a simultaneous increase (not so easily assumed) in the 'inner exchange values' of all goods traded.

The more the movements of prices of various goods diverge in direction and degree, the less does mere observation of statistical facts permit an even fairly reliable conclusion like the above. Being only a probabilistic conclusion to start with, it fails almost completely in many observable instances. The question, very important in practice, whether an observed price movement [89] is caused by a change in the 'inner value' of money or of the individual goods or rather by a combination of both – which is really the question whether in the particular case the factors determining the price movement were connected with money or with the goods or with both sides – may never be answered in the above manner with full certainty, in many cases only with some degree of probability, and occasionally not at all. To say nothing of the question of measuring fluctuations of the 'inner values' of money and of the individual goods, especially in those cases in which the price movement represents the result of the combined activity of price-changing influences on both sides! What share of the price movement belongs to the change in the 'inner value of money' in such cases, and what share to the 'inner value' of the goods traded? The above procedure will provide no definite answers to questions like these.

Similar difficulties, although naturally in most cases not as great, arise (if the same procedure is employed) when we investigate the causes of interlocal differences in prices and especially of the share that possible interlocal differences in the inner exchange value of money have in them.

12. Whether the inner exchange value of money and its movements can be measured. The fact that the inner exchange value of money shows no constancy, uninfluenced by the diversity of conditions of place and time, has prompted efforts to measure its movements (and also its interlocal differences!). That this has been attempted almost without exception on the basis of price statistics could at first glance be interpreted as a misunderstanding about the true nature of the problem under discussion here. In general, the movement of prices of goods is the result of determining factors operating on the side of the goods traded just as much as on that of money. How then are we to identify from the interlocal differences or the movements of goods prices the differences and changes in the inner exchange value of money, let alone to measure it on this basis? There is, however, one possible exception to the obvious unreliability of a solution to this question on the basis of price statistics. [90] So far as the factors determining price movements operate on the side of the goods traded, they work partly in the positive and partly in the negative direction, or on some of the goods in a predominantly positive and on others in a predominantly negative direction (partly raising prices, partly reducing prices). Now it is not utterly unthinkable that in certain summary accounts of the price movements of a multiplicity of goods, the positive and the negative influences of factors determining price movements on the side of the goods traded (whether quite generally or at least by and large!) cancel out; so that in such cases the summary accounts of price movements for all or at least a large number of goods would basically show us only the direction and degree of the effects of the factors determining the price movement on the side of money (that is, the movement of the inner exchange value of money). All attempts at solving the above problem on the basis of price statistics start from this assumption.[50]

The above presupposition (the presupposition that in summary accounts of interlocal differences and of movements of prices of suitably chosen commodities or of quantities consumed, the effects of the negative and positive factors of price formation on the side of the traded goods cancel out, so that the price-changing influences on the side of money find unequivocal expression) is so far-fetched, however, and also so hard to test that even the most sensible methods of applying [91] this idea cannot lead to an entirely satisfactory result. All methods of identifying interlocal differences and the movement of the inner exchange value of money that are based on this presupposition are even basically arbitrary and unsupported.

The problem in measuring interlocal differences and the movement of the inner exchange value of money is how to separate the factors determining price formation and price movements on the side of money from those on the side of the goods traded. Moreover, the influence of price-movement determinants on the side of money is to be identified in direction and degree. A problem of this kind is by its very nature an analytical one; it cannot be solved by resorting exclusively to even the most exact statistical observation of price fluctuations, which, after all, result from price-movement determinants on both sides, nor by resorting exclusively to averages or other summary representations of price movements and conclusions based on them. Only an investigation that would make us recognize the factors actually determining price formation and price movements with regard to both money and goods traded and that would at the same time teach us to trace the effects of the various influences on price movements by direction and degree could clarify the above problem theoretically. But even then, answering the question whether and in what degree a movement of the inner exchange value of money had actually taken place in a given instance would still crucially depend on knowledge of the statistical relations involved, that is to say, on a careful and comprehensive statistical analysis not only of prices and their movements, but also of the (statistically representable) causes of the price movements.

Until then, any conclusion about the movement of the inner exchange value of money will be the result of freely assessing price statistics on the basis of pertinent theoretical understanding and our knowledge of the factors causing the movement of goods prices and of their magnitude.

[92]

# XII. THE CONCEPT OF MONEY AS DERIVED FROM ITS FUNCTIONS

The essence and concept of money are determined by its position in the national economy and by its functions in goods trade. No thing is in itself money because, for example, of its material and its technical properties or its external form, let alone because of mere acts of will of rulers (simply because of these circumstances!). On the other hand, a good of whatever kind, be it a commodity previously serving consumption or technical production, a raw material or a finished product, a metal weighed out, or a document capable of circulating, becomes money when and insofar as in the historical development of a people's trade in goods it actually acquires the function of a generally used intermediary of exchanges (or the functions deriving from that) and thus assumes that distinctive position in trade and in the national economy by virtue of which it becomes something unlike all other objects of trade whose exchange it mediates: an object of trade mediating the exchange of goods.

For the general concept of money it makes no difference whether a traded object performs the above functions more or less perfectly or inadequately. If it functions at all in the general way assumed here, then the object is money in any case, whether it functions well or badly, whether it is sound or pathological. The *assignats* and *mandats* of the French government and the bank notes, redemption bills, and anticipation bills of the Austrian government at the end of the eighteenth and beginning of the nineteenth centuries certainly functioned badly in the later phases of their circulation and were pathological money, which circulated, moreover, only because of unjust compulsion and abuse of both the note-issue prerogative and legal authority; still, so long as they actually performed the above functions in trade, they were undoubtedly money.

[93] It is likewise irrelevant for the general concept of money whether an object of trade has acquired the above functions automatically or by some sort of compulsion. Whether it is money that emerged automatically or money created and influenced in its development by government – in particular, money developed and perfected (or corrupted!) automatically or by government – in either case it is money when and insofar as it actually performs the functions of a generally used intermediary of trade in goods and capital (or the functions deriving from that), just as law, whether common law or statute law, is law in either case, that is, falls under the general concept of law.

For the same reasons, too, an object of trade becomes money – not, to be sure, in abstract generality, but always only within those limits of place and time in which it actually performs the functions under discussion here. What is money for one people is not necessarily money for other peoples, and what previously used to be money is nowadays often a commodity like any other on its markets. Indeed, experience shows that specific goods may even function as money only in certain strata of a country's population and even for certain transactions only, while in other strata of the population and for other transactions other kinds of goods perform the functions of a generally used (in this limited sense) intermediary of exchange, measure of value, etc., in other words, are money.

But neither the insight that it is not the technical nature of an object of trade or external influences in themselves but rather its actual functions in trade that cause it to become money (from the economic point of view!) nor the knowledge, no matter how exact, of the functions of money suffices for an understanding of its essence. We would gain only a very inadequate understanding of the essence of money if we were to consider its functions only in their outward coexistence and not their inner relations, particularly their genetic linkage, especially so if we did not take care to distinguish the original functions of money from the merely derivative ones, the essential from the merely accidental. All those definitions of money that are nothing other than a superficial stringing together of the functions and forms of money derived from observing the trade of modern civilized nations, [94] or nothing other than an arbitrary selection from these, fail to recognize the problem of the development of the concept of money and must be regarded as both inexact and, since they are mostly limited to the mere observation of money in its most modern manifestations, as ahistorical.

The original (primary) function of money, common to all its manifestations and stages of development, is that of a generally used intermediary of exchange. Already by itself, this function gives an object of trade the distinctive, exceptional position in goods trade and in the national economy that separates it, as an object of trade mediating the exchange of goods, from all other market goods and substantiates that peculiar and striking distinction between itself and all other objects of trade which in common speech is called the contrast between money and commodities (more precisely, between an intermediary of exchange and merchandise).

With a developing and intensifying trade in goods, however, this original function of money does not remain the only one. Precisely the objects of trade that have become generally used media of exchange tend also to take on a series of other functions in the economy, partly as a necessary consequence of their medium-of-exchange function and partly accidentally. As soon as essentially all or nearly all prices are in fact money prices, the valuation of goods at their exchange values expressed in money becomes a matter of course; hence the function of money as 'price indicator and standard of exchange value' (see chapter XI, section 1). The fact that in the developing money economy precisely the generally used media of exchange are adopted more and more for unilateral transfers and substitute performances is no accident either, but a natural consequence of the function of money as the generally used medium of exchange. It is not true that an object of trade functioning as the general intermediary of exchange only becomes money by assuming these derivative functions. On the contrary, the above derivative functions and kinds of use are merely a historical feature; they accompany the development of money but are not constituent elements in its emergence.

[95] This fact should not be overlooked in the development of the concept of money. It runs counter to the principles of accurate thinking to include the consequences of a phenomenon in its general concept and also to name, along with the essential characteristics of a phenomenon, derivative ones that may have their place only in its development. This is an error of definition even if it is assumed that the derivative phenomena are a necessary consequence of the phenomenon whose nature is to be defined, and all the more so when they accompany the phenomenon in question only usually or even only accidentally or when they appear only as artificial developments, perhaps brought about by government. Yet this error is committed by those economic theorists to whom both the fact that objects of trade that have become generally used media of exchange also regularly take on other functions in the economy in the course of their development, and the fact that a number of different coequal functions and uses are observable in historical moneys, justify their mechanically listing, even in the definition of the general concept of money, all the functions of the moneys of highly developed nations as coequal features or for making an arbitrary selection from them in this connection.[51]

[96] What distinguishes money from all other market goods (what may be observed of money in all its manifestations and phases of development but not of any other object of trade) and what thus determines its general concept is its function as a generally used intermediary of exchange of goods. All

other features that we can observe only in specific manifestations of money or indeed only in money of specific stages of civilization (that is, functions deriving from the intermediary-of-exchange function of money!), are phenomena only of the development and designs of money (or accidental features of them) that are not part of its general and essential concept.[52]

Only the fact that the function of money as 'standard of exchange value' (and 'measure of price') evolves by necessity from the original function of money as an intermediary on the commodity market and so appears wherever media of exchange emerge, and that the functions of money as an intermediary of exchange and 'measure of value' also influence each other in their development and appearance in many ways and in this sense may be considered as correlates explains **[97]** the popularity of and even to some extent justifies the usual conceptual identification of money as the generally used medium of exchange and as the standard of value of goods (or more exactly as the general intermediary of commodity and capital transactions and indicator of the value of goods).[53]

The inclusion of the 'function of general medium of payment' in the definition of money is due to a misunderstanding (see chapter VII), while the inclusion of some other merely occasional functions and kinds of use of money in the definition of money is to be avoided, if only on technical grounds; the exposition of the latter has its systematic place rather in discussions of the evolution of money.

**[98]**

## XIII. IS LEGAL TENDER PART OF THE CONCEPT OF MONEY OR IS THE LATTER MERELY PERFECTED BY LEGAL TENDER?

(A) <u>The juridical point of view.</u> The doctrine that legal tender belongs (is essential to) the concept of 'money in the legal sense' and that, accordingly, only those circulating media are to be regarded as 'money' or 'perfect money' 'in the legal sense' that government has declared legal tender is put forth by jurists on the grounds that 'Every legal system requires regulations regarding what shall be a (legal) medium of payment, that is, what the creditor shall be required to accept as settlement of a money debt or ultimately of any obligation and to nonacceptance of which are attached the consequences of default (in acceptance). Only thus is the ultimate implication drawn from those notions of which the concept of money is composed. Perfect money is only that which has been invested with the property of legal medium of payment by statute or by common law.'[54]

One certainly must admit that there are practical reasons in cases concerning disputed money debts, especially debts of sums of money, why the administration of justice should require not only that the amount of money to be awarded to the plaintiff be decided upon, but also possibly (namely, in case of doubt or dispute) **[99]** the medium of payment, and why it should also require a legal basis for such decisions that precludes (as far as possible) the arbitrary discretion of the judge. Still, it seems to me that the above argument goes much too far, even from the standpoint of judicature, when it infers from this need, which arises only in certain cases, the necessity of legal tender for money as such.

Wherever a generally accepted medium of exchange (or a generally used intermediary on commodity and capital markets) circulates in a country, money debts are, as a rule, expressed in the usual money (no matter whether the monetary system of the country in question is the result of automatic development or of government regulation). In all countries with a monetary system to which the population has become accustomed, it is the payment of amounts of the customary money that normally constitutes the substance, expressly or tacitly agreed upon, of the claims in question. Thus, as a rule, such money is the medium of payment in the legal sense without having been declared legal tender: a medium of payment that the claim-holder must accept since it corresponds to the substance of the claim, expressly or tacitly agreed upon; otherwise, he has to bear the consequences of default of acceptance. In the above case, which is to be taken as the normal one, the generally accepted medium of exchange, customary money, becomes the medium of payment in the legal sense, and not by virtue of its having been declared 'legal tender'.

This holds true above all if essentially only one kind of money circulates in a country. When several kinds of money circulate side by side in a country, however, and are valued differently by the contracting parties, whether because of some special interest operating in an individual case or because of general economic causes, then it will as a rule be either trade usage or, if necessary, the specific agreement of the contracting parties about the kind of medium of settlement (for example, 1000 talers payable in talers of which 30 pieces are coined from one pound of fine silver, and the like) that tends to provide the judge with a sound basis for a decision not only about the amount of money to be paid but also about the specific medium of settlement. Legal tender is not a necessity, not even in the last-mentioned case, let alone so unconditional a necessity as seems to follow from the above argument and **[100]** as most economists in fact assume.

What really follows from the above argument is not a need to make money legal tender on principle but something quite different: the need, with a view to trade, for a uniform national currency (for a uniform generally used intermediary of commodity and capital transactions); for in this way trade is substantially facilitated and freed from numerous awkward complications and many kinds of uncertainty about the substance of money debts; all these are advantages that benefit not only trade but equally the administration of justice. Yet this purpose, which aims first of all at facilitating trade, is served not by having the state indiscriminately declare money as such to be legal tender but rather, as I have already emphasized (see chapter V, p. [42]), by a system of government regulations including, when necessary in certain cases, the declaration of specified sorts of money as legal tender. Thus, from the legal point of view also, legal tender is by its nature an exceptional regulation; it is not part of the general concept of money.

Likewise, the opinion widely held among jurists and economists that money is simply perfected by being declared legal tender, or 'is perfected in its concept', is based on a misunderstanding. When the state declares a specific sort of money or a number of sorts legal tender (makes the creditor's obligation to accept them at their face values as settlement of money debts a legal rule), it undoubtedly does perfect these kinds of money in their function as media of payment (from the standpoint of the judicature). The *assignats* and *mandats* of the French Revolution, whose status as legal tender was backed up by the guillotine and a series of legal regulations intended to thwart any attempts by creditors to escape the effects of legal tender, undoubtedly were quite ideal 'media of payment' from the standpoint of the administration of justice and perhaps also of debtors who had already satisfied their credit requirements. But were they also ideal money? That is not a legal but an economic question, which the history of money has answered: we know from it that despite all laws and all government regulations involving force, these 'legal media of payment', [101] which were so splendid from the standpoint of the judicature and of debtors, eventually ceased altogether, and indeed for reasons of the 'convenience of trade', to be generally used media of exchange (usual money!), that is, money in the economic sense of the word.

The declaration of legal tender, a measure intended in the great majority of cases to force into or maintain in circulation, against the will of the population and by an abuse of legal authority, pathological (thus exceptional!) forms of circulating media originating mostly through abuse of the coinage prerogative or the note-issue prerogative, cannot possibly be part of the general concept of money, let alone of perfect money ('perfected in its concept').

Even when considering the monetary system from the juridical point of view, it is an inordinate generalization from what occasionally is an actual need of trade and of the administration of justice to maintain that legal tender is a necessary and general prerequisite of a legally effective medium of payment; but it is a much more far-reaching error to assert (confusing the concepts of money and of legal medium of payment) that legal tender is a general attribute of money (of the concept embracing all manifestations and stages of development of money) or of perfect money, 'money perfected in its concept'.

The above error may be explained only by the fact that in jurisprudence the usual object of investigation is not at all the concept of money in all its manifestations and stages of development, that is, the general empirical concept of money in the economic sense of the word. The jurist is interested not in the phenomenon of money as such but quite particularly in the developed money of highly civilized countries, which is already influenced and regulated by government in many ways, or in most cases even only in the money of the country whose law he has to interpret or apply. On the contrary, the historical-empirical concept of money (the concept of money in the sense of economic theory) is somewhat remote from the jurists' field of interest and obviously also from their analyses of money. It is not the general nature of money but rather the requirements of a medium of payment suitable for the administration of justice, and as a rule only the currently valid legal rules applying to a particular country's system of payments, [102] that are in the foreground of the jurist's interest in investigating the 'concept of money'.

These notions of jurists about the nature of a medium of payment appropriate for the administration of justice, which derive partly from observation of a particular phase of development of a country's monetary system and of legal rules pertaining to its monetary and payments system and partly from the practical requirements of the administration of justice, or the definitely (even in this regard) inordinate generalizations on the part of some jurists cannot be definitive for the economists' theoretical analysis of the general historical-empirical concept of money that comprises all its manifestations and stages of development.

Even the great importance attributed in inquiries into the above question to the fact that money is 'the legal medium of payment' for substitute performances of contract and 'thus in the last analysis for all obligations'[55] seems to me to be disputable in more than one respect. It is not correct that money is in the last analysis the means of fulfilling all obligations; for at least in modern legal systems the fulfilment of the substance of obligations, as far as it is legally enforceable, will be enforced also if the substance of the obligation is not money but some other object.[56] Only extreme prejudice will interpret it as compulsion when a creditor is awarded, in place of an otherwise impossible or unenforceable fulfilment, a sum of money 'equivalent' to the omitted fulfilment, in other words, the most appropriate form of compensation [103] (see p. [48]) for the claim-holder (and indeed awarded that in his own interest), and will see such compulsion on the creditor to accept as a substitute the sum of money awarded to him as an argument for considering legal tender a part of the concept of money in the legal sense. This would imply that money really lacks legal-tender status only when (or that no compulsion is exercised on the creditor only when) the creditor in the above case receives either no compensation at all or merely something less suitable for him than what is offered him in the form of a sum of money.

(B) The economic point of view. In the historical development of the economy, money, as distinct from the goods traded, makes its appearance as soon as some object of trade or a number of them become the generally used intermediaries of exchange for goods and a distinction is made on a country's markets between the goods that mediate the exchange of goods and all other goods whose exchanges are mediated by the former (the distinction appears between the money good and the goods offered for sale for money). If one adds to this distinctive position of money (as compared to that of the goods traded) as intermediary of exchange the striking fact that within individual economic units money is also visibly separated from all other goods and acquires a trade form distinguishing it from all other goods, as regularly happens in the development of the monetary system even without government influence, one would have to be more than a little prejudiced, it seems to me, to assert that money does not yet exist in this situation and that it first appears as a state's legal tender. Only the erroneous idea, widespread among some jurists but especially among economists, that money's legal tender is a prerequisite of the administration of justice, not only in certain cases demanding special regulations but quite simply in all cases of controversial money debts, was able to secure for this misleading doctrine the popularity that it enjoys even today in some learned circles, surely to the detriment of a natural conception of money. To cite only one example, what an unnatural conception of money it is [104] to deny the character of money to the notes of a solvent bank, redeemable at any time and readily accepted by everyone not only in cash transactions but for payments of all kinds, while immediately acknowledging as money the notes of the same bank once it has gone bankrupt and its notes have been declared legal tender – indeed as perfect money, perfected in its concept.

Even the opinion that money simply is perfected or undergoes an advantageous development by being declared legal tender must in this general formulation be definitely rejected from the economic point of view. Widest experience has taught that, by and large – that is, apart from exceptional cases requiring special regulation in view of their peculiarity (see chapter VI, sections 2 and 3) – the monetary system of a country is the more perfect the less it depends on legal tender. Insofar as it is not merely of technical-juridical significance, legal tender, in the main cases considered here, amounts to legal compulsion exercised on claim-holders to accept as payment for debts of sums of money (occasionally also for debts of other kinds) such kinds of money as do not correspond to the expressly or tacitly agreed-on substance of the claims or to force upon them their acceptance at a value not equal to their value in free transactions. It appears chiefly for bank notes and state treasury notes that are depreciated against the national coin and occasionally for subsidiary coins issued in excess and even for standard coins whose value has declined on the open market. In these cases legal tender is a means of forcing into circulation or coercively maintaining in circulation, through abuse of legal authority, kinds of money that have become pathological through abuse of the coinage and note-issue prerogatives; in most cases it is a measure complementary to and supportive of those acts of government by which the pathological state of the monetary system had been brought about.

In these cases, the legal-tender declaration surely aims not at creating a normally functioning uniform monetary system or at promoting its emergence and development but rather (sacrificing the purposes that a normal monetary system serves and mostly even sacrificing the stability of legal relations) at forcing certain kinds of money that have become pathological onto the market at a fictitious value exceeding their true value. [105] The view that a country's monetary system is perfected or even 'perfected in its concept' in such cases, which are in no way exceptional but rather the chief cases of legal tender, is simply untenable.

If only these cases are taken into consideration (the ones that do attract the attention of the population above all), then it could in fact be asserted that legal tender, far from being a perfection of money, implies the opposite instead and that a country's monetary system is all the more perfect and sound, the less legal tender figures in it, that is, the higher the degree to which the national coin carries its value in itself and so need not be made legal tender, and that the same is true for any bank notes and state treasury notes circulating side by side with the national coin (because of their assured redeemability or their strictly guaranteed limited amount). For as a rule the above kinds of money, which form the major part of the monetary circulation in most countries, are in fact more perfect the more readily they are accepted by everyone as payment in transactions without having been declared legal tender.

To conclude from this, however, that legal tender is simply reprehensible and that government should not intervene in the monetary system at all or should do so only in the interest of individuals is just as erroneous as the view that legal tender is part of the concept of money or signifies simply a perfection of money. For if one considers not only the above-mentioned main cases in which legal tender is usual, but also all the complications occurring in a country's monetary system, then it turns out that in certain cases the needs of trade seem to permit and occasionally downright to require not only some sort of government intervention but specifically the declaring of particular kinds of money as legal tender.

In discussing government influence on the monetary system, I already pointed out a number of cases in which government compulsion in the above sense proves necessary or seems justified precisely in the interest of free, unhampered trade (see chapter V). Given certain obstacles to an appropriate organization of the monetary system that could otherwise be overcome either not at all or only with disproportionately great economic sacrifices, rejecting legal tender on principle [106] is likewise an error.

But even in these cases it should not be overlooked that legal compulsion of trade can never be an end in itself. Here, any compulsion is itself an evil; its application may be regarded as justified only insofar as it eliminates or prevents greater evils or as it serves a mostly expedient organization of trade by overcoming certain obstacles inherent in the habits or prejudices of the population. That holds true especially for the legal tender of money. This too is itself undoubtedly an evil, but one that is outweighed in a number of cases by the advantages that legal tender brings. To reject legal tender on principle is just as much an error as to demand it on principle. It seems to me, though, that the former involves the lesser error. For while it may rightly be held against those who oppose legal tender on principle that they generalize what is a rule (on the whole, with justified exceptions) of practical economic policy into a law without exception, it may be held against those who advocate legal tender on principle that they turn something that proves useful or necessary only in certain exceptional cases into a general rule – indeed, by including legal tender in the very concept of money, into a law without exception.

[107]

# XIV. THE DEMAND FOR MONEY

(A) The demand for money of individual economic units. As soon as one commodity or a number of commodities have become generally used media of exchange for a people, there arises in every individual economic unit that participates in the division of labour, in addition to the demand that may have existed previously for these commodities for purposes of consumption and technical production, a further and different demand for medium-of-exchange purposes. From now on, every economic unit needs to hold a stock of these commodities ready especially for the purpose of mediating exchange and subsequently also for other purposes connected with the medium-of-exchange function of the commodity in question – a small inventory, so to speak, of the commodities in question[57] – at first it probably is not separated from the stock intended, for example, for consumption purposes, but subsequently it becomes a separate stock, especially if the part of the commodity that has become money acquires a special form in trade or a special name and even a different look. If a people has advanced to precious-metal money and a money economy, then every earning and spending unit requires a certain cash balance (a business or household cash balance), which is not an accidental or transitory but a permanent prerequisite of orderly and prudent economic management.

The size of the money stock that an economic agent in the age of the money economy must hold to meet the requirements of his earning and spending activities under normal circumstances and to be able safely to carry on his economic activities in a secure manner even under abnormal circumstances depends in the first place on the nature and [108] scope of his economic activities: on his gainful occupation and on his household. The cash balance to be held by a larger or more market-dependent unit is in general larger than that of the smaller or less market-dependent unit (for which, e.g., barter predominates); as a rule, the cash balance of a spending unit with more frequent receipts and payments (for example, with wages paid daily, dwelling rent paid daily, etc.) is smaller than that of a spending unit for which the opposite prevails under otherwise the same circumstances. The cash balance to be held by an earning unit in which circulating capital predominates will, under otherwise the same circumstances, exceed that of an earning unit whose capital is larger but is predominantly invested in fixed form. Also, the smaller economic unit that hoards or that conducts a credit business will easily absorb more cash than the incomparably larger unit in which money is used only as medium of exchange.

The nature of its economic management also materially influences a unit's demand for money. Not infrequently, units of the same kind and size have very different cash balances depending on whether their executives consider a larger or smaller degree of hedging against economic disturbances necessary and are willing to make the sacrifices necessary for conducting their business safely. (Think of the interest lost on rather large cash balances and especially also of the zero or relatively low interest paid on bank deposits; think how large cash balances necessarily curtail the funds otherwise available for expanding the business or for many other desirable expenditures, etc.).

The size of the cash balances necessary to assure a firm's orderly conduct of business is above all notably affected by the business acumen of its managers, by correct foresight and timing of receipts and payments (especially of the maturities of claims and of payments to be made), and by the greater or lesser mastery of the technical and legal difficulties of making payments. The inexperience, lack of proficiency, and clumsiness of most economic agents in the above respects lead, on the one hand, **[109]** to uneconomically large cash balances and, on the other hand, to disruptions of the conduct of business because of inadequate cash balances, especially in firms needing different amounts of money in different time periods.

With the progressive development of trade, it was chiefly these shortcomings that everywhere brought about the emergence of collectively organized institutions for the groups involved and independent enterprises that undertake and expertly conduct the payments business of individual economic units. This side of bank activity not only has the beneficial effect of substantially relieving bank clients of the difficult, arduous, and responsible payments business; it also, as experience shows, has highly useful educational effects on the money management and indeed the general economic conduct of the participants. It tends to adapt the volume of cash balances of individual economic units to their correctly calculated particular requirements and to manage them in that way.

(B) The demand for money of the national economy. Analysis of the economy's demand for money has often started from misleading premises.

The view that it is especially advantageous for a nation to accumulate the largest possible stock of cash resources and the view that the total amount of money required by a nation and the 'value' of all goods offered for sale must be kept in equilibrium, and so forth, are, to be sure, errors already refuted. Yet those who try to calculate the demand for money of a national economy on the one hand from the value of the quantities of goods to be traded within a certain time period or from the maximum sum of payments to be made during a period (simultaneously!) and on the other hand from the 'velocity' of money (from the larger or smaller number of times during the period in question in which payments tend to be made by the same pieces of money) – they too fail to recognize the true determinants of an economy's demand for money.[58] They ignore the fact that the quantity of money used for payments at any time **[110]** forms only a part, indeed only a relatively small part, of the cash resources required by a nation, while another part must be held in the form of reserves of various kinds to provide for uncertain payments that in fact in many cases never take place at all (for the sake of the undisturbed functioning of the economy!). The amounts of cash found in the metallic reserves of banks of issue and in the coffers of state and public bodies, of savings banks, of credit institutions, but especially also of private economic units, and held with a view to uncertain needs, rare and extraordinary dangers, and in fact partly for extreme emergencies only, although not regularly used for payments, still are just as much a part of an economy's demand for money as the small amounts of subsidiary coins found in the possession of every economic unit and changing hands several times a day. The amounts of money hoarded by private persons and occasionally even today by public economic units are also to be considered here, since they must be taken into account in calculating a nation's demand for money for specified periods, even though they are not regularly used for payments in the period in question.

The demand for money of a national economy, like that of private households, is far from correctly expressed by the payments that are to be made within a certain period or 'at the same time', even if the calculation is based on the largest possible volume of these.

Likewise, in classical and post-classical economic theory, the influence of the velocity of circulation of money on a nation's demand for cash resources is often greatly overestimated.

The theory that the velocity of circulation of money has a quite decisive influence on a nation's demand for money rests chiefly on the assumption that in every economy and in every time period, a definite amount of existing debts has to be paid back and a certain number of transactions in goods (mediated by money) have to be accomplished and that these require the less money the more frequently individual pieces of money perform their function as media of payment in every time period. But this argument ignores the fact that the cash balances of individual economic units are intended not to be spent **[111]** at once or with all possible speed but rather to assure the orderly operation of these units. Only a small part of the cash balance of an economic unit is intended to be spent at once, while the far greater part is intended for purchases and payments some time later and as a reserve for extraordinary occasions. For part of the cash balances, the immediate spending of money might be as economically sensible as it would be uneconomic and inappropriate for the other parts. Imagine the state of the national economy if all private economic units, public bodies, banks, especially also the banks of issue, and the state were to circulate their cash balances as quickly as possible. Although part of the money in the tills of individual economic units is put into circulation only very gradually and another part only after a long period, possibly only after decades – not circulating in the meantime –, these amounts of money nevertheless perform their economic function just as much as, say, the standard and subsidiary coins in a little industrial town that continually move from the tills of entrepreneurs into the hands of workers and from there into the hands of grocers and innkeepers, to return to the tills of entrepreneurs in exchange for notes, then to resume anew their restless circulation.

Even if a general upswing or slowdown in trade is to be observed in a certain period (for example, during a generally favourable or unfavourable trend of business), it still tends, as a rule, not to show itself mainly, let alone exclusively, in the quicker or slower circulation of individual pieces of money but mainly in the use of existing cash balances as reserves for payments to a greater or lesser degree than before.

The above doctrine, which in its usual formulation is an error that classical economics took over from late mercantilism, is comparable to that of an economist who would calculate a nation's total demand for pliers, hammers, or other tools from the number and duration of instances of their uses and the greater or lesser speed with which these tools were used, while overlooking that the latter are useful to us chiefly **[112]** by being on hand in the household and available for use at any time.[59]

A realistic theory of an economy's cash requirements presupposes an analysis that starts from the cash requirements of the individual and collective economic units that compose a 'national economy', which is the ultimate measure of an economy's demand for money, and then seeks to assess the economy's total demand for cash, taking due account of the functions of its institutions that provide substitutes for coined money and economize on cash.

First to be considered here are the banks of issue: because of their well-known organization and business practices, they are in a position, as experience shows, to put into circulation an amount of document money that considerably exceeds their metallic reserves and that circulates freely like coined money, into which it is redeemable at any time.

Although the banks of issue mostly issue notes in amounts exceeding their metallic reserves and although these acquire the character of (document) money, there still does not necessarily occur a corresponding lasting increase in the monetary circulation. Because the bank notes placed in circulation drive out of circulation a part of the country's coined money circulating in the population, so that part of the precious metals that were needed for circulation becomes available for other uses or for export, the banks of issue operate as institutions that replace part of the otherwise necessary coined money with document money and thus organize a country's monetary system more economically to a certain extent; but they do not necessarily permanently increase the circulation of money or reduce the economy's total demand for circulating media at all. They are essentially institutions that replace coined money with document money but do not necessarily reduce the economy's total demand for circulating media. [113] Because of their lending and investing and especially because of their usually extensive discounting of bills of exchange, however, they are in a position to satisfy the public's temporarily increased demand for circulating media the more easily as this is usually accompanied by an increased demand for credit also. Owing to the elasticity of note issue, the banks of issue thus effectively perform the important function of adapting the monetary circulation to the economy's varying requirements for circulating media. Normally, however, they do not exert any other influence, except perhaps an indirect one, on the monetary circulation and the economy's total demand for circulating media.

The circulation of state treasury notes also tends to drive part of the circulating coined money of the country or part of the circulating bank notes out of general circulation; they too are by nature document money that economizes on coins, which is a means of lessening the sacrifices demanded of the population with a view to maintaining the national currency (possibly, though, at the cost of its security) without, under normal conditions, necessarily having any substantial influence on the monetary circulation or the economy's total demand for circulating media in the long run.

While the above institutions of the economy essentially replace coined money with document money and thus normally tend not to reduce (but rather indirectly to increase) a country's total circulation of cash, a number of other, different, institutions do not put document money into circulation and yet considerably reduce the economy's total demand for cash (for coins, bank notes, and state treasury notes taken together), so that they may be described as cash-economizing institutions of the economy: commercial banks and deposit banks, especially when they are connected with clearing houses, and also savings banks. What these institutions have in common is that they take into their safekeeping and administration the cash balances or cash holdings that serve other purposes for many economic agents and that, because of their organization, they are in a position, with an amount of cash that is smaller than the total of deposits, to let every individual depositor have his balance at his disposal at any time or at short notice. They can do this chiefly because they know from experience that deposits will not all be withdrawn at the same time by all depositors, but rather at different [114] points in time and also mostly only in partial amounts, and that, moreover, what is paid out will also mostly be replaced by new deposits and in many cases will take the form of mere book transfers. Thus, the deposit bank or the savings bank is actually in a position to repay individual depositors their balances in full or in part on demand at any time or at short notice without having to hold the total amount of the deposits in cash in their tills. Both types of institution are thus normally in a position to use a considerable part of the deposits for credit operations, to put into circulation sums of money that would otherwise have to remain in the depositors' strong-boxes, and so initially and directly to increase the circulation, but gradually to enable the national economy to get along with less cash than otherwise.

Note that the above institutions do not substantially reduce individual depositors' requirements for available cash, but their cash balances take the place of those of the depositors in a certain sense; so through economizing on cash, these institutions bring about the above result for the depositors as a whole and for the national economy.

To sum up: the demand for money of a national economy is the total of the money holdings required by a nation's individual and collective economic units organized on the basis of the division of labour, this total thus being its ultimate measure. It is a quantity whose significance lies not only in the total figure alone but also importantly in its distribution among the nation's individual economic units. But a national economy's demand for money is found not by mechanically summing the cash requirements of individual units. In addition, one has to take account of the functions of those institutions of the economy that provide substitutes for coin and that economize on cash.

The distinctive character of money as compared to other goods means that with every change in the outer exchange value of money (as a consequence of influences on the side either of money or of the goods traded), the demand for money of the individual economic units (and so too of the economy) changes: every increase in the outer exchange value of money **[115]** tends to reduce and every decline to increase the demand for money. Growing prosperity tends to increase a nation's demand for money for two reasons: first, because of increased turnover of goods, increased payments, increased capital accumulation in money, and the expansion of the 'money market'; second, because individual economic units gradually become accustomed to holding larger amounts of money available (either directly or indirectly in the form of bank accounts) to satisfy their economic need for cash more completely, which serves the convenience and security of economic management. This tendency is resisted in a mature credit economy by clearing procedures of many kinds, credit in general, and the emergence of institutions whose function of economizing on coined money or cash in general has been explained above. Speeding up payment procedures (because of increasing density of population and improvement of means of transport and methods of payment) also has the effect of reducing numerous avoidable and thus uneconomic cash balances of individual economic units to the required size and so relatively reducing the national economy's demand for cash.

# NOTES

\*   Translation of the article 'Geld', *Handwörterbuch der Staatswissenschaften*, 3rd edition, vol. IV, Jena 1909, as reprinted in Carl Menger, *Gesammelte Werke* (F.A. Hayek, ed.), 2nd edition, vol. IV, Tübingen 1970, pp. 1–116. For convenience of comparison with the German original, its page numbers have been retained; they appear in brackets, bold, in the running text.

1.  The expression 'intermediary of exchange' is far more exact for denoting the mediating function of money in exchanges of goods than the expression 'medium of exchange', a term which in German may refer to any good whatsoever intended for exchange. Since in scientific language, however, the term 'medium of exchange' has come to be used for both of the above concepts, and since the expression 'intermediary of exchange' is rarely used in everyday language and proves clumsy when frequently repeated, the following exposition will retain the manner of expression so far customary wherever there is no need of a precise distinction between the above concepts.

2.  Obligationenrecht, I, §40.

3.  Cf. W. Lexis, 'Geldwirtschaft', in Elster's *Wörterbuch der Volkswirtschaft*, 1898, I, pp. 805 ff.

4.  On the most primitive phenomena of trade in goods in the form of extensive voluntary and semivoluntary hospitality, mutual gift-giving, and probably in part also of robbery and so forth, cf. Herbert Spencer's *Princ. of Sociology*, Part IV, ch. IV, §368 ff., and Part VIII, ch. VII, §754 ff.; also Bücher, *Die Entstehung d. Volkswirtsch.*, 1898, pp. 78, 83 ff., with regard to specifically economic aspects, and G. Schmoller, *Grundriss d. allg. V. W. L.*, passim, esp. II, p. 668 ff., with regard to the administrative-legal aspects of the development of the economy. Nearly all peoples that Spencer cites (in his *Descriptive Sociology,* Division I, Part I. A, 1874) as types of the lowest-standing races knew certain forms of the division of labour and were acquainted with barter, and some of them even with media of exchange. Where reports of individual travellers say otherwise, it may be suspected that the tribes in question only shied away, as it were, from open barter with strangers, being accustomed to so-called silent trade or other forms of trade in goods. H. Spencer has recently reported, however, on some peoples that, down to our own days, were not even acquainted with barter: *Principl. of Sociol.*, Part VIII, ch. VII, §754 ff. On the point that more primitive stages of economic development, even a stage of the crudest search for food, must necessarily have preceded the oldest historically documented stages of civilization see Spencer, *loc. cit.*, Part III, ch. IX, §319.

5.  If the origin of money is dated back to earlier stages of development, as has been attempted in fact, this is due to a misunderstanding, as I shall argue below.

6.  V.L. Cameron, *Across Africa*, 1877, I, pp. 246 f.

7.  Heinr. Barth, *Reisen u. Entdeckungen in Nord- und Zentralafrika* (1849-1855), 1857, II, p. 396.

8.  One-sidedly emphasized by Karl Bücher, *Die Entsteh. d. Volksw.* 1901, p. 81: 'How simple it is to explain', says Bücher, 'the emergence of the different kinds of money: For every tribe, money is that commodity which it does not produce itself but regularly obtains in exchange from outside the tribe, for naturally [!] it becomes for it the general medium of exchange against which it trades away its own products; it is for it the standard of value in which to measure its own assets,

which cannot be realized in any other way; in it it sees its wealth, for it cannot increase it at will, etc.'

9. On money among peoples of primitive culture and on the oldest forms of money, cf. especially Theodor Mommsen, *Gesch. d. röm. Münzwesens*, 1860, introduction and pp. 169 ff.; v. Carnap, 'Zur Geschichte d. Münzwissenschaft u. d. Wertzeichen', *Tüb. Zschr.* 1869, pp. 348 ff.; Kenner, 'Die Anfänge des Geldwesens im Alterthume' (*Wiener Akad. Schriften, Phil.-hist. Sect.*, 1863, pp. 385 ff.); Soetbeer, *Forschungen z. deutschen Gesch.*, I, pp. 207 ff.; W. Roscher, *System* (I, §118 ff.); Johannes Brandis, *Das Münz-, Mass- und Gewichtswesen in Vorderasien* (pp. 72 ff.); Fr. Lenormand, *La monnaie dans l'antiquité*, 1878, passim; A. Delmar, *History of Monetary Systems*, 1894. From an essentially ethnographic angle: Richard Andree, *Ethnographische Parallelen*, 1878 and 1889; F. Ilwof, *Tauschhandel und Geldsurrogate*, 1882; Osk. Lenz, *Ueber Geld bei Naturvölkern* (Virchow-Wattenbachsche Sammlung g. Vort., 1893, no. 226); W. Ridgeway, *The Origin of Metallic Currency and Weight Standards*, 1892 (mainly metrological); H. Schurtz, *Grundriss einer Entstehungsgeschichte des Geldes*, 1898.

10. As long as only a part of the population of a country uses media of exchange, while the other, as a rule the more numerous, part of the population uses the media of exchange – which the former employ to effect their trading in goods – only as favourite consumption goods, the media of exchange of the country in question are still so undeveloped that it may seem doubtful whether they may be called money yet. He who exchanges his commodities on the market first for glass beads, tea bricks, salt slabs, etc. in order to obtain, by means of them, the goods he directly needs in an easier, cheaper, and surer way than would be the case with direct exchange of his commodities for the latter, may nevertheless already consider as money the above-mentioned commodities intermediating his transactions. But as long as a large or the greater part of the population, though readily accepting these commodities for the goods they bring to market, use them only for their own consumption (adorn themselves with the acquired glass beads, consume tea and salt, etc.), these are indeed especially popular and favourite consumption goods for this part of the population, but they are not yet money. The phenomenon of money in the sense of a generally employed intermediary of exchange does not yet exist in these cases. One may speak of money in the sense of a generally used intermediary of exchange only when not only those classes of the population that are naturally active in economic progress but also the naturally passive classes, through imitation and accommodation, use a commodity as intermediary of exchange, i.e. readily accept it as payment for their commodities and services even when they do not need those goods or are already sufficiently supplied with them, and when in consequence thereof the media of exchange quite regularly do not go into consumption but circulate.

11. Investigation into the origin and changing usage of the word 'money', which is an important question regarding the evolution of the concept of money, has lagged far behind, up to now. Among most peoples the name for money was first taken from the coined form of money; e.g. the Latin and Italian *moneta* (belonging to the postclassical and poetical vocabulary), the French *monnaie*, the Spanish *moneda*, the Portuguese *moeda*, the Russian *dengi* (denga = stamp, originally probably stamped, minted), the Arabic *fulus* (coins), etc. – In many languages the name (mostly in the plural) of the most common types of coin (*denare, Pfennige,*

etc.) came to designate 'money'; e.g. Italian *danaro*, Spanish *dinero*(s), Portuguese *dinheiro*, Slovenian *dnár* and *penegi*, Polish *pieniadze* , Czech *penize*, Danish-Norwegian *penge*, Swedish *penningar*, Hungarian *penz*, modern Greek *aspra* (*asper*: a small Turkish coin). (As to the word *Pfennig* it is not certain whether the meaning 'coin' is not the older one.) Cf. the article 'Pfennig' in Kluge's *Etymol. Wörterb. d. deutsch. Spr.* (1889), 1905, and also J.H. Müller's *Deutsche Münzgeschichte*, I, pp. 259 ff. Of course, some peoples already took the name of 'money' from that of the monetary material or that of the commodity that had become the medium of exchange: Hebrew *Keseph* (silver), ancient Greek *argyrion* (diminutive of *argyros* = small silver) and *chrysion* (diminutive of *chrysos*), Latin *argentum, aurum, aes* and French *argent* belong here (*etiam aureos nummos aes dicimus*, in Ulpian, L. 1959, Dig. 50, 16; also common in classical times in the combination *aes alienum* = money debt. Among the Greeks and Romans, money was commonly called *argyrion* and *argentum* without regard to the metal). The German and Dutch word 'geld' (verbal noun of 'gelten' = to pay, to make a return gift or compensation) originally means: performance, compensation of any kind. (Gothic: *gild* = tax, rent, due, Old English: *gilt* = replacement, sacrifice; Old Norse: *gjald* = payment, due, etc.) Cf. J. Grimm, *Rechtsaltertümer*, 3rd edn, pp. 601 and 649; as to restriction of the concept of money to goods and chattle (movable possessions) in contrast to landed property, see Grimm, *loc. cit.*, p. 565; Schröder, *Deutsche Rechtsgesch.*, 1898, p. 270; as to the restriction to fungible things (movable fungible possessions = money, means of payment), *ibid.* p. 277. In the present-day sense first in Middle High German and correspondingly in some other German dialects. (According to Arnolds, *Zur Geschichte des Eigentums in den deutschen Städten*, p. 89, already in a document of 1327.) This linguistic usage has gained the upper hand in German especially since the 16th century (with the prevalence of the money economy) and gradually displaced the older usage almost completely. The original barter-economy meaning of the word (= performance, even the performance of a prayer, compensation in general) turned into the newer money-economy meaning (performance consisting of money – in today's sense – or simply 'money'). Roscher's opinion (*System*, I. §116, n. 4) that 'Geld' derives from 'gelten' [to be valid] (because it is valid everywhere) is disputable. Cf. already my *Grunds. d. VL.*, 1871, pp. 263 ff.) Tileman Friesen ('Münzspiegel', 1592, in *Acta publica monetaria*, 1692, p. 3) has this interesting observation: 'Hence coins also were called money, *ab effectu*, because one pays and buys with them. In some places coins also are called little hellers – the name of the species for the genus – and likewise the word pennies is used for money.'

** Translator's note: In this text, Menger uses 'automatisch' (both as adjective, in 'automatic development', and as adverb) no less than ten times; in his usage, the word corresponds exactly to what later Austrians, above all F.A. Hayek, were to denote as 'spontaneous'.

12. Cf. my *Grunds. d. Volkswirthschaftslehre*, 1871, pp. 250 ff. – Wilhelm Roscher: 'The cleverer economic agents gradually arrange on their own to have themselves paid in whatever are the most marketable goods at the time' (*System*, I. §116, since the 10th edn., 1873) and Knies, *Geld und Kredit*, Section I: Das Geld, 1873, pp. 67 ff. – Likewise with a number of recent authors: 'People overcame the chief difficulty (of barter) only when someone wanting the animal, slave, or sword of his trading partner was willing and able to give a good in exchange that was

generally wanted, easily saleable again and again, generally acceptable and marketable'. '... There thus emerged, very early, certain groups of particularly desired goods as general media of payment and exchange' (Schmoller, *Grundriss d. allg. V.L.*, 1904, II, p. 65). 'In the progress of trade, the population sees itself driven by compelling necessity to look for an object that may be used for the intermediation of exchanges, i.e. an object is chosen for that purpose which is in fact used everywhere, which everyone therefore gladly accepts, and which thus possesses the greatest marketability.' J. Conrad, *Grundr. d. Pol. Oek.*, 4th edn I, §25. 'The difficulties' (that even under the most primitive conditions impeded direct exchange) 'could be overcome only when people with a surplus of certain goods first accepted in exchange for them such goods as could be expected to exchange at any time for the things that they actually needed.' (Karl Helfferich, *Geld und Banken*, 1903, I: Das Geld, p. 15.) 'Through every individual's doing what seemed appropriate in his personal circumstances, the community gradually came to the exclusive use of the precious metals for mediating exchanges.' *Ibid.*, p. 27. The error that suggested itself and has prevailed ever since Plato and Aristotle, namely, that money is the product of a general convention or of positive legislation (thus the result of government and social measures undertaken in awareness, from the outset, of both end and means), may be considered as refuted (cf. Karl Helfferich, *Geld und Banken*, 1903, I, pp. 6 ff., and Adolph Wagner, *Sozialökon. Theorie des Geldes*, 1909, p. 116). The most recent attempts at solving the above problem, undertaken on an ethnographic basis, arrive at this result: '... it is apparent, that the doctrine of a primal convention with regard to the use of any one particular article as a medium of exchange is just as false as the old belief in an original convention at the first beginning of Language or Law'. (W. Ridgeway, *The Origin of Metallic Currency etc.*, 1892, p. 47.) Similarly Heinrich Schurtz, *Grundriss einer Entstehung des Geldes*, 1898, p. 175. Those authors who still cling to the counterhistorical opinion that the origin of money may be traced back to positive legislation or a social contract for the most part confuse the problem of the emergence of money and that of legal provisions for settlement of money debts. They fail to see that while the latter are indeed often the result of positive legislation, they already presuppose the existence and function of money. Investigating the medium-of-exchange function of money, Adolph Wagner, in his excellent *Sozialökonom. Theorie des Geldes* (1909, pp. 110 ff.), is guided, like many earlier theorists of money, by the idea that the money good is accepted as compensation only because of the confidence that it will also be accepted (because of the same confidence!) by the other members of the trading community in exchange for their goods. This confidence factor, regarded from the standpoints both of individual psychology and (because of established custom!) of mass psychology, is taken to be essential and decisive for understanding the medium-of-exchange function of money. This view rests on the prejudice, even today often prevailing among monetary theorists, that money – in contrast to all other goods – will be accepted by us as equivalent for the goods given up for it only because we have the prospect of (or confidence in) being able to dispose of it in the same way and because of the same confidence of other persons. What is overlooked here is that this is no peculiarity of money. The merchant, the speculator, etc. also acquire the goods that they subsequently offer for sale again only in 'confidence' that they will be able to sell them again, and – as to the critical point here! – it is a matter of complete indifference to them whether the eventual buyers of the goods intend to consume them or sell them, in their turn. The same is true for money, which we acquire (regularly, but not without exception!) just as the merchant does with his goods: only with a view to its exchange value, i.e. to dispose of it again. The distinctiveness of money, as compared with other goods, rests not on any special 'confidence' manifesting itself, as it were, only with money but in truth on the relatively wide marketability, which is further increased by custom and subsequently by government measures, of the money commodity: it is into this that everyone is interested in first exchanging his own less marketable commodities. This simple and obvious situation (the fact that on all markets certain goods become generally used intermediaries of exchange because of their relatively wide marketability) has been obscured by theory, often to the point of unrecognizability, because of the many complications of the monetary system. The true insignificance, however, of this confidence factor (in the sense of the above theory) particularly with respect to money becomes clear when we recall that indeed all commodities are regularly offered for money, so that we are sure that for money we can acquire appropriate quantities of all goods offered on the markets according to our needs and preferences. Confidence (confidence in persons previously quite unknown to us and in no contractual relation whatever with us!) is both inadequate for explaining the distinctiveness of money and superfluous, especially with money. Only in the special case of document money does the confidence factor enter the question, although in a quite different sense from the one that is crucial here. The attempt by some recent authors to relate the phenomenon of money to certain value relations already characteristic of the barter economy (on this see chapter XI, pp. [47] ff.) culminates in the idea that even on barter markets there existed value relations fixed either by custom or by authoritative pronouncement among a number of goods, which together originally functioned as money; from these money in the narrower sense was supposed subsequently to have developed. Albert Hermann Post, *Afrikanische Jurisprudenz*, 1887, II, p. 185, explains African conditions: 'Trade goods appearing relatively often gradually became standards of value for goods traded regularly. Such standards of value were originally still very unstable but were then fixed from time to time by royal decree and gradually became media of exchange that to some extent took the place of coined money.' W. Lotz in *Conrads Jahrbücher*, 1894, 3rd series, vol. 7, pp. 344 ff., generalizes this idea: 'The first objects of private property are traded for one another at fixed rates.... At first a range of different commodities functions as money: Collectively, they make up money. Each individual commodity is only a component of this range of commodity-money.' Page 346: 'The first commodities that were traded at all became money at the same time. Since trade reckoned these commodities at conventional exchange ratios, these exchange ratios among different commodities continued to be considered a monetary system, even after the objects originally serving as the only market commodities in their turn had become the standard of value for other, additional, objects of market trading, i.e. had become money.' And p. 352: 'As a good that wanders from country to country, gold was traded as a commodity at an early stage and later became money, the commodity *par excellence* (especially since gold was the first good that was weighed). The main shortcoming of the above theory of the origin of money – apart from the assumption that the standard-of-value function of money is the primary function of money – consists in the complete failure to recognize the essential difficulty that hinders the development of trading on barter markets (see chapter I, section 2). Even if it were true that on all barter markets on which generally used media of exchange had emerged, fixed value ratios (fixed by authority) among a number of goods originally existed in the degree of generality assumed by Lotz and that these price ratios had everywhere had the stability ascribed to them by Lotz, one still should not ignore the question of how those difficulties of barter, pointed out above (chapter I, section 2) could be overcome in this way, since these are rooted not in price formation (chapter X) but rather in the fact that not everyone needs every commodity. These difficulties were not to be overcome by any sort of value ratios but only by a good, or a number of these, intermediating trade in goods. Only because Lotz presupposes a kind of commodity currency on the barter markets, which he thinks of as analogous to our coined currencies (*loc. cit.*, p. 346), in other words, because he assumes that insofar as fixed prices exist on a market, commodities may be exchanged against one another at will, just as in money-changing (*loc. cit.*, p. 346), could he be misled into putting forward a theory of the origin of money that already presupposes the existence of a proper currency analogous to our modern currencies and that consequently leads him to assume that 'the milking of a goat throughout summer and fall' and the like had originally been money, for which all the other goods brought to market could be exchanged as easily as is currently the case 'in changing two 10-mark pieces for one 20-mark piece'.

13. The diminishing importance of barter is emphasized by H. Dernburg, *Pandekten*, §§94 and 103.

14. See chapter V, pp. [44] ff.

15. *Ut aliud est vendere aliud emere, alius emptor alius venditor: sic aliud est pretium, aliud merx, quod in permutatione discerni non potest, uter emptor, uter venditor sit* (L. 1 Dig. XVIII, 1). Likewise more recent jurists: 'Metallic money, as the general exchange good and means of payment, is the counterpart of the particular object of an exchange or payment. On the recognition of this contrast rests the distinction of purchase from barter, of money price (pretium) from commodity (merx)' (Goldschmidt, Handelsrecht I, §103; cf. also H. Dernburg, *Pandekten*, §103). – Only where money, by way of exception, is actually intended to be sold for money, where specific pieces of money (specie) are held ready, as e.g. in professional sales, can these become objects of purchase and sale and acquire the character of commodities in the juridical sense.

16. As a rule, the acquisition of ownership of (other people's) money is effected by its being mixed with one's own (H. Dernburg, *Pandekten,* I, §210; Bernhard Windscheid, *Pandekt.*, II, §189); validating a claim to money is in many cases out of the question; in many cases of purchase and sale the principles of *periculum* and *commodum* are not applied to the money price; the sums of money transferred (economically!) by the creditor to the debtor to be used for a limited period of time only (as loans!) legally become the property of the debtor (in contrast to objects loaned or leased), and so forth.

17. The contrast between money price (*pretium*) and merchandise (*merx*) in jurisprudence does not amount to the contrast between money and other assets; this may already be deduced from the fact that for Roman jurists *pecunia* comprises all (movable and immovable) assets, and indeed both physical objects

and rights, and thus there can be no question of any fundamental contrast in Roman law between money and assets. *Pecuniae verbum non solum numeratam pecuniam complectitur, verum omnem omnino pecuniam, hoc est, omnia corpora, nam corpora quoque pecuniae appellatione contineri, nemo ambigat.* 1.178 pr. D. 50. 16 de verb. sign. (Ulpianus). *Pecunia nomine non solum numerata pecunia, sed omnes res, tam soli quam mobiles et tam corpora quam jura continentur.* 1. 222 pr. D. 50. 16 de verb. sign. (Hermogenianus).

18. For modern man, especially the city-dweller, it is somewhat strange that the precious metals (gold, silver, copper, bronze) should have circulated in worked-up form (as rings, clasps, weapons, bronze and in ancient China as knives, spades, etc.) only in the very beginnings of metallic money, and even then not generally, while later they should have functioned as media of exchange above all in the shape of raw materials and semi-finished products (in the form of wires, sheets, rods, bars, etc.). This is explained by the incomparably more general and relatively greater need of individual economic agents for raw materials at a time when trade was only little developed. In the more or less closed-off and self-sufficient domestic household economy, every economic agent must possess stocks of raw materials of all kinds, especially also of metals, if his need for the corresponding consumption goods is to be satisfied. Even later, with trade still undeveloped, mostly raw materials, especially metals, are handed over to craftsmen to be made into goods that we are accustomed to buy ready-made so that many of us see none of the numerous raw materials that are objects generally in demand in lower stages of civilization. In mountainous regions (e.g. in the mountainous parts of Styria) even today the owners of remote farms tend to possess not only the necessary stocks of metals but also their own smithies.

19. When Karl Knies, *Das Geld*, 1885, Section 1, Geld und Kredit, p. 261, traces the distinctive character of precious-metal money as compared with other goods to a 'special' value, a 'specific precious-metal value', whence he infers 'that objects of another kind of value should not function as money', this follows from that conception which sees in money primarily not a medium of exchange but a 'standard of value' and so is inclined to explain the distinctiveness of metallic money as compared with other goods not by its high marketability but by the peculiar nature of the 'value' of the precious metals. Similarly already Lorenz von Stein, *System der Staatswiss.* 1852, I, pp. 217 ff., *Nat-Oek.* 3rd edn 1887, pp. 140 ff.

20. Note that these drawbacks do not affect all classes of the population to the same degree. The merchant who always has scales and weights at hand and has the necessary equipment and assistants at his disposal for assaying the fineness of the precious metals also possesses the requisite expertise and therefore, in troublesome situations in trade, ordinarily is not the injured party; of course, he will feel no such pressing need for coinage of the precious metals as, say, the multitude of market participants for whom the above does not hold. Even today, for the reasons cited, the banker in many cases prefers weighing coins to counting them, since the former is usually less troublesome and time-consuming for him than the latter, and in addition, when it is a question of exactly determining the quantity of the precious metal, also more reliable. In international wholesale trade among knowledgeable merchants, especially bankers, the costly coining of the precious metals is in many cases quite uneconomic because unnecessary. – It is illustrative of what has just been said that it was not the great trading nation of

antiquity, the Phoenicians, but only the Greeks or Lydians who first began to mint coins and that, up to modern times, the Chinese used coins only in retail trade, but otherwise used scales.

21. The concept of coin is defined too broadly, on the one hand, too narrowly, on the other, in the main probably because the concept of coin in the technical sense is not distinguished precisely enough from that of coined money. There are coins (exhibition, souvenir, commemorative, and memorial pieces, etc.) that are not money, and conversely numerous forms of money (livestock money, shell money, weighed precious-metal money, etc.) that are not coins. Coins in the economic sense, coined money, are only those coins that serve as money. If this is recognized, it is clear that, e.g., obsolete or recalled coins, although formerly coined money and although still coins in the technical sense, are not coined money because they no longer serve as money. Foreign coins and trade coins are undoubtedly coins in the technical sense; the former, however, are coined money regularly only in their home country, the latter, on the other hand, only within the area where they actually circulate as money. Bars of precious metal, bank notes, and state treasury notes are money insofar as they perform the functions of money, but not coined money; bills of exchange are neither money nor coins, etc. In my opinion, a legitimate controversy can arise only over two questions: first, over the question whether bars of precious metal become coined money merely because their gross weight and fineness have been determined and certified in a reliable manner, as by government, and second, whether coined money (in the sense defined above) is to be recognized as coins in the economic sense only when it is minted by the state (or in its name and according to its regulations) and its value is guaranteed by it.

The first question must be answered in the negative. For if it were true that bars of precious metal or some other piece of precious metal become coins or coined money merely because their gross weight and their fineness have been ascertained in a reliable manner, as by government, then bars of precious metal put in circulation for technical purposes by mining companies (at least by the administrations of state-owned gold and silver mines) – insofar as their weight and fineness have been authenticated in a reliable manner, as by government – would also have to be recognized as coins. Coins are thus not 'lingots, dont le poids et le titre sont certifiés, rien d'autre et rien de plus' (Michel Chevalier, *Cours d'E. P.*, 1866, III, La Monnaie, pp. 39 f.); neither are they just bars whose fine content (gross weight and fineness) has been certified by government (Levin Goldschmidt, *Handbuch des Handelsrechts*, 1868, I, 2nd part, p. 1093). Pieces of metal authenticated as to fineness and weight (as distinct from metal bars) may in any case be described as coins in the economic sense (as coined money!) only if they serve the purpose of money.

On the other hand, it seems to me that the concept of coin is defined too narrowly by those who recognize as coins in the economic sense only those coins in the technical sense that 'in order to serve as money have been minted in the name of and according to the regulations of the state and whose value has been guaranteed by the state' (cf. Lexis, vol. V, p. 898 of the 2nd edition of this Handwörterbuch). The minted pieces issued by private mints (if they become generally used media of exchange and actually take on all the functions of coined money) are undoubtedly coins in the economic sense (coined money), just like the foreign trade coins circulating even today among many peoples. From the recent past I still remember the California private coinages in the fifties of the last century, the private coinages of the two Bechtlers in Rutherfordton (North Carolina), those of the Mormons, etc.

The above definition refers only to state coins (a particular historical form of coined money).

22. Cf. Friedrich Noback, *Münz-, Mass- und Gewichtsbuch* 1879, pp. 158 ff., 422, etc., for cases in which coins are in fact cut into pieces in trade.

23. Note how difficult it would be in ordinary trade to weigh out with scales the quantities of precious metal contained in our present coins (e.g. 7.96495 grams of 900/1000 fine gold – the German 20-mark piece – or 6.775067 grams of gold of the same fineness – the Austro-Hungarian 20-kronen piece), while, on the other hand, the quantities of gold easily measurable with the usual commercial scales and weights, e.g. of 1000, 100, or 10 grams of weight, do not necessarily answer the needs of trade (think of the gold krone of the German-Austrian coinage treaty of 21 January 1857, which never managed to become really accepted in international trade!).

24. Consider how much less complicated contracting and especially settling a debt is when this involves not a quantity of bullion specified by weight but rather a specified number of pieces of definite (identically minted) types of coin or even a specified number of coinage units.

25. In the course of the historical evolution of the coinage system in most countries, the original quantities, specified by weight, of coins and coinage units (pounds, marks, and their fractions, etc.), understandable by everyone, were replaced by coin names that likewise express certain weights and certain grades of fineness for the expert but are not understood by the greater part of the population; and, to be sure, this fact was one of the main reasons why monetary units which, in the respect relevant here, are nothing but specified quantities of coin metals of specified fineness, have come to appear as abstract 'quanta of value'.

26. The precious metals, considered as primal substances (elements), are of course fully homogeneous and in this sense, without regard to their places of origin, completely fungible. But in reality they do not serve as 'kinds' or 'elements'; rather, individual pieces of precious metals serve as money. These can be exceedingly different, however, in weight, fineness, and shape (that is, in the respects decisive for the function as money). There are few things indeed that in practice could exhibit such sizeable differences (that tend to be fungible to such a slight degree) with respect to their monetary purpose as different pieces of the same precious metal. Only when the precious metals are coined in such a way that the individual coins or coin types are identical (within the limits of technical feasibility) in gross weight, fineness, and shape do individual pieces of the monetary metals become fungible in the fullest sense for practical economic life.

27. Generic obligations (in contrast to obligations whose objects are individually specified, e.g. a specific house, a specific horse) are obligations whose object is specified only by a generic name or by general features (e.g. a horse unspecified, a certain quantity of wheat of average quality, hectolitres of wine or of wine of a specific sort). The great importance that these obligations have for trade, especially when they extend over time, need not be remarked upon. But it must be emphasized here that their object, by the nature of the case, is not specified perfectly precisely. By exact determination of the 'genus', i.e. by adding characteristic features, the object of the obligation gains in precision. But in the

end its precision depends also on the more or less strict fungibility of the individual units comprised by the 'type'. Now what quite especially distinguishes the coined metals and eminently qualifies them as objects of generic obligations is their strict fungibility (depending on the technical capabilities of the mints).

28. See footnote 20.

29. The coins of 50, 1, 0.5, and 0.25 dollars put into circulation by the many private mints in California as late as the early 1850s proved to be smaller on average than those minted by government (in some cases by up to 2 percent) and since 1854 have been more and more displaced by those of the national mint in San Francisco (Fr. Noback, *Münz-, Mass- u. Gewichtsbuch*, 1879, p. 792). – The 5-dollar pieces minted for a while by the Bechtlers in North Carolina (Rutherfordton) were in part smaller by up to 1.5 percent; the 5-dollar pieces examined in 1849 in Philadelphia turned out to be 4 dollars and 94 cents, and even if the silver alloy is taken into account, were worth only 4 dollars 96.5 cents. The earlier 5-dollar pieces of C. Bechtler were issued even 1 to 6 percent below their face value, on average 3 percent, the one-dollar pieces of A. Bechtler 2 percent below. The gold pieces of 20, 10, 5 and 2.5 dollars minted by the Mormons in the state of Utah also proved to be very irregular in fineness and weight. The value of the 10-dollar piece was 8 dollars 52 cents on average, those of the other denominations were in proportion (*ibid.*, p. 647). On private mintages in other trade areas, cf. also *ibid.*, pp. 158 f. (Bogota), p. 169 (Bombay), p. 620 (Montreal), p. 754 (Rangoon), p. 821 (local coins in Singapore), p. 860 (Australia), p. 866 (Tahiti), etc.; see also Chr. u. Fr. Noback, *Vollst. Taschenb. d. Münzverhältnisse*, 1850, p. 1630 (California).

30. In a Carolingian addendum to Lex Ripuar. 36, c.11, value schedules are specified in all sorts of assets for the case of compensation for a killing. Similar value schedules in Lex Saxon. 66 and in the Capitulare Saxonicum of 797, c.11 (Schroeder, *Deutsche Rechtsgesch.*, 3rd edn, §26, also §12, note 46); see also Inama-Sternegg, 'Deutsche Wirtschaftsgesch.', I, 1879, pp. 195 ff., for a list of the livestock values specified in money of the ancient common laws see *ibid.*, p. 512. In addition: Schmoller, *Grundriss d. V. L.* II, 1904, p. 66.

31. Cf. Windscheid, *Lehrb. d. Pandektenrechts*, II, §256.

32. For the question (much discussed in jurisprudence) of the standard (expressed in money) of substitute performances, the economic theory of exchange equivalents (e.g. x hundredweights of iron = y hundredweights of coal = z pounds of silver) has become of great importance (see, on the other hand, already my *Grunds. d. V. L.*, pp. 172 and 272 ff.). Goldschmidt (*Handelsrecht*, II, 1883, p. 88, n. 20) shares my opinion that in reality there are no 'objective equivalents' in the sense assumed by both economic theory and jurisprudence. 'At any rate', he says, 'all exchange rests on equating a specified quantity of good x and a specified quantity of good y with regard to their overall economic usefulness and insofar as (e.g.) 100x has the same value as (is equivalent to) 50y.' Against this it must be objected that an 'overall economic' usefulness (abstracting from the subjective relation of the goods to economizing individuals!), as assumed by Goldschmidt and some economic theorists, exists just as little, in fact, as the quantity relation assumed by them of 100x = 50y, etc. There is no market where 100x could be exchanged for 50y and vice versa (bought and resold at the same price, ad libitum). Moreover, this is a fiction that jurisprudence not only has no need of but that it should reject outright with regard to the problems chiefly being

considered here of substitute performances in general and compensation for damages in particular.

There is an important consequence to be drawn from a correct interpretation of exchange ratios among goods: when valuing goods, these should not be dissociated from the economy in which they are found and should not be valued in money without regard to the economic purpose that the valuation serves; rather, the above-mentioned circumstances should be taken into account, as is in fact done in the advanced practice of appraisal of goods. It makes a difference e.g. for the estimated price ('the money equivalent') of a good whether it is in the possession of a person who needs the good directly for his consumption or his production or in the possession of someone for whom it has only 'exchange value'. Consider the damages which the owner may claim for a collection of books intended for his own use and those that his widow, say, would be justified in claiming for the same object after his death. Lest he suffer a loss, the former must receive as compensation a sum of money for which he could again acquire, that is buy, a library of the same sort; the latter must be paid the money price for which she could sell the same library – which, as everyone knows, makes a very big difference in the amount of compensation. Valuation of goods by their overall economic usefulness is a fiction which, even if it were feasible, would be unsuited to the requirements of both economic life and the administration of justice.

33. Without delivery of the commodities or of the purchase price or without counting out and settling sums of debt, transactions on commodity and capital markets would be economically purposeless and quite unthinkable as normal phenomena of economic life. Payment of the purchase price is as essential a component of purchase and sale as delivery of the commodity. Just as one cannot ascribe a special function as means of settlement to the commodities (e.g. the grain or the iron which the seller has to deliver), one cannot do this in the case of the money to be paid as purchase price. The same holds for the settlement of loans.

34. For jurisprudence, the theory of the settlement of money debts is of special importance if only because the decision about the quantity and kind of means of payment by which money debts may be settled with legal effect in a particular case forms a very extensive and important part of the administration of justice. In economic analysis, the act of payment is far less important than the analysis of the causes of transactions of goods and of influences on price formation. On this compare my remarks in the sections on the 'Influence of Government on the Shaping of the Monetary System' and on the 'Concept of Money' (chapters V and XIII).

35. This explains why, with an advancing money economy, hoarding tends to be more and more replaced by capital accumulation. In the economic conditions of peoples of advanced civilization, putting money aside for an emergency (the income that might be derived from it playing a minor role among the economic considerations) is analogous to hoarding, once so important. A war treasure put aside in hard cash (emergency money of the state in the strict sense of the words) is a case in point.

36. The explanation of the fact that in an exchange of goods – both in an exchange of goods for consumption purposes and in one between entrepreneurs (producers and merchants) – both contracting parties seek to gain an economic advantage (an improvement in their economic position) or profit, and with proper economizing

normally in fact do gain it, follows above all from the consideration that they do not undertake an exchange mechanically and under any and all circumstances (perhaps at the fictitious ratio of x hundredweights of coal = y pounds of copper = z bushels of wheat) but rather enter into an exchange only if and when a profit results for both parties. Especially in the first case the mutual gain is explained by the different use values that the different goods may have (even on the same market and the same point in time) for two different economic agents (the two contracting parties) because, e.g., good *a* in possession of economic agent A has less use value for him than good *b* in possession of B, while for B the opposite value relation holds. From an exchange occurring on this or a similar basis both sides can in fact obtain an economic advantage, as is self-evident; both of them may improve their economic positions by the exchange. Indeed, the prices may be agreed on between the contracting parties at different levels (within certain price limits) without the economic advantage for either one being necessarily nullified thereby. Wherever the precondition for mutual gain of the contracting parties is not satisfied, an economic exchange of goods cannot take place at all and indeed normally does not take place.

The profit (or entrepreneurial profit) on both sides gained from such transactions occurring between merchants and other entrepreneurs is to be explained likewise. Here, too, it must first of all be observed that the above economizing individuals conclude a deal not under any and all circumstances but only when it promises a profit to both parties. Now, if there existed at every point in time on the same market exchange ratios fixed in advance, as by the typical formula given above, then in transactions between merchants a profit for both parties, when it in fact occurs, would in many cases be truly unexplainable. If it is kept in mind, however, that the above exchange ratio of goods in its strict mathematical formulation, supposedly prevailing on the markets already before the acts of exchange are performed, is only a fiction (if it is kept in mind that the exchange ratio of goods on our markets is not the precondition but the result of the interplay of the economic interests of the contracting parties), then the traders' mutual entrepreneurial profit from exchanges of goods is explained in a way both natural and illuminating. – Cf. my *Grundsätze d. V. L.*, pp. 160 ff.; E. v. Boehm-Bawerk, Grundzüge der Theorie des wirtschaftlichen Güterwertes (*Jahrb. f. Nat. u. Stat.*, 1886, N.S. XIII, pp. 483 ff., esp. 489 ff.); E. Sax, *Grundlegung der theoretischen Staatswirtschaft*, 1887, pp. 271 ff. and 276 ff.; Fr. v. Wieser, *Der natürliche Wert*, 1889, pp. 300 ff., 352 ff., references *ibid.* pp. 44 ff., 88 ff.; R. Zuckerkandl, *Zur Theorie des Preises*, 1889, passim; E. v. Philippovich, *Grundriss*, 3rd edn, pp. 204 and 221.

37. While Plato (*Politeia*, II, 11 ff.; *The Laws/ Gesetze /*, V, 9 ff., VIII, 9 ff.) restricts himself to emphasizing the necessity of the division of labour, exchange of goods, money, and merchants and allowing the latter a 'fair profit' on the basis of strictly fixed prices, Aristotle (in conformity with his ethical doctrine) puts forth the principle that in an exchange of goods each of the contracting parties should receive equal amounts, wherefore the goods to be exchanged should be measured in money beforehand: 'Just as a community would not be possible without exchange, so exchange would not be possible without equality nor equality without a common standard' (*Nik. Eth.* V, 7 ff., *Polit*, I, 6). 'If relative equality is determined first and compensation or equalization takes place accordingly, this is what we mean ... Therefore, all things to be exchanged must be comparable in a

certain sense. That is what money is intended for: to be, as it were, the intermediary; for it measures everything, therefore also surplus and deficiency, e.g., how many shoes are equal to a house or a certain quantity of foodstuffs' (*Nikom. Eth.*, V, 8). – Note that Aristotle, as Plato had already done in part, repeatedly emphasizes that need is the true cause of the exchange of goods and the measure of everything. By agreement, however, money has become the proxy of need and accordingly the measure of the goods to be exchanged (Plato, *Politeia*, II, 11 and 12; Aristotle, *Nik. Eth.*, V, 8).

38. The authors who follow the doctrine contested here, or who at least are more or less unconsciously influenced by it, have been misled chiefly by the fact that on reasonably developed markets, the individual pairs of contracting parties are influenced in the establishment of prices not only by their subjective evaluations of the goods but also by the competition in supply and demand of other market participants (or by the market prices resulting from their competition). (Cf. my *Grunds. d. V. L.*, pp. 201 ff.) Whoever on a market for his goods, e.g., could exchange these with a fellow market participant for goods having a higher (subjective) value for him than the former would nevertheless regularly reject this exchange (although he could improve his economic situation by it!) if he could obtain the goods offered to him from another market participant for a smaller quantity of his own good. Likewise, as a rule, no one trades away his commodity to persons who offer him otherwise satisfactory prices if still better buyers of his commodity are to be found. In exchanging goods, the contracting parties in fact take account not only of their subjective value judgments but also, in pursuit of their economic interests, of the market prices (in no way uniform!) being formed (through the interplay of the individual interests of the other market participants). The more trade develops and especially as it becomes concentrated through the organization of exchange on the individual markets and by connecting different markets (through commodity shipments and arbitrage), the greater and more continuous becomes the influence exerted on individual economic units by the competing efforts of other units (even of those who are economically precluded by the price struggle from the acquisition or sale of the goods in question!) and by the market prices being formed. But even on the markets so organized, the prices of goods always vary within more or less wide limits of price formation. Commodities of the same kind and quality, indeed of the same origin, are, as is known, sold at noticeably different prices at different points of sale, and even at the same points of sale at the same time to different customers. This phenomenon is to be observed even with the most ordinary articles of retail trade but far more so in the sale of goods of low marketability (rare old books, copperplate engravings, old coins, etc.), which, as experience shows, are sold, even at the same time and in the same place, at different points of sale, at grossly different prices, indeed in individual cases at double and triple of what they can be acquired for and in fact are acquired for at other points of sale.

Nowhere, however, can the above phenomena be more exactly and reliably observed than in wholesale trade, and precisely on those markets where the greatest concentration of supply and demand occurs: on the organized exchanges. Here, of course, price formation takes place in normal times within far narrower limits than in retail trade or the not equally tightly organized branches of wholesale trade. Anyway, it is precisely on the securities and commodity

exchanges that we may observe how the prices that actually evolve are formed
between the limits of supply price and demand price, and indeed at the same
point in time and on the same exchange, at noticeably different levels. If the level
of price goes down, hitherto latent demand appears; if it rises, hitherto latent
supply appears (they are turned into effective demand and effective supply,
respectively); the effective prices move, however, within the limits of those
prices listed in the price sheets under the rubrics *bid* and *asked* (*Geld* and*Ware* in
Vienna, *Geld* and *Brief* on the German exchanges). Even on the securities and
commodity exchanges, the well-known formula $7x = 10y = 20z$, etc. is not
applicable; and even here the effective prices agreed on between specific pairs of
contracting parties are still the result of the respective economic agents' profit
motives, however much they are also influenced by the competing efforts of
other market participants and by the transactions concluded between other parties
on the exchange. Even here the 'exchange values' of the items traded are not first
measured by the exchange value of the money unit, with trade then taking place
on this basis. It is clear, rather, that even in these cases the effective prices are the
results of the interplay of the evident and mutually influencing economic interests
of the economic agents. Yet the fact that the levels of the prices actually being
formed at any time have no compelling influence, as a rule, on the individual
contracting parties is explained by the fact that the latter, according to what their
economic interests require, buy and sell or hold back their purchase and sale or
altogether abstain from trading.

39. Cf. the article 'Price' (general part) [in *Handwörterbuch der Staats-
    wissenschaften*, 3rd edition].
40. Note that 'exchange value' in this sense is no definite magnitude, a fact that is
    taken into account only partly in practical life and usually not at all in theory
    because of the prevailing deficient price theory (on this see section X).
41. The doctrine of money as measure of the exchange value of goods was set on an
    unrealistic (fictitious) foundation only when a number of economic theorists
    failed to appreciate that the 'exchange value' expressed in money – the 'money
    value' – of goods represents only an exchange relation between tradable goods
    and money, which accordingly cannot appear in the individual good and is,
    moreover, a variable and not precisely determined relation, being mainly
    determined by the interplay of the individual interests of the market participants,
    and when they interpreted the 'exchange value' of goods as something inherent in
    the individual goods (in commodities as well as in money), as a 'quantity of
    exchange value' inherent in them (and not only figuratively but quite seriously as
    'exchange power inherent in the individual goods'), and the act of assessment of
    goods in money units as 'measurement of this quantity of exchange value by the
    quantity of exchange value inherent in money or the money unit' (in this sense
    still Knies, *Das Geld*, 2nd edn, 1885, pp. 146 ff.).

    'To measure easily and conveniently the relative values of all commodities,
    compared one with another, and to enable all dealers to estimate the profits which
    they make upon their sales: this purpose is completely [!] answered by money'
    (R. Malthus, *Princ. of P. E.*, 2nd edn, 1836, p. 84).
42. E. v. Philippovich, *Grundriss d. P. Oek.*, I, §91, 4, 7th edn, 1908, p. 233.
43. On proposals for overcoming the fluctuations of commodity prices: Jos. Lowe,
    *The present state of England*, etc., 1822 (German transl. by L.H. v. Jacob, 1823,
    pp. 445 ff., esp. 486 ff.); G. Poulett Scrope, *Princ. of P. E.*, 1833, Ch. XVI, pp.

397 ff., 405 ff., 413, 421 ff.; St. Jevons, *A serious fall in the value of gold*, 1863, esp. Chs. II and V; idem, *Money and the mechanism of exchange* (1875), esp. Ch. XXV in the edition of 1882; H.S. Foxwell, *Irregularity of employment and fluctuations of prices*, 1886, pp. 25 ff., 37 ff.; Alfr. Marshall, 'Remedies for fluctuations of general prices' (*Contempor. Rev.* 1887, March, pp. 355, 368 ff.); L. Walras, *Théorie de la monnaie*, 1889, passim; Aneurin Williams, 'A "fixed value of bullion" standard', *Econ. Journ.* II, 1892, pp. 280 ff.; cf. also J. Nicholson, *A treatise on money*, 1888, Part I, Ch. II, §§10-12 and Part II, Sect. 7; idem, *Princ. o. P. E.*, I, 1893, pp. 327, 337 ff. (On various interesting phenomena of the Austro-Hungarian currency, see B. Földes *J. f. N. u. St.*, 1882, N.S. IV, pp. 141 ff., 245 ff.) See the bibliography of the article on 'Preis' ('Statistische Bestimmung des Preisniveaus' [in *Handwörterbuch der Staatswissenschaften*, 3rd edition].

44. See bibliography of the article on 'Preis' [in *Handwörterbuch der Staatswissenschaften*, 3rd edition]. – Periodical reports on price movements by Soetbeer, Conrad et al. in *Conrads Jahrbücher*, passim; esp. in the volume for 1899, pp. 642 seq.

45. Nothing is more usual than to say that wealth or a capital has doubled when its outer exchange value (its 'money equivalent') has doubled over time. The same holds true for income. Likewise, people speak of a rise or fall in the value of a commodity when its 'money-economy market equivalent' has become larger or smaller, without noticing the movement in the inner exchange value of money. (Cf. A. Marshall, *Principles of Economics*, 3rd edn, 1895, pp. 673 seq.)

46. See already Xenophon, *De Vectigalib. Atheniens.* 4.

47. Je trouve, que la charté que nous voyons, viens [sic] quasi pour quatre ou cinq causes. La principale et presque seule (que personne iusques icy n'a touchée) est l'abondance d'or et d'argent, qui est aujourd'huy en ce royaume plus grande, qu'elle n'a esté il y a quatre cens ans ... La principale cause (de la charté), en quelque lieu que ce soit, est l'abondance de ce qui donne estimation et prix aux choses.' (*Discours de Jean Bodin sur le rehaussement et diminution des monayes*. Paris, chez Jacques du Pays, 1578 4°, fol. f. seq.; in the Latin translation by Herm. Contrin, *Joh. Bodini respons. ad paradoxa Malestretti de caritate rerum*, Helmstad, 1671, pp. 11 ff.). But cf. already Aristotle (*Ethic. Nic.*, V, 8): 'To be sure, money also is subject to change, for it does not always have the same value, but it tends to be more nearly unchangeable than everything else.'

48. 'There has been no more fruitful source of error in the very elements of political economy, than the not distinguishing between the power of purchasing generally and the power of purchasing from intrinsic causes; and it is of the highest importance to be fully aware that, practically, when the rise or fall in the value of a commodity is referred to, its power of purchasing arising from extrinsic causes is always excluded' (R. Malthus, *Princ. of P. E.*, 2nd edn, 1836, p. 60).

49. See W. Bagehot, 'A new standard of value' (*Economist*, Nov. 1875 and again in the *Econ. Journ.*, II, 1892, pp. 472 ff.); R. Giffen, 'Fancy monetary standards' (*Econ. Journ.*, ibid, pp. 463 ff.). – If no small number of students of monetary theory regard the present state of the monetary system of countries with a pure gold standard – under which regime government is essentially only the people's mintmaster for full-valued coins (the basis of the entire monetary system) – as the peak of attainable perfection and development of money, it must be pointed out

that even this form of monetary system, with all due recognition of the advantages that it has for the economy in general in some respects and for certain groups of the population in others, may nevertheless be regarded only as a stage in the evolution of money and is of far from absolute significance.

50. Going beyond previously used methods, W. Lexis attempts to identify movement of the 'inner value of money'. Basically, he relies on the observation that quantity prices (the trade values of the quantities consumed) show special stability, both for individual economic units and in the national economy. When a commodity becomes cheaper the quantity consumed rises, as experience shows, and when it becomes more expensive the quantity declines; therefore, movements of unit prices would be at least partly evened out in the above-mentioned quantity prices; also, the income saved by one commodity's becoming cheaper would be used for the consumption of other goods; so that for this reason, too, the sum total of the prices of the quantities consumed of various commodities in a national economy (with quantities varying in different periods of observation, depending on varying needs) would exhibit relatively greater stability than the average of the unit prices of the same commodities. The elasticity of circulation of the means of payment would also contribute to this. On the use of these observations for identifying the movement of the inner value of money, see W. Lexis, 'Über gewisse Wertgesamtheiten und deren Beziehung zum Geldwert'. *Tübinger Ztschr. f. d. ges. Staatsw.*, vol. 44, 1888, pp. 225 ff. See also Nasse-Lexis in *Schönbergs Handbuch*, 4th edn, 1896, vol. 1, pp. 342 ff.

51. Failure to appreciate the above facts has been the cause of many errors. Long before the developing and increasingly complex trade in goods led to the emergence of generally used media of exchange, indeed long before there was any exchange of goods at all in human societies, unilateral transfers of various kinds (gifts, contributions, fines, compensation for damages, etc.), especially also hoarding, and in no few cases even rough valuations of goods by means of other goods (not, of course, according to their exchange values but according to their use values for the economic agents!) (see chapter VI) were already common. These are economic transactions that can scarcely be conceived of in advanced economies, especially in present-day civilized nations, without the use of money, at least, in part, or some reference to it, transactions with which, accordingly, we are in any case used to associating money payments, while in the earlier periods of cultural evolution these transactions took place entirely as barter – they were phenomena not of the money economy, but of the barter economy. If the functions of money are registered not in their proper genetic linkage but only mechanically side-by-side, then the idea suggests itself to regard already as money those goods that in the era of barter (i.e. in the phase of economic development in which truly there cannot be any question of 'money' yet) were used or preferred for purposes which today are served almost exclusively by money payments – an error that we encounter often enough indeed among economists and historians. (It is a palpable error, e.g., to infer the money character of certain goods in the periods in question from the fact that these goods were once used for contributions, fines, etc. in kind or that estimates and valuations for barter purposes were carried out in them.)

52. Here we must attend especially to a fact that is important not for identifying the nature of money but for forming the popular notion and in part even the scientific concept of it. At the beginnings of trade, especially with the division of labour

only slightly developed, that part of a good intended by an individual economic unit to be traded away is not strictly separated, not even quantitatively, let alone by individual units, from the part held back for its own use; rather it is influenced by particular changes in needs and the changing market situation. This also holds true, of course, especially at the beginnings of money, of goods that subsequently become generally used media of exchange. A strict separation of the stock of goods that particularly serve to mediate exchanges from consumption goods, on the one hand, and other goods intended for the market, on the other hand, first occurs in individual economic units when their growing dependence on the market creates a need for special stocks of media of exchange, but especially when those goods become generally used media of exchange for which many economic units have no direct need and when requirements of trade demand that those goods be given a special trading form that facilitates the exchange of goods. Only thereby does the intrinsic (economic) contrast between money and the market goods offered for money show itself outwardly also in the individual economies. The development of the concept of money among different peoples offers noteworthy evidence of how important this fact has been, especially for the popular idea of money (see footnote 11).

53. A. Wagner (*Theor. Sozialökonomie*, part II, vol. 2: 'Geld und Geldwesen', pp. 116 ff.) also describes the functions of money to be observed, apart from its functions as medium of exchange and measure of value (price), as only secondary (derivative) functions; but he sticks to the view that the function of money as standard of value (price) (like that of medium of exchange) is a 'primary or chief function' of money. It is to be noted, however, that both the function of money as 'standard of value' and the separate function of money as measure of price (as price indicator!) necessarily presuppose the phenomenon of money prices, indeed in their developed form even the comprehensive function of money as intermediary of exchanges (on this see chapters X and XI, Introduction), and accordingly must be described as derivative functions of money.

54. R. Koch in Endemann's *Handb. d. deutsch. Handelsrechts*, 1882, II, p. 115; cf. L. Goldschmidt's *Handb. d. Handelsr.*, 1868, II, part I, pp. 1069 and 1079, note 28; idem, *System d. Handelsr.*, 1889, p. 126; G. Hartmann, *Über d. rechtl. Begriff des Geldes usw.* 1868, pp. 12 ff.; Dernburg, *Pandekt.* Book III, §26; idem, *Lehrb. d. preuss. Privatrechts,* 5th edn (1897), II, §32. Qualifications of the above interpretation in Goldschmidt, *loc. cit.*, pp. 1069 ff.; Koch, *loc. cit.*, p. 115; F. Regelsberger *Pandekt.* I, §104, note 4.

55. It is characteristic of the development of economic views in the 19th century that, almost without exception, the predominantly Manchester-liberal writers of its first half regard legal tender as a symptom of the corruption of money (a fact that reacts upon the monetary doctrines of jurists also), while economists of the second half of the 19th century (influenced by jurists!) are inclined to see in legal tender an attribute of perfect money.

56. §883 (new numbering) of the Rules of Civil Procedure of the German Empire, section 1, reads: 'If the debtor is to deliver a movable object or a quantity of specified movable objects, these are to be taken from him by the bailiff and transferred to the creditor.' §884: 'If the debtor is to deliver a specified quantity of fungible objects or securities, the provision of §883, section 1, is to be applied accordingly.' Similarly §346 of the Austrian Rules of Execution. (Cf. v.

Schrutka, *Zeitschr. f. deutsch. Zivilproz.*, vol. 11, 1887, p. 164, who suggests the term 'executory substitute delivery' for the procedure covered by the above regulations.)

57. With regard to money, all of us find ourselves in a certain sense in the position of the merchant: we regularly acquire money not to consume or process it but to part with it again. Our stock of cash is thus somewhat similar to a commodity inventory. The difference between the two cases is that we acquire and spend money (as such) not only from a profit motive, which in the age of the money economy shows itself mainly in buying and selling, but essentially to facilitate exchanges of goods. (See, however, R. Hildebrand, *Theorie des Geldes*, p. 10.)

58. Cf. A. Smith, *W. o. N.*, IV. i, passim; Ricardo, 'High price of bullion', *Works*, 1871, p. 234; J. S. Mill, *Princ. of P. E.*, III, Ch. VIII, §3; some earlier references in Roscher, *System* I, §123, 5.

59. Despite the misunderstandings on which they are based, the above theories do contain a correct element of monetary theory insofar as they make us aware that in a money economy even the mere technicalities of goods trading and of payments require a considerable amount of cash and that, accordingly, every avoidable obstacle to and delay of the circulation of money and payment procedures causes an avoidable (uneconomic) demand for circulating media, involving economic sacrifices, in individual economic units and indirectly in the national economy.

# REFERENCES

Literature on the monetary system is overabundant. It includes – apart from works on numismatics – (according to estimates that I have undertaken with J. Stammhammer on the basis of comprehensive bibliographical compilations to date) far more than 5000 to 6000 separate writings and articles published in scientific journals. A complete bibliography on the monetary system would fill an octavo volume of about 300 pages. Here I limit myself to a survey of the more important bibliographical publications and collective works about the monetary system published so far.

Bibliographical works: **Philippus Labbe**, Bibliotheca numaria ex theologis, jurisconsultis, medicis ac philologis concinnata, octavo [8°] Paris: 1664 and later. – **Anselm. Bandurus**, Bibliotheca numismatica, II. Lutet. Paris. 1718, fol., published in quarto [4°] by Fabricius, Hamburg: 1719. – **F. E. Brückmann**, Bibliotheca numismatica, oder Verzeichnis der mehresten Schriften, so vom Münzwesen handeln was hiervon sowol Historici, Physici, Chymici, Medici, als auch Juristen und Theologi geschrieben, octavo [8°], Wolffenb.: 1729, with supplements of 1732 and 1741. – **Joh. Christ. Hirsch**, Bibliotheca numismatica (omnium gentium) exhibens catalogum auctorum, qui de re monetaria et numis tam antiquis quam recentioribus scripsere, collecta et indice rerum instructa, folio, Nürnberg: 1760. – **J. G. Lipsius**, Bibliotheca numaria, sive catalogus auctorum, qui usque ad finem seculi XVIII de re monetaria aut numis scripserunt, II, octavo, Leipzig: 1801.

Collections of treatises: **Math. Boyss**, Tractatus varii atque utiles de monetis earumque mutatione ac falsitate, octavo, Köln, 1574. – **Rener. Budelius**, Tractatus varii atque utiles, nec non consilia singularesque additiones tam veterum quam neotericorum authorum, qui de monetis, earundemque valore, liga, pondere, postestate, etc. scripserunt (appendix to his De monetis et re nummaria libr. II, quarto, Köln, 1591 – De monetarum augmento **[116]** variatione et diminutione tractatus varii, octavo, Augsburg, 1609. – Zwanzig Tractate, das schlechte Münzwesen und dem Wucher bey den Kippern und Wippern betreffend, quarto, 1659. – **Dav. Thom. v. Hagelstein**, Acta publica monetaria (also including many treatises, among others ones by Nic. Oresmius, Gab. Byel, Joh. Aquila), folio, Augsburg: 1692. – **Lord Overstone** and **J. R. McCulloch**, A select collection of scarce and valuable tracts on monney [sic] (Vaughan, Cotton, Petty, Lowndes, Newton, Prior, Harris and others), London: 1856. – **Idem**, A select collection of scarce and valuable tracts and other publications on Paper-Currency and Banking (Hume, Wallace, Thornton, Ricardo, Blake, Huskisson and others), London: 1857.

Older valuable literature surveys: Dictionnaire de l'Econ. Pol. by Coquelin and Guillaumin, II, 1853, article 'Monnaie' (extending to around the middle of the 19th century). – **McCulloch**, The literature of polit. economy, London, 1845, pp. 155-91 (chiefly English literature).

More recent literature surveys: **Dona** [recte: Dana] **Horton**, appendix to the International Monetary Conference Held in Paris in August 1878, Washington: 1879, pp. 854 ff. (chiefly literature of the 19th century up to 1879). – **H.** [recte: W.] **St. Jevons**, bibliography of books and articles on money and coinage systems, appendix to his Investigations in Currency and Finance, ed. by H. S. Foxwell, London: 1884, pp. 363-414 (rather extensive information on the literature of the monetary system from the middle of the 16th century up to 1882). – **Ad. Soetbeer**, Literaturnachweis über Geld- u. Münzwesen insbesondere über den Währungsstreit, 1871-1891, Berlin: 1892. – Extended by the bibliographer **Lippert** up to and including 1902 in **K. Helfferich**, Geld und Banken, 'Das Geld', vol. I, pp. 532 ff., 1903. – **R. H. Inglis Palgrave**, Dictionary of Political Economy, vol. II, pp. 795 ff., London: 1896 (literature survey up to 1896). – Continuing reports on new literature (books and articles) and legislation concerning the monetary system in *Jahrbücher für Nationalökonomie und Statistik* (Jena), beginning in 1882 (N.S. vol. IV). – Also see the references in the articles 'Gold-', 'Silber-', 'Doppel-', 'Parallelwährung', 'Preis', etc. in this work.

# TRANSLATOR'S NOTES BY LELAND B. YEAGER

Carl Menger wrote long compound-complex sentences, almost as if he feared being quoted out of context and wanted to leave no supporting considerations, no examples, and no qualifications go unrepeated, even within single sentences. The temptation is strong to split up Menger's sentences and curtail his repetitions. Dr Monika Streissler and I agree, however, that a translator, even more so than a copy-editor, has the duty to resist what H. G. Wells called the strongest of all human passions, the

passion to improve on someone else's text. The very different word orders in German and English offer scope enough for a translator's creativity. (Some trifling improvements were legitimate, however, like supplying some opening or closing parentheses or dashes forgotten by Menger or by the printer.) It may be true that prolixity is a vice of German and Austrian professors, but the German language does not impose it. Menger could have written otherwise, but he preferred a complicated, verbose, and old-fashioned style; and he is the author.

The word 'government', noun and adjective, is almost always 'Staat' and the derived adjective in the original; and 'state' would have been an equally acceptable translation.

I had begun expanding the abbreviated titles and publication data of the books and articles cited, but it was decided further to preserve Menger's style by leaving these pretty much unchanged. Menger occasionally misspells an author's name, for example, Dona [for S. Dana] Horton in the references at the end.

Menger's persuasive account of how money evolved 'spontaneously' from the most convenient articles of barter, not being a contrivance of the state, does not dictate our understanding of its role in the modern world. Modern money, as well as the emerging electronic payments systems analysed in this volume by Lawrence White, George Selgin, and Stefan Schmitz, has become a device for monitoring transactions, keeping records, calculating economic benefits and costs, and accomplishing multilateral clearing. Money enables people conveniently to use entitlements acquired by delivering goods and services and securities to some trading partners to obtain others of these from other trading partners. The tickets and memoranda employed in these operations need not take the form of little disks of precious metal or 100-percent-backed warehouse receipts for these or other kinds of base money. Despite the assertions of one small sect of 'Austrian' economists, nothing in economics, morality, or law so requires.

PART II


Perspectives on the Evolution of Electronic
Money

# 3.    Carl Menger's 'Money' and the current neoclassical models of money

## Stefan W. Schmitz[*]

The following chapter briefly summarizes the current neoclassical models of money and contrasts them with Menger's institutional approach.[1] The models were motivated by an attempt to reconcile Walrasian value theory with monetary theory. In a frictionless market where agents trade multilaterally and simultaneously based on equilibrium prices there is no 'absence of a double coincidence of wants' constraint to barter. Consequently, there is no role for money as a medium of exchange.[2] In order to explain why rational agents exchange goods for intrinsically worthless money, various frictions have to be introduced in the models. The Mengerian approach is contrasted with current neoclassical models of money in order to point out the narrow scope of the latter in particular with regard to their treatment of the social institution[3] of money.

The selection of current neoclassical models is restricted to those that satisfy Wallace's (1998) 'Dictum for Monetary Theory': as examples of the eligible models I discuss Kiyotaki and Wright's (1992) search model, Samuelson's (1958) overlapping generations model, and Townsend's (1980) spatial separation model. To satisfy the dictum, a theory has to specify assets by their physical properties (that is, their explicit payoffs) and embed the economy in an environment in which the asset's role in exchange is determined endogenously. I will briefly describe the three models, although the main focus is on the equilibrium concepts employed and their suitability to study the fundamental questions in the theory of the origin of money.

> That a good is given up by its possessor in exchange for another one more useful to him is an occurrence plausible even to the meanest intelligence. But that among all somewhat civilized peoples every economic agent should be willing, indeed eager, to trade away his goods intended for exchange for small metal disks that seem useless in themselves or for documents representing these: this is an occurrence so contrary to the ordinary course of things that we must not be surprised if it seems downright 'mysterious'. [...] How did money come about? (Menger, 1909, p. 3)

Menger emphasizes two questions: (*i*) the individual rationality of accepting intrinsically worthless objects in exchange for goods,[4] and (*ii*) the emergence of the social institution of money. I will argue that the three models discussed in the chapter focus only on the question of individual rationality and its welfare implications taking the social institution of money as given. Moreover, they are static in the sense that the expectations of the agents in the economies concerning the acceptability of money are constant over time and determined exogenously. Therefore, the models do not address the question of how the social institution of money came about or why agents prefer monetary exchange to indirect barter.

In addition, the chapter argues that the Mengerian method of institutional analysis is suitable to investigate current institutional change in the monetary system due to the emergence of new electronic payment systems.

Due to the exogeneity of expectations, the use of static equilibrium concepts and the neglect of the evolution of the institution of money, the models are of limited use in the analysis of new electronic payment systems. An understanding of the formation of expectations is crucial for the analysis of new electronic payments systems. Positive irreversible fixed costs (such as terminals, acquisition of technology competence and so on) are frequently associated with joining a new electronic payment system. Furthermore, the realized marginal utility due to transaction cost savings associated with an individual transaction is relatively low. Consequently, the decision to join a new electronic payment system can be interpreted as an investment decision. The expected return on investment is influenced by the individuals' expectations with regard to the acceptability of the new medium of exchange (for example some form of electronic money).[5]

The emergence of new electronic payment systems is an instant of institutional change in the financial system. Current neoclassical models of money assume the institutional setup (including the social institution of money) to be exogenously given. In order to analyse the emergence of new electronic payment systems a different method is required – the Mengerian method of institutional analysis.

Moreover, a very short translation of Menger's 'Money'[6] is one of the most quoted early papers in the theory of the origin of money. A critical assessment of the models from a Mengerian viewpoint thus sheds light on the differences in economic approaches to the role of money.

The paper is structured along the following lines: first, the three current neoclassical models of money are briefly described – search models, overlapping generations models, and spatial separations models. Secondly, their common methodological characteristics are contrasted with the Mengerian method of institutional analysis. The final section provides a conclusion and summary.

# 1. SEARCH MODELS

Search models base the argument for the origin of money on the absence of a double coincidence of wants. Due to specialization of production and preferences that do not allow agents to consume their own product, trade is necessary to consumption. The absence of a centralized market imposes high search costs on the agents. The mutual acceptance of a medium of exchange can overcome some of the restrictions imposed by the trading technology and the economic environment by reducing search costs. A double coincidence of wants is no longer necessary. The description in Table 3.1 of a search model follows Kiyotaki and Wright (1992). Other examples include Kiyotaki and Wright (1989, 1991) and Wallace (1997).

*Table 3.1: Assumptions of a typical search model of money (Kiyotaki and Wright, 1992)*

| The Economy |
|---|
| ➢ A very large number of agents all of whom live indefinitely[7] and maximize discounted utility $U$. |
| ➢ Agents' discount expected future consumption at a constant rate $0 < \beta < 1$ or $1/(1 + r)$ where $r$ is the real rate of interest. |
| ➢ There is a large number of goods that are indivisible and storable at no cost. |
| ➢ Furthermore, the agents do not know the economy's full history of transactions (see Kocherlakota, 1998a, b) nor can they commit to future actions (see Wallace, 1997). |

| Consumption |
|---|
| ➢ All goods are consumed by a fraction $x$ of all agents. |
| ➢ Each agent consumes the fraction $x$ of all goods.[8] |
| ➢ No agent consumes the good he produces. |
| ➢ Utility derived from the consumption of one unit of a consumption good is $u$. |

| Production |
|---|
| ➢ All goods are produced by an equal number of agents, the fraction $x$ of all agents. |
| ➢ Before an agent can produce a unit of a good he has to consume. Production takes place immediately after consumption. |
| ➢ The costs per unit produced are $c$ (in terms of disutility). The quantity produced is one unit. |

| **Endowment** |
| --- |
| ➢ The fraction *M* of all agents is endowed with one unit of an intrinsically worthless object called money.<br>➢ Money is indivisible.<br>➢ The fraction *(1 – M)* is endowed with one unit of a good. |
| **Trading technology** |
| ➢ In each period two agents are randomly matched.<br>➢ They trade iff it is beneficial for both of them.<br>➢ One makes a take-it-or-leave-it offer. Trade leads to an equal distribution of the gains of trade.[9]<br>➢ Accepting one unit of a good other than money in exchange involves a transaction cost $\varepsilon$ (in terms of disutility). |
| **Equilibrium** |
| ➢ The equilibrium concept employed is a symmetric, steady state Nash equilibrium. |

The frictions in the market due to the trading technology are of crucial importance: if we presume the existence of a centralized market with zero search costs of indirect exchange via a Walrasian auctioneer, consumption and production would take place in each period. A double-coincidence-of-wants constraint on bilateral barter would not pose any trading restrictions. Under the assumption of a zero search cost trading technology, no medium of exchange would be necessary.

Because there are a large number of agents in the economy it is unlikely that agents will meet more than once. Credit arrangements to facilitate trade are therefore not an option. The very low probability of ever meeting a certain agent and the restrictions on credible commitment technologies rule out the circulation of credit certificates as the probability of redemption is low. Consequently, the incentive structure would not be sufficient to constrain the issue of individual credit certificates in relation to individual future production.[10]

The equilibrium concept employed by Kiyotaki and Wright (1992) is restricted to symmetric, steady state Nash equilibria. This implies that agents are treated identically and treat each other identically. Furthermore, it implies that given the symmetry of consumption and production of all goods the acceptability of each good is identical. An equilibrium consists of the optimal trading strategies for all agents based on their belief about the strategies of all others that assign a specific trading decision to each current holding (of either money or the good produced) conditioned on the holding (of either money or the good produced) of each possible trading partner. The strategies must be consistent with maximization of discounted expected utility and rational expectations.[11] Since the analysis is restricted to steady state equilibria, the optimal strategy is independent of time.

**Solving the Model**

Because of the symmetry of the model, the distinction between different goods with respect to whether or not they have been produced by the agent is not necessary. Each agent might therefore hold either (*i*) money or (*ii*) a good which the agent does not himself consume at the end of the initial period. In each period each agent randomly meets someone who holds either money or a good he does not himself want to consume.

First consider the case in which two agents meet, both of whom hold goods. If they trade goods they do not themselves want to consume, both of them have to bear the transaction cost $\varepsilon$. What are the benefits derived from accepting a good one does not want to consume? Holding a good that is more likely to be accepted in exchange for the desired consumption good would increase the discounted expected utility of future consumption. But, due to the symmetry of the model, the acceptability of all goods in trade is equal. No gain in terms of discounted expected utility is associated with the exchange but the transaction cost of $\varepsilon$ is incurred by each agent.

Consequently, no agent accepts a consumption good in equilibrium he does not himself consume. Therefore, two agents holding goods trade if and only if both of them receive their desired consumption goods. Since each good is consumed by the fraction $x$ of all agents, the probability for such a double coincidence of wants to occur is $x^2$. The equilibrium strategy in meetings with agents who hold goods, therefore, is: accept a good in exchange for another good if and only if it is your desired consumption good. An agent derives utility $U = u - c - \varepsilon$ with probability $(1 - M)x^2$.

After having resolved the acceptability of goods through meetings, the acceptability of money has to be determined endogenously in line with Wallace's dictum. The probability of accepting money is $\pi$ and the expectations concerning the acceptability of money by others is denoted $\Pi$. In order to determine the conditions for the acceptance of money being an equilibrium strategy, we have to analyse the relative values of holding (*i*) a good at the end of a period ($V_c$) and (*ii*) of holding money at the end of the period ($V_m$). The agent accepts money in exchange for goods if and only if $V_m \geq V_c$. The value of holding a good at the end of the period is defined by:

$$V_c = \beta\left\{(1 - M)x^2 U + Mx\pi V_m + (1 - Mx\pi)V_c\right\} \qquad (1)$$

It is the discounted sum of: (*i*) the expected utility derived from a double coincidence of wants which leads to an exchange, consumption and immediate production $(1 - M)x^2 U$ and the expected value of holding a good at the end of the period $(1 - M)x^2 V_c$. (*ii*) the probability of exchanging the good for money and deriving the value $V_m$ which results in an expected value of $Mx\pi V_m$. (*iii*) the expected value of holding a good at the end of the period because the agent meets someone who holds money, who desires the good the agent holds but the agent does not accept money $Mx(1 - \pi)V_c$. (*iv*) the expected value of holding a good at the end of the period because the agent meets someone who holds a good the agent does not consume and, therefore, does not accept in exchange $(1 - M)(1 - x)V_c$. (*v*) the expected value of holding a good at the end of the period because the agent meets a trading partner who does hold the agent's desired consumption good but does not consume the good the agent holds and is not willing to accept it in exchange $(1 - M)x(1 - x)V_c$.

The value of holding money at the end of the period is given by:

$$V_m = \beta\left\{(1 - M)x\Pi(V_c + U) + [1 - (1 - M)x\Pi]V_m\right\} \qquad (2)$$

It is the discounted sum of: (*i*) the expected utility of consumption net of transaction and production costs and the value of holding a good at the end of the period $(1 - M)x\Pi(U + V_c)$. (ii) the expected value of holding money at the end of the period $[1 - (1 - M)x\Pi]V_m$. Agents end up holding money in all matches other than when they can exchange money for their consumption good. In equilibrium, agents do not accept any good in exchange for money other than their consumption good.

In order to determine the optimal strategy with respect to the acceptance of money $\pi$, Kiyotaki and Wright express $V_c$ in terms of $V_m$ in equations (1) and (2) and substitute $1/(1 + r)$ for $\beta$:

$$V_c = \frac{(1 - M)x^2 U}{(r + Mx\pi)} + \frac{Mx\pi}{(r + Mx\pi)} V_m \qquad (3)$$

$$V_c = -U + \left[1 + \frac{r}{(1 - M)x\Pi}\right]V_m \qquad (4)$$

The algebraic solution is derived by a reformulation of (3) and (4) and the subtraction of (4) from (3) to yield:

$$\left[r + Mx\pi + (1 - M)x\Pi\right](V_c - V_m) = (1 - M)xU(x - \Pi) \qquad (5)$$

As the terms $[r + Mx\pi + (1 - M)x\Pi]$ and $(1 - M)xU$ are always positive, the sign of the left hand side of equation (5) depends on $(x - \Pi)$. If and only if it is expected that money is more likely to be accepted in exchange than goods $(x < \Pi)$, then it is the medium of exchange in the model. In this case it is the optimal strategy for the agent to always accept money in exchange for goods $(\pi = 1)$. However, the expected acceptability of money $\Pi$ is not determined endogenously in the model. Therefore, Kiyotaki and Wright (1992) show that (*i*) it is indeed individually rational to accept money given the social institution of money, and (*ii*) that the resulting allocation Pareto dominates the allocation in a setting without that social institution.

## 2. OVERLAPPING GENERATIONS MODELS

In overlapping generations models, the age structure of the population and the physical characteristics of the consumption good in the model mean that certain markets do not exist. The exposition builds on Blanchard and Fischer (1989). Original contributions of OLG models of money include Samuelson (1958) and Diamond (1965).[12]

*Table 3.2: Assumptions of a typical overlapping generations model of money (Blanchard and Fischer, 1989)*

| The Economy |
| --- |
| ➤ Agents live for two consecutive periods and maximize lifetime utility $u(c_{1t}, c_{2t+1})$ which is a twice differentiable, continuous, strictly concave, and either separable or homothetic function[13] increasing in its arguments. |
| ➤ There is only one homogeneous good that is not storable. |
| ➤ Population grows at the rate $n$ such that $N_t = N_0(1 + n)^t$. |
| ➤ There is no intrinsic uncertainty in the model. Individuals are assumed to have perfect foresight. |
| **Consumption** |
| ➤ Agents born in period $t$ consume $c_{1t}$ when young and $c_{2t+1}$ when old. |
| **Endowment** |
| ➤ Each agent is endowed with one unit of the good when young and zero units when old. |
| ➤ At $t = 0$ the old are endowed with $M_s$ units of money which is divisible and can be stored and exchanged at no cost. |
| **Trading technology** |
| ➤ Agents can exchange money and the consumption good or engage in barter at competitive terms. Agents are price takers. There are no frictions in the money or good market (no information, transaction, or search costs). |

---

**Equilibrium**

➢ Market clearing in the money market implies market clearing in the good market (Walras' Law). In all markets all agents are price takers. The analysis is constrained to steady-state equilibria. All generations of young agents are treated identically as are all generations of old agents.

---

In an economy – characterized by the assumptions in Table 3.2 – without money, the young consume their entire endowment and the old cannot consume at all. The decentralized equilibrium is not Pareto optimal as both, the old and the young, would profit from intertemporal (or intergenerational) exchange of goods. But the young cannot exchange with the current old because the latter can neither offer any consumption goods in exchange nor commit to settle their debt in the following period as they would then already be dead. Equally, the current young cannot exchange goods with the future young because these have not yet been born. Intertemporal barter is impossible. Agents of each generation could only engage in barter amongst themselves within each time period. Intratemporal barter among agents of one generation is not necessary as there is only one homogeneous good and the identical endowments and preferences of all agents.

The introduction of money in this economy can lead to the creation of a market for intertemporal exchange. This can have the following implications: (*i*) An intrinsically worthless object (money) can have positive value as a store of value since it dominates the other good in its rate of return. (*ii*) Once money is valued, steady state equilibria involving trade between three generations are possible and, thus, can lead to a Pareto optimal allocation of resources between generations.[14]

### Solving the Model

Agents face the following maximization problem:

$$\max_{c_{1t}, c_{2t+1}} u(c_{1t}, c_{2t+1}) \tag{6}$$

subject to

$$P_t(1 - c_{1t}) = M_t^d$$

$$P_{t+1}c_{2t+1} = M_t^d$$

The first order condition is

$$\frac{\dfrac{\partial u(c_{2t+1})}{\partial c_{2t+1}}}{\dfrac{\partial u(c_{1t})}{\partial c_{1t}}} = \frac{P_{t+1}}{P_t} \tag{7}$$

The savings function of the young is given by $(1 - c_t) = M_t^d/P_t$: their savings are equal to their real money demand. From the first order condition we know that optimal savings imply that the marginal rate of intertemporal substitution is equal to the real gross return on money holdings $(P_{t+1}/P_t)$.[15, 16]

In OLG models money serves solely as a store of value and not as a medium of exchange (see McCallum, 1983 and Hoover, 1988). This is particularly interesting from a Mengerian point of view since in Menger's 'Money' the role of money as a store of value is only an incidental function derived from its central, defining role as the generally accepted medium of exchange. Wicksell (1935) emphasizes that only the medium of exchange function is fundamental to the role of money. This, he argues, implies the store of value function for short periods of time, that is between accepting money in exchange and spending it again. The decision to engage in monetary exchange rather than indirect barter is not influenced – at the margin – by changes in the real rate of interest over this short period of time. In defending the store of value function of money, Wallace (1978) argues that there cannot be any other asset with a rate of return distribution dominating that of money since the demand for money would then immediately drop to zero. Anything else would violate the intrinsic uselessness of money, which is a defining characteristic of fiat money. This implies that the 'use' of money as a medium of exchange would be incompatible with its intrinsic uselessness, and seems to be a rather narrow definition of the latter. Wallace (1988) emphasizes that – given the absence of legal restrictions – the value of all assets could be explained by their store of value function. This store of value, however, could be anything that supports the expectations of the young to receive compensation for forgone consumption when old, for example social security and not necessarily money.[17]

Since money is intrinsically worthless, the old offer their entire holdings $M_s$ at the going price. The young demand money according to their savings function. Therefore, equilibrium in period $t$ is given by:

$$(1+n)^t M_t^d = M_s \qquad (8)$$

In the previous period the old have determined their real money holdings according to their own savings function $L(P_{t-1}/P_t)$. Therefore, we can rewrite (8) in terms of supply and demand in the market for intertemporal exchange between two consecutive generations by:

$$(1+n)L\left(\frac{P_t}{P_{t+1}}\right)P_t = L\left(\frac{P_{t-1}}{P_t}\right)P_{t-1} \qquad (9)$$

$$(1+n)\frac{P_t}{P_{t-1}} = \frac{L\left(\dfrac{P_{t-1}}{P_t}\right)}{L\left(\dfrac{P_t}{P_{t+1}}\right)} \qquad (10)$$

As the savings of the old and the young must be mutually consistent in steady state (for example, $c_{1,t} = c_{2,t+1}$) and $n$ and $(P_t/P_{t-1})$ are constant over time, it follows that the price level must decrease at the rate of population growth. As the nominal supply of money is fixed at $M_s$ but the real demand for money increases with the growth of the population, the price level must fall in order for the real supply of money $M_s/P_t$ to increase as well.

The crucial point is that equation (10) involves the price levels of three consecutive periods. Since the equation must hold in steady state, the expected value of money must be positive in all periods. 'Suppose that the old and every generation thereafter believe that they will be able to exchange money for goods, at price $P_t$ in period $t$.' (Blanchard and Fischer, 1989, p. 158.) The expectations concerning the future acceptability of money are not determined endogenously.[18] Given the social institution of money, the additional endowment of $M_s$ units of an intrinsically worthless good can have the positive effects cited above: (*i*) It is individually rational to accept money in exchange for goods. (*ii*) The allocation in the monetary economy Pareto dominates the allocation in an economy without money.

## 3. SPATIAL SEPARATION MODELS

In models with spatially separated agents, like in OLG models, certain markets do not exist. While in OLG models different lifetime spans are the source of the frictions, it is spatial separation between different markets, the impossibility of transfers and communication between markets, and the fact that the consumption good is not storable that render certain bilateral exchanges impossible in an economy without money. The exposition of a typical spatial separation model (Table 3.3) builds on Townsend (1980).

*Table 3.3: Assumptions of a typical spatial separation model of money (Townsend, 1980)*

| **The Economy** |
|---|
| ➤ Two groups of countably infinite numbers of agents (type A and B) – all of whom live indefinitely and maximize discounted lifetime utility – are situated along two turnpikes. |
| ➤ They move along the two turnpikes in opposite directions. |
| ➤ All agents are born at the same time and live forever. |
| ➤ One agent of each group is born into each market. |
| ➤ The utility of consumption is $U(c_t^{A,B})$ which is a twice differentiable, continuous, strictly concave, and time separable function with $U'(0) = \infty$, increasing in its arguments. |
| ➤ There is no communication or transaction between markets. |

> Agents discount expected future consumption at a constant rate $0 < \beta < 1$ or $1/(1 + r)$ where $r$ is the real rate of interest.
> There is no intrinsic uncertainty in the model. Agents have perfect foresight.
> At the beginning of each period a lump-sum tax $z_t^{A,B}$ (positive or negative) on money holdings can be imposed by a central planner.
> Furthermore, the agents do not know the economy's full history of transactions (see Kocherlakota, 1998a, b) nor can they commit to future actions (see Wallace, 1997).

## Consumption

> All agents consume the single consumption good.
> The consumption good cannot be stored.

## Endowment

> One group of agents receives one unit of the consumption good in odd periods ($y_t^A = 1$ for all odd $t$). The other group receives one unit of the consumption good in even periods ($y_t^B = 1$ for all even $t$).
> Agents of both groups are endowed with initial money balances of $M_o^{A,B} \geq 0$.
> Money can be stored and carried costlessly. Money holdings cannot be negative.

## Trading technology

> Each period two agents belonging to the two groups are paired at any one market.
> Agents cannot choose their direction and/or trading partners.
> They trade iff it is beneficial for both of them.
> Each market enables agents to exchange money and the consumption good or engage in barter at competitive terms. Agents are price takers. There are no information, transaction, or search costs.

## Equilibrium

> Symmetry conditions: All agents are treated identically, independent of their initial positions. The price of a unit of the consumption good in terms of money $p_t$ is the same across all markets in each time period.
> A monetary equilibrium is defined as a set of sequences of positive finite prices, consumption, money holdings and lump-sum taxes for each type of agent such that agents maximize lifetime utility and each market clears in each period.

Due to the fact that both groups move along their respective turnpikes in opposite directions each pair meets only once in a lifetime and shares no third persons as trading partners. As one trading partner has an endowment of zero units, he cannot offer anything in barter. Therefore, the situation constitutes a special form of an absence of double coincidence of wants. Intratemporal barter is impossible as transfers and communication between markets are ruled out.

Private debt cannot circulate since any transfer of such debt could only take place with those agents who are situated 'behind' the issuer. Therefore, debt would not be redeemable, no link between future wealth and debt could be enforced (there would be no limitation on the issue of private debt) and, consequently, the price level would not be determined. Bilateral intertemporal trade is impossible unless individuals assume money to be accepted by all future trading partners. The consumption good cannot serve to facilitate intertemporal trade as it is perishable while money is storable and transferable at no cost. Thus, money enables the creation of a market for intertemporal and intratemporal exchange.

### Solving the Model

The agents' problem for types A and B takes the following form:

$$\max_{c_t^{A,B}, M_t^{A,B}} \sum_{t=0}^{\infty} \beta^t U\left(c_t^{A,B}\right) \tag{11}$$

subject to

$$c_t^{A,B} \geq 0 \qquad\qquad \forall t \geq 0.$$

$$M_t^{A,B} \geq 0 \qquad\qquad \forall t \geq 0.$$

$$p_t c_t^{A,B} + M_{t+1}^{A,B} \leq p_t y_t^{A,B} + M_t^{A,B} - z_t^{A,B} \qquad \forall t \geq 0.$$

with $M_0^{A,B} \geq 0$ and $z_0^{A,B} = 0$ given.

This yields the first order condition for a maximum:

$$\frac{\dfrac{\partial U\left(c_{t-1}^{A,B}\right)}{\partial c_{t-1}^{A,B}}}{\beta \dfrac{\partial U\left(c_t^{A,B}\right)}{\partial c_t^{A,B}}} \geq \frac{p_{t-1}}{p_t} \qquad \forall t \geq 1. \tag{12}$$

The FOC holds as an equality iff money holdings are positive and non-zero (the constraint on $M_t$ is non-binding). Again, the rate of deflation must be $1 - \beta$. Money yields a positive rate of return and dominates the rate of return on consumption goods.[19] The maximized discounted lifetime utility yields a sequence of consumption $c_t^{A,B}$ and a sequence of 'savings' $M_t^{A,B}$ for all $t$.

The equilibrium of the monetary economy involves positive money holdings and non-finite positive prices of consumption goods in terms of money consistent with the agents' maximization problem. Therefore, the model shows that (*i*) the acceptance of intrinsically worthless money is individually rational given the social institution of money.

As a benchmark for the monetary economy Townsend (1980, p. 271) derives a solution for a centrally planned economy based on the maximization of a weighted average of the utility functions of types A and B in an economy without money. The exercise yields $c_t^A = \lambda$ and $c_t^B = 1 - \lambda$ for all *t*. Townsend (1980, p. 272) establishes the following results: (*ii*) The optimal allocation $c_t^A = \lambda$ and $c_t^B = 1 - \lambda$ for all *t* cannot be attained without intervention ($z_t^{A,B} = 0$). (*iii*) A monetary equilibrium without intervention exists and, although non-optimal relative to the benchmark allocation, it is Pareto superior to autarky.[20]

# 4. CURRENT NEOCLASSICAL MODELS OF MONEY AND MENGERIAN INSTITUTIONAL ANALYSIS

The neoclassical models focus on equilibrium allocations under different institutional arrangements and comparative statics of their welfare implications.[21] In a certain period (for example, $t = 0$) agents maximize expected lifetime utility *given* the institutional arrangement and *fully anticipating* the other agents' optimal strategies. The equilibrium concepts adopted imply rational expectations[22] including perfect knowledge about preferences, expectations, and (future) optimal strategies of all agents, the technology and the institutional setting. The equilibrium allocation is derived under these restrictive informational assumptions and the additional assumption that money is expected to be accepted by all other agents in all future periods (that is, in OLG models), at all spatially separated markets in all future periods.[23] It is shown that it is individually rational to accept money, and that the allocation in the monetary economy Pareto-dominates the allocation in the economy without money. Equilibrium and co-ordination are achieved instantaneously and at no cost. Wallace (1998) uses the notion of endogeneity in a strictly model theoretical context. The individual rationality of accepting money is not simply postulated exogenously by including money in the utility or production function or by imposing a cash in advance constraint but it is determined endogenously given the social institution of money. The scope of the models is to account for money in various examples of modified Walrasian settings.[24] The emergence of the latter, of course, remains determined exogenously. An endogenous theory of money, though, has to deal with both questions raised by Menger: (*i*) the individual rationality of accepting intrinsically worthless objects in exchange for goods, and (*ii*) the emergence of the social institution of money.

The formation of expectations concerning its acceptability and, thus, the emergence of the social institution of money are excluded from the analysis in the neoclassical models of money. Due to the fact that the equilibrium concepts focus on steady state (or stationary) equilibria, changes to the (simple) monetary systems are *ex definitionem* impossible, since the institutional arrangements, preferences, and technologies are exogenously given and institutional change is not an issue.

Menger interprets money itself as a social institution. Its emergence is the *unintended consequence of purposeful, individual action* (pp. 6, 9 and 17[25]). In Menger's article the institutional arrangement itself is the scope of analysis. The formation of expectations concerning the acceptability of different forms of money is crucial because (*i*) indirect exchange involves the passage of a time period between accepting and spending money, and (*ii*) money exhibits network effects. The demand schedule for participation in a network is downward sloping but shifts outwards with increases in the (expected) number of participants. Menger describes the process of the formation of expectations concerning the acceptability of money. Menger's institutional analysis of the origin of money emphasizes the following points:

Agents engage in exchange iff both of them expect to profit from the transaction, iff *mutual gains from trade* are expected (p. 33). Due to the division of labour and search costs, there is an *absence of a double coincidence of wants* (p. 3).

*Goods are heterogeneous with respect to demand for them and, consequently, with respect to their acceptability in trade* (p. 4).[26] Although he provides a number of potential explanations (for example, different goods are affected differently by habit or prevailing power structures and unilaterally imposed liabilities such as taxes, and so on (p. 6)), this heterogeneity is exogenous to Menger's analysis. Iway (1996, p. 471) criticizes the assumption of different acceptability of goods and reaches different conclusions about the evolution of monetary equilibrium: 'Contrary to what Menger said, we can find no "natural" tendency for the evolution from a barter to a monetary economy.' According to Iway, the acceptability of goods is not a 'fundamental' of the economy but the result of individual trading strategies based on (symmetric) endowment-need frequencies (defined as the proportion of individuals endowed with a certain good *i* while demanding another one *j*). The acceptability of money is endogenized in terms of endowment-need frequencies and increases in the proportion of the economy that demands money as medium of exchange. The use of an arbitrary good as a medium of exchange increases its acceptability and reinforces its role as 'money'. Thus, equilibrium in any good (for example, fiat money) is sustainable. However, the sustainability of equilibrium is different from the proposition that this equilibrium evolves naturally. Based on symmetric endowment-need frequencies the barter economy is shown to be locally stable. Consequently, only an exogenous disturbance that decreases the transaction costs of one good relative to the others such that indirect exchange becomes more efficient for individuals shifts the economy to a monetary equilibrium. By assuming symmetric endowment-need frequencies, however, Iway's critique of Menger's analysis fails to take into account the differences in demand for different goods. Furthermore, Menger explicitly emphasizes the reinforcing effect of the emergence of indirect trade on the relative acceptability of different goods (p. 10) and thus implicitly distinguishes between (exogenous) demand and (endogenous) acceptability of different goods. Menger offers a rational reconstruction[27] of the evolution of monetary exchange through indirect barter based on the fundamentals of the economy, i.e. the heterogeneity of goods with respect to individual demand.

The question '... why agents [in a monetary economy] engage in indirect exchange through money rather than general indirect barter ...' (Hellwig, 1993, p. 236) cannot be addressed by the neoclassical models of money. Indirect barter is ruled out in the Kiyotaki and Wright (1992) model by imposing symmetry of goods with respect to individual demand.[28] In the overlapping generations and spatial separation models discussed there is only a single consumption good, and endowments and preferences are identical such that there is no intratemporal barter at all. Intertemporal (direct and indirect) barter is impossible due to the absence of markets and the structure of endowment and demand sequences. In Menger's account the singular position of money as the only medium of exchange is the result of indirect barter and the increasing acceptability of some of the goods that were used in indirect barter at early stages of the evolutionary process.

*The advantages of indirect barter and indirect exchange (by exploiting the heterogeneity of goods with respect to their acceptability) are not understood by all agents at once* (p. 5). Initially, only a few agents understand the heterogeneity of goods with respect to their acceptability on the respective market and the related profit opportunities.[29] They engage in indirect barter at first, as this strategy increases their discounted expected utility (pp. 5, 7) (independently of whether or not others accept the respective commodity as a medium of exchange (!) – rather, based on the supply/demand conditions of the good under consideration). This increases their chances to trade the goods they bring to market for the goods they wish to buy on the market.

*The process of learning about the different degrees of acceptability* (p. 5) is the driving force of the emergence of the social institution of money, the formation of expectations concerning the behaviour of other agents. Instead of focusing on symmetric, steady-state equilibria in which agents take the expectations and strategies of all others as given, Menger focuses on the evolution of indirect exchange based on the heterogeneity of both goods and individuals. Moreover, he emphasizes the process of learning about the different degrees of acceptability of goods and about the strategies and expectations of the other agents.[30] Due to the structure of supply and demand curves, some goods are more likely to be accepted in exchange in a certain market at a certain time than others. Gradually, more agents learn about the higher degree of acceptability of certain goods through the economic success of those agents who have recognized the role of indirect barter first. They learn about the others' strategies in exchange and their expectations and adapt their own strategies and expectations. In particular, practice, imitation, and the formation of habit facilitate the assessment of these expectations. The acceptability of the goods with the highest degree of acceptability thereby increases even further. Finally, a certain good evolves into the generally accepted medium of exchange (p. 8). The process does not end at this point as technological, legal, and institutional arrangements might emerge that economize on certain aspects of the medium of exchange. Examples of early media of exchange were domestic animals, furs and slaves. In order to reduce transaction costs (for example, costs of evaluating quality and quantity of those goods) media of exchange evolved that were more fungible, divisible, marketable in wider boundaries of time and space, transportable, and preservable (p. 8). The imperfections of early monies led to their gradual displacement by coined precious metals (for example gold and silver) in many societies. Selgin and Klein (2000) analyse a related dynamic process in computer simulations based on imperfect knowledge about the different degrees of marketability of different goods. They argue that, in Menger's approach, at least some individuals are assumed to recognize the single most marketable good and fully understand the benefits of indirect barter at once. Were this recognition shared by everyone, Menger's dynamic process would imply immediate convergence to a commodity money equilibrium (with the single most marketable good becoming the generally accepted medium of exchange). In fact Menger does not assume that all individuals learn immediately about the individual desirability of indirect exchange (Klein and Selgin refer to this assumption as ad hoc). In Menger's approach only a small fraction of the total population initially learns about different degrees of marketability while the rest regards all goods as equally saleable. Furthermore, the decisions to adopt indirect barter and, at a later stage, indirect monetary exchange involve expectations about future marketability, risk and time preferences, opportunity costs, and wealth constraints. The more general assumption, therefore, is that adoption patterns vary among individuals. Those who refrain from indirect barter and indirect monetary exchange are gradually convinced by the economic success of early adopters.

*The medium of exchange function of money is central* (p. 52). All other functions of money – such as store of value (p. 31), unit of account (measure of price p. 32) etc. – are only derived from the core function of money as the generally accepted medium of exchange. In OLG and spatial separation models money is modelled solely as store of value, facilitating intertemporal transfers.

*Transaction costs, state involvement and institutional change play a role in the perfection of the social institution of money* (pp. 9, 17–25, 65–67). The total economic costs (transaction, information, opportunity costs and so on) associated with the operation and use of the payment system can be reduced by continuously adapting its institutional structure: (*i*) The state can have a role in ensuring the uniformity of the unit of account or declaring – in some circumstances – a legal tender. (*ii*) Private note issue economizes on the opportunity costs associated with the use of coined money.[31] (*iii*) Financial institutions can reduce the demand for money in an economy by consulting their clients on optimal cash management and by substituting book money for notes and coins.

*The emergence of the social institution of money has positive real effects on the economy.* (*i*) It is individually rational to exchange goods for intrinsically worthless money (p. 7). (*ii*) The emergence of a generally accepted medium of exchange leads to a move from bilateral monopsony to increased competition. Consequently, prices reflect market conditions (supply/demand) rather than the – more arbitrary – outcome of a bargaining process with a small number of buyers/sellers and sellers/buyers (p. 11).[32] In simple OLG and spatial separation models there is no exchange without money. Consequently, before the introduction of money, there are no meaningful market prices that could be compared with those in the monetary economy. The prices quoted by a Walrasian auctioneer are not affected by the introduction of money. In search models, agents do engage in exchange if there is a double coincidence of wants. The simple take-it-or-leave-it bargaining mechanism, indivisibility of goods, the symmetry of agents, and the absence of time discounting within bargaining periods mean that prices in bilateral monopsony are identical to hypothetical competitive prices. (*iii*) The emergence and evolution of the social institution of money facilitates trade, the division of labour, and contributes to economic growth (p. 4).

# 5. CONCLUSION

The neoclassical models of money focus on symmetric equilibria and simultaneous decisions. Menger emphasizes the heterogeneity of agents with respect to their understanding of the heterogeneity of goods with respect to their acceptability in trade. Agents do not possess perfect knowledge about each other's preferences and expectations. They cannot fully anticipate each other's optimal strategies. Thus, they have to learn about these and adapt their own strategies accordingly. The neoclassical models assume the existence of the social institution of money as exogenously given. Their attempt to explain the rational acceptance of money in (modified) Walrasian structures cannot be successful as long as the emergence of the social institution of money is not endogenized either. The scope of Menger's paper is the rational reconstruction of the development of the social institution of a generally accepted medium of exchange from barter via indirect barter.

Moreover, the differences between the Mengerian contribution to the institutional analysis of money and the current neoclassical models of money make it worthwhile for 'Mengerians' to reconsider the original contribution of Carl Menger's 'Money'.

The emergence of new electronic payment systems is an example of institutional change in the financial system. Current neoclassical models of money are essentially static and assume that a specific institutional arrangement is given exogenously. Thus, there is no endogenous institutional change. The formation of expectations concerning the acceptability of money is crucial for the understanding of the social institution of money. Current neoclassical models do not endogenously model expectations and changes to expectations. They are assumed to be exogenously determined. The current neoclassical models of the origin of money are therefore of limited use in the understanding and analysis of new electronic payment systems.

Menger's method of institutional analysis, on the other hand, focuses on the process of the formation of expectations. Money is interpreted as a social institution that is subject to constant change. Selgin and White (1987, 1994) and Selgin (1997) discuss further examples of institutional change within the institution of money, such as (among others) the introduction of fiat money and the evolution of a complex financial systems inspired by Menger's approach. The emergence of new electronic payment systems is yet another example of institutional change. Thus, Menger's method of institutional analysis is well suited to analysing new electronic payment systems.

## NOTES

\* The author thanks the participants of the workshop 'The Analysis of New Electronic Payments Systems based on Carl Menger's Institutional Theory of the Origin of Money', Vienna, 20–21 October 2000, as well as B. Weber, for helpful comments. The usual disclaimer applies.

1. For a discussion of Menger's institutional approach see the Introduction and Streissler's contribution to this volume. For a recent survey of New Institutional Economics (NIE) see Williamson (2000).

2. See Hellwig (1993). For a historical account of attempts to reconcile value and monetary theory see Hoover (1988).

3. Menger interprets money as a social institution, that is, a system of norms, expectations, and conventions that influence the decisions of the participants (for example financial intermediaries, firms, households and so on). In particular, the mutual consistency of expectations that other individuals accept money as the generally accepted medium of exchange with near certainty is the result of a complex learning, co-ordination, and development process (for a discussion see Furubotn and Richter, 1997).

4. Hellwig (1993) refers to the same question as the Hahn problem.

5. See Osterberg and Thomson (1998) and Sheehan (1998). The demand curve for a good exhibiting network externalities (for example joining a payment system) still slopes downward but it is shifted outwards if its expected number of units sold (for example its expected acceptability) increases (see Economides, 1995 and 1996).

6. See Menger (1892). Goodhart (1998, p. 408) calls the theorists who base their explanation of the positive value of intrinsically worthless money on individually

rational decisions to overcome the costs of an absence of double coincidence of wants Mengerians.

7. In all three classes of models discussed an infinite horizon is necessary in order to ensure that accepting money is individually rational (see Kocherlakota, 1998a, p. 244).

8. Due to the symmetry between the fraction $x$ of agents consuming each consumption good and the fraction $x$ of consumption goods consumed by each agent and complete specialization (each agent always produces the same consumption good after having himself consumed) the expected fractions of all consumption goods supplied and demanded remain constant throughout all periods.

9. See Kreps (1990), p. 556.

10. See Wallace (1997) and Townsend (1980), p. 269 n. 10.

11. See also Kiyotaki and Wright (1989).

12. For critical discussions of OLG models see McCallum (1983) and Hoover (1988).

13. See Shone (1997), p. 497.

14. See Blanchard and Fischer (1989), p. 159.

15. Future prices are equal to expected future prices due to perfect foresight and the absence of intrinsic uncertainty.

16. If the economy has a finite horizon, the younger generation in the final period will not accept money in exchange since they would not reach old age to spend it again. By backward induction it can be shown that no generation would accept money in such a setting.

17. See Hoover (1988).

18. Also Samuelson (1958, p. 481) presupposes a 'grand consensus' on the acceptability of (fiat) money.

19. Again, the expected rate of return is equal to the rate of return due to perfect foresight and the absence of intrinsic uncertainty (see Blanchard and Fischer, 1989).

20. Autarky refers to the allocation achieved by the decentralized economy without money such that agents can only consume their endowments.

21. See Green (1999).

22. In many models there is no intrinsic uncertainty such that rational expectations correspond to perfect foresight.

23. In search models the assumption that money has a higher acceptability than consumption goods often suffices.

24. 'More or less all the models of monetary economics that are being used in practice proceed in this way, using artificial adaptations of the Walrasian centralized-markets to accommodate money without actually giving an account of what the role of money in the economy is' (Hellwig, 1993, p. 215).

25. In the following paragraphs all page numbers refer to Menger (1909).

26. The differences in individual endowments are only discussed implicitly (p. 6).

27. I borrow the terminology from Selgin and White's contribution to this volume.

28. In their 1989 paper, indirect barter and monetary exchange are identical due to the structure of the model.

29. For an attempt to endogenize investments in information about the qualities of goods offered on the market, exchange opportunities, or relative prices to explain the use of money see Brunner and Meltzer (1971). They criticize models of the origin of money that focus on stationary states. In their model, as information

becomes abundant (at least in the limit) in a stationary state the *raison d'être* for a medium of exchange disappears.

30. Selgin (1997) criticizes current search models of the Kiyotaki and Wright type along similar lines. Jones (1976) analyses a simplification of the evolutionary process described by Menger. He focuses on the different degrees of acceptability and learning about changes in the acceptability of an emerging medium of exchange but abstracts from differences between individuals.

31. Today this private note issue can take place in electronic form (for example new electronic payment systems) to economize on central bank money. The reduction of resource costs at a given money stock due to the development of a fractional reserve money system is also emphasized by Smith (1776) and Brunner and Meltzer (1971). Both works emphasize coinage and the latter also bank credit cards as examples of institutional change within the monetary system to reduce the marginal costs of information.

32. Streissler in his contribution to this volume emphasizes the role of a medium of exchange in creating an information network among market participants in Menger's approach.

# REFERENCES

Blanchard, O. J. and S. Fischer (1989), *Lectures on Macroeconomics*, Cambridge, MA: MIT Press.

Brunner, K. and A. H. Meltzer (1971), 'The Uses of Money: Money in the Theory of an Exchange Economy', *American Economic Review*, **61**, pp. 784-805.

Diamond, P. (1965), 'National Debt in a Neo-Classical Growth Model', *American Economic Review*, **55**, pp. 1125-50.

Economides, N. (1995), 'Commentary', *Federal Reserve Bank of St Louis Review, November/December*, pp. 60-63.

Economides, N. (1996), 'The Economics of Networks', *International Journal of Industrial Organization*, **14**, pp. 673-99.

Furubotn, E. G. and R. Richter (1997), *Institutions and Economic Theory: An Introduction to and Assessment of the New Institutional Economics*, Ann Arbor: University of Michigan Press.

Goodhart, C. A. E. (1998), 'The Two Concepts of Money: Implications for the Analysis of Optimal Currency Areas', *European Journal of Political Economy*, **14**, pp. 407-32.

Green, E. J. (1999), 'We Need to Think Straight about Electronic Payments', *Journal of Money, Credit and Banking*, **31**, Part 2, pp. 668-70.

Hellwig, M. F. (1993), 'The Challenge of Monetary Theory', *European Economic Review*, **37**, pp. 215-42.

Hoover, K. D. (1988), *The New Classical Macroeconomics*, Cheltenham: Edward Elgar.

Iway, K. (1996), 'The Bootstrap Theory of Money: A Search-theoretic Foundation of Monetary Economics', *Structural Change and Economic Dynamics*, 7, pp. 451-77.

Jones, R. A. (1976), 'The Origin and Development of Media of Exchange', *Journal of Political Economy*, **84**, pp. 757-75.

Kiyotaki, N. and R. Wright (1989), 'On Money as a Medium of Exchange', *Journal of Political Economy*, **97**, pp. 927-54.

Kiyotaki, N. and R. Wright (1991), 'A Contribution to the Pure Theory of Money', *Journal of Economic Theory*, **53**, pp. 215-35.

Kiyotaki, N. and R. Wright (1992), 'Acceptability, Means of Payment, and Media of Exchange', *Federal Reserve Bank of Minneapolis Quarterly Review*, pp. 2-10.

Kocherlakota, N. R. (1998a), 'Money is Memory', *Journal of Economic Theory*, **81**, pp. 232-51.

Kocherlakota, N. R. (1998b), 'The Technological Role of Fiat Money', *Federal Reserve Bank of Minneapolis Quarterly Review*, **22**, pp. 18-21.

Kreps, D. M. (1990), *A Course in Microeconomic Theory*, New York: Harvester, Wheatsheaf.

McCallum, B. T. (1983), 'The Role of Overlapping-Generations Models in Monetary Economics', *Carnegie-Rochester Conference Series on Public Policy 18*, pp. 9-44, reprinted in: K. D. Hoover (1992), *The New Classical Economics Vol. II*, Cheltenham, UK and Northampton, MA, USA: Edward Elgar, pp. 472-507.

Menger, C. (1892), 'On the Origin of Money', *Economic Journal*, 2, pp. 238-55, translated by C. A. Foley.

Menger, C. (1909), 'Money', translated by L. B. Yeager with M. Streissler, in this volume; translation of 'Geld', *Handwörterbuch der Staatswissenschaften*, 3rd edn, J. Conrad et al. (eds), IV. Volume, Fischer, Jena, pp. 555-610; reprinted in: Hayek, F. A. (ed.) (1970), *Carl Menger Gesammelte Werke*, Band IV Schriften über Geld und Währungspolitik, Tübingen: J. C. B. Mohr (Siebeck), pp. 1-116.

Osterberg, W. P. and J. B. Thomson (1998), 'Network Externalities: The Catch-22 of Retail Payments Innovations', *Federal Reserve Bank of Cleveland Economic Commentary*, pp. 1-4.

Samuelson, P. A. (1958), 'An Exact Consumption-Loan Model of Interest with or without the Social Contrivance of Money', *Journal of Political Economy*, **LXVI**, pp. 467-82.

Selgin, G. (1997), 'Network Effects, Adaptive Learning, and the Transition to Fiat Money', *Manuscript, Department of Economics, University of Georgia*, Athens.

Selgin, G. A. and P. G. Klein (2000), 'Menger's Theory of Money: Some Experimental Evidence', in: J. Smithin (ed.), *What is Money?*, London and New York: Routledge, pp. 217-34.

Selgin, G. A. and L. H. White (1987), 'The Evolution of a Free Banking System', *Economic Inquiry*, **25**, pp. 439-57.

Selgin, G. A. and L. H. White (1994), 'How Would the Invisible Hand Handle Money?', *Journal of Economic Literature,* **32**, pp. 1718-49.

Sheehan, K. P. (1998), 'Electronic Cash', *FDIC Banking Review*, pp. 1-8.

Shone, R. (1997), *Economic Dynamics*, Cambridge: Cambridge University Press.

Smith, A. (1776), *An Inquiry into the Nature and Causes of the Wealth of Nations*, Düsseldorf: Verlag Wirtschaft und Finanzen (1986) (facsimile edition of the London edition 1776).

Townsend, R. M. (1980), 'Models of Money with Spatially Separated Agents', in: J. H. Kareken and N. Wallace (eds), *Models of Monetary Economics*, Minneapolis: Federal Reserve Bank of Minneapolis, pp. 265-313.

Wallace, N. (1978), 'The Overlapping Generations Model of Fiat Money', *Staff Report # 37, University of Minnesota and Federal Reserve Bank of Minneapolis*, Minneapolis.

Wallace, N. (1988), 'A Suggestion for Oversimplifying the Theory of Money', *Economic Journal,* **98**, pp. 25-36.

Wallace, N. (1997), 'Absence-of-Double-Coincidence Models of Money: A Progress Report', *Federal Reserve Bank of Minneapolis Quarterly Review,* **21**, pp. 2-20.

Wallace, N. (1998), 'A Dictum for Monetary Theory', *Federal Reserve Bank of Minneapolis Quarterly Review,* **22**, pp. 20-26.

Wicksell, K. (1935), *Lectures on Political Economy, Volume II – Money*, Edited with an Introduction by Lionel Robbins, London: Routledge & Kegan Paul.

Williamson, O. E. (2000), 'The New Institutional Economics: Taking Stock, Looking Ahead', *Journal of Economic Literature,* **38**, pp. 595-613.

# 4. Mengerian perspectives on the future of money

## George A. Selgin
## Lawrence H. White[*]

---

## 1. MENGER'S PROJECT AND OURS

Carl Menger (1909) offered a logical evolutionary account or 'rational reconstruction' of the development of money out of barter. He explained how money had emerged incrementally and spontaneously from individuals' efforts to economize on their costs of achieving desired trades. Here we use Mengerian analysis to envision *future* developments in the payments system.

Menger had to rationally reconstruct the origins of commodity money because the events he wanted to explain took place prehistorically, before written evidence. His theory is consistent with the anthropological and experimental evidence we do have. Just as importantly, the theory is grounded in the behaviour of decentralized, self-interested, and modestly informed individuals. These features favour Menger's theory over theories that imagine money to be the creature of general equilibrium, central design, or heroic invention.

In 'The Evolution of a Free Banking System' (Selgin and White, 1987) we offered a logical evolutionary account of an unregulated payments system, using Menger's account of the evolution of commodity money as our starting point. We argued that, absent legal restrictions, private bank notes and transferable deposits would largely displace full-bodied coins and bullion (except in interbank payments), but the underlying specie standard would persist. Market forces would *not* promote the spontaneous emergence of a monopoly bank of issue or a fiat money.

In extending Menger's analysis to address past developments in banking, we could refer to historical evidence. We had to use rational reconstruction, however, to disentangle spontaneous developments from the results of government interference. The evolution of an idealized *free* banking system is only approximated by the history of any actual banking system.

Projecting the development of the payments system into the future poses new challenges in addition to those faced by Menger and by our earlier paper. The historical record helps insofar as we extrapolate historical trends, but the value of simple extrapolation is doubtful. The future development of the payments system will depend on future entrepreneurial innovations that can neither be extrapolated nor predicted in detail (without implying implausibly that we know where unexploited profit opportunities lie waiting). Our predictions must also be conditioned by assumptions about the future role of government in the payments system. An invisible-hand Mengerian explanation will be relevant to future developments only to the extent that governments choose (or are compelled) to allow spontaneous market processes to operate.

## 2. THE RISE AND FALL OF MONETARY NATIONALISM: RETAIL PAYMENTS

When Menger wrote, the payments systems of most countries remained largely the products of market processes. Commodity standards prevailed. Private commercial banks issued the currency notes in everyday use. Clearing and settlement, having grown from agreements between pairs of banks into system-wide arrangements, remained in the private sector. National governments were largely limited to producing coins – an ancient role that had become less important with the advent of bank-issued money – and to regulating the private commercial banking industry.

The century that followed Menger's essay saw governments sharply expand their involvement in monetary affairs, and might in retrospect be dubbed the 'era of monetary nationalism'.[1] National governments monopolized the issue of bank notes and thereby created national central banks, suspended the gold convertibility of their notes and thereby substituted fiat monies for commodity base monies, and instituted exchange controls ostensibly to protect the value of their fiat monies. Market institutions were forced into a smaller role in the payments system.

Today, monetary nationalism appears to be waning. Driven by technological and ideological change, the market has begun to re-emerge as a major ordering force for both bank-issued money and base money.

In banking, several factors are contributing to the resurgence of market forces. The ideological current that has promoted deregulation and privatization of other industries around the globe – the growing acceptance of market liberalism – operates as well in banking and finance. Most importantly, ongoing advances in information processing and communications technology bring financial-market innovations that progressively erode legal restrictions on banks. The process of financial markets eroding restrictions is not new: since the late 1950s the growth of the 'offshore' banking market (once known as the 'Eurodollar' market) has allowed at least large players to bypass anti-competitive domestic restrictions on deposit interest rates. Since the mid-1970s the development of money-market mutual funds has done the same for small savers. Today the computerization of 'sweep' accounts is rendering reserve requirements (where reserves earn subcompetitive rates) unenforceable. Banking by phone, fax, and internet is making geographic restrictions on banks increasingly less effective. As the price of remote access to offshore banking services falls toward zero, depositors both large and small can, ever more cheaply, avoid *all* kinds of inefficient restrictions on banks. To prevent the banking business they regulate from moving abroad, domestic regulators must abandon inefficient restrictions: interest rate ceilings, geographic limits, reserve requirements, lending quotas and other portfolio restraints, binding capital requirements, and mispriced deposit insurance.[2]

For the moment, governments face little direct competition from domestic banks in the issue of hand-to-hand currency. But emerging 'smart card' systems like Mastercard's Mondex have the potential to return the issue of currency to the private banking sector. Mondex card balances are functionally private bank notes: they are redeemable bearer claims that (unlike Visa Cash or GeldKarte balances) can circulate from card to card without passing through the clearing system.

Because trade and technology are making it increasingly easy for transactors to switch currencies, nation-states are losing their local monopoly powers in supplying base money. The trend is especially evident in smaller and poorer nations with weak currencies. As Benjamin J. Cohen (1998) has emphasized, the world is moving away from the pattern of one monetary standard per nation-state. Nations around the world have undergone unofficial 'dollarization' as their citizens switch their savings and even their transactions balances to US dollars from weak domestic currencies. Several nations have conceded their monetary independence by tying the domestic money to the dollar or the euro through a 'currency board' arrangement. In September 2000 the government of Ecuador abolished its domestic currency unit and adopted the US dollar outright as the official currency.[3] The emerging pattern recalls classical and medieval arrangements in which silver and gold were international monetary standards, and respected large-value coins circulated beyond national borders.

The fiscal (profit) motive that originally led ancient and medieval sovereigns to impose national monopolies in money production (see Selgin and White, 1999) has not disappeared. But with citizens finding it increasingly easy to acquire and use stronger foreign currency, governments can no longer so effectively exploit their domestic currency as source of revenue. Some may even discover that imposing the inflation tax on domestic currency is no longer worthwhile, especially if inflation seriously diminishes the real revenue from other taxes. By officially dollarizing, the government of Ecuador bowed to the market, and adopted the currency that the country's private sector had already adopted. In general, the further opening of currency choice in all nations points toward a world of fewer monetary standards. Much as in the Mengerian convergence from many to few commodity media of exchange, the more widely accepted and more trusted fiat currencies will increase their global market shares.

Though the main impetus for change has been technological, opinion among academics and policy-makers has also moved in the last 25 years toward supporting the reduction of government's involvement in money and banking. At the edge of this opinion movement has been a flourishing of research on monetary *laissez-faire* that Friedman and Schwartz (1986) have attributed to the influence of rational expectations, public choice, and modern Austrian economics, all of which emphasize the fundamental importance of monetary regimes. (If they are correct about the third of these influences, then Carl Menger's work on money has itself played at least an indirect role in fostering the developments that we are using it to analyse.) Elsewhere (Selgin and White, 1994) we have surveyed recent *laissez-faire* monetary thought. Closer to the mainstream of professional opinion, numerous economists have provided persuasive evidence that particular banking regulations are inefficient and destabilizing, both in developed countries (for an overview of US evidence see Benston, 1991) and in developing countries (see Fry, 1988).

In what follows we will argue that there are good reasons for expecting governments to remove the remaining significant legal restrictions on money and banking, and we will envision the implications for the future development of the payments system. We begin with the implications for the monetary standard.

### Should we Expect Private Monetary Standards?

Drawing inspiration from Hayek (1978), some writers (for example Macintosh 1998) suggest that competitive monetary innovation will lead to the emergence of new private monetary standards, that is, base monies and accounting units distinct from the fiat monies that central banks currently administer. We find such scenarios implausible. Mengerian theory and historical experience indicate that, while commodity money evolved spontaneously from barter, the same forces of convergence (or network effects) that drove that evolution strongly favour an established money over any would-be alternative. A new money initially lacks a critical mass of users, and that fact itself discourages people from using it. Even if the incumbent is a fiat money and the newcomer is a commodity money, spontaneous switching is not to be expected unless the incumbent currency standard is expected to be highly unstable.[4] Outside of such hyperinflationary economies, where the incumbent currency becomes so bad that we do see spontaneous 'dollarization', there is too little incentive to go first in switching to a novel standard. A switch to some kind of commodity standard will therefore not happen spontaneously (absent hyperinflation). It would require a public debate and a co-ordinated public decision, much like a decision to switch the side of the road on which we will all drive.

Another group of writers (for example Browne and Cronin, 1995, Dowd, 1998, Rahn, 1999), drawing inspiration from the 'New Monetary Economics' of Fama (1980) and others, suggest that financial innovation will lead to the emergence of a moneyless world relying on a kind of sophisticated barter. Base monies will disappear, and a 'pure accounting system of exchange' will prevail, potentially using units of any arbitrary standardized commodity or commodity bundle as the unit of account. We find such scenarios equally implausible. Mengerian analysis implies that, notwithstanding financial innovation, monetary exchange will continue to pose lower transactions costs than barter and thus will persist (on this see Krueger, 2000), and that accounting units will continue to be linked to actual base money or media of redemption (White, 1984). Network effects work against the emergence of new commodity units of account 'separated' from any base money, notwithstanding the fact that such units may represent more stable standards of value.[5]

Writers who imagine that market forces will deliver the *best imaginable* or an *ideal* standard of value seem to be engaged in utopian thinking. They wishfully think that most money users, despite being habituated to an inherited monetary standard, will know and demand the standard that would be best for macroeconomic stability. (We note that these writers themselves disagree about what that ideal standard is.) With network effects, however, the result of individuals' pursuit of self-interest does not necessarily produce the monetary standard that a benevolent economist or social planner would select for society as a whole. Menger was well aware of this. From barter, the convergence process can select a commodity that ranks first in suitability as a medium of exchange but less than first as a standard of value. Once a monetary standard has been selected, network effects make that standard difficult to dislodge without coercion, especially by an imagined money with no base of current users.

Although it is unlikely that market forces alone will give rise to brand-new monetary standards, so long as at least one existing standard is tolerably stable, a wider scope for choice among existing currencies will influence future monetary standards as already noted. People opting for more trustworthy currency will break the link between monetary standards and nation-states, reducing the number of nations administering their own standards, and reducing the number of distinct standards in the world. Monetary denationalization and monetary consolidation will go hand in hand.

## The Future of Retail Payments

Government central banks issue currency today not because they have outcompeted private firms at attracting loyal customers but because they have outlawed private competition. Legislation from the eighteenth to the twentieth centuries increasingly restricted private note-issue and finally gave central banks a monopoly of note-issue.[6] Today, private firms are introducing non-paper substitutes for central bank currency in the form of smart cards and other electronic media for conveying digital cash balances. If the new media are not legally repressed, and can exceed the convenience or interest yield (and match the anonymity) of paper money, they may eventually lead to a substantial reduction in the real demand for government currency.

The familiar types of electronic payment today are not currency-like but are forms of deposit transfer. Wire transfer has for many years accounted for the vast majority of the volume of payments (by value) in advanced economies, because it is how large-value payments are made in financial markets. (Paper currency is the most common payment method by number of transactions per day, but the average value per transaction is small.)

In recent years the introduction of retail (or 'point-of-sale') electronic funds transfer, using a 'debit card' and phone line to access the spender's bank account, has brought the key features of wiring money down to the level of the retail transaction. Like a wire transfer but unlike a paper cheque payment, retail electronic funds transfer is paperless, fully remote (neither spender nor recipient need convey any paper to the bank), and bounce-proof (the seller phones the bank for payment verification before finalizing the sale).[7] Automated clearinghouse payments, 'direct deposit' of paycheques, and bill-paying by personal computer have the same advantages. The most obvious result of these technologies is a reduction (at least *ceteris paribus*) in the frequency of writing paper cheques.

A different type of electronic payment – digital or electronic money – is now on the horizon. (Accordingly we below call paper notes and coins 'analogue currency'.)[8] Software on an electronic device in the consumer's possession holds a specific amount of money, encoded as a string of digits. It may be stored on a 'smart' plastic card with an implanted microchip ('electronic purse'), or on a personal computer hard drive ('digital cash'). Like a traveller's cheque or a private bank note, a bank-issued electronic money balance is not base money or legal tender. It is a claim on a bank or other financial institution that is denominated in and redeemable for base money or legal tender.

Like an analogue currency payment, but unlike a deposit transfer, an electronic money payment does not require the spender to have a bank account. For a \$10 purchase, a card-reading device subtracts \$10 from the card's balance and adds \$10 to the balance stored in the memory of the seller's terminal or recipient card. A card's balance can be increased by purchasing or borrowing balances from an issuing bank, or by placing the card in an automatic teller machine and transferring funds from a bank account, or (under the Mondex card system) by receiving funds from another card. A balance stored on a personal computer can similarly be increased by getting on-line with the issuing bank, or by receiving a payment through electronic mail or other internet transfer.

In contrast to analogue currency, electronic money is easy to carry even in large amounts. It avoids the need to carry the correct coins for parking or public transportation. It reduces the vulnerability of vending machines to theft. It eliminates the need to count notes and coins or wait for change at a retail checkout. In an increasingly fast-paced world, a store with faster-moving queues offers shoppers an increasingly attractive advantage over its competitors. The acceptor must, however, have special hardware that analogue currency does not require. In contrast to a debit or credit card, a currency card does not require the recipient to make a phone call before payment. In contrast to a cheque card, it does not require the acceptor to make a phone call at the end of the day, or even to have a phone line.

Currency smartcards themselves are fairly cheap to produce, and consumer resistance to carrying yet another card can be overcome by putting the purse-carrying microchip on a card the consumer would carry anyway, such as a debit or cheque card. The chief barrier to the spread of currency-card payments is the cost of the hardware for accepting the cards.[9] Will many retailers anticipate enough additional sales (or retention of sales that would otherwise have gone elsewhere) to justify the incremental cost of attaching currency-card readers to their sales registers? Will many consumers have enough occasions for receiving card-to-card payments to invest in and carry 'digital wallets'?

The best evidence on the prospects for electronic money comes from the world's largest installed smartcard base today, Germany's GeldKarte system developed by the commercial banks' industry association (the Zentraler Kreditausschuss or ZKA). Germans carry an estimated 60 million GeldKarte-capable cards, mostly microchip-equipped EuroCheque cards issued in the last few years. Transactions volume is still small compared to cash and cheque use. Universal use has not been immediate, because many retailers naturally hesitate to invest in card-reading terminals before many of their customers ask to pay by currency card, and many customers wait to see more retail terminals before they switch to customarily using the cards. At present GeldKarte use appears to have caught on in parking garages and a few other uses, but it remains to be seen whether its use will widen to achieve a self-feeding growth trajectory.[10]

The forces of global convergence are at work in smartcard systems. Europay (owned by MasterCard) has made an agreement with the ZKA to integrate GeldKarte into Europay's electronic purse product Clip, thus promising at least trans-European par acceptance of GeldKarte balances in years to come. Ironically arriving almost simultaneously with the final stages of European currency unification, the trans-European acceptance of currency cards will eliminate the hassle and expense of changing analogue currencies at the border, which was one of the leading rationales for undertaking the expenses and risks of unification. The technology for securely loading the GeldKarte via the internet, using a home computer and a relatively inexpensive peripheral device, exists in prototype and may soon be generally available. Paying by internet should not be far off.[11]

The German experience suggests that the adoption of currency cards will be slow, but it should be noted that in important ways the GeldKarte is not a true currency card. When a user loads a GeldKarte with balances from her bank account (recall that the GeldKarte chip is typically on a personal cheque card), the bank simultaneously creates a 'shadow account balance' in her name against which card payments are reconciled. Alice cannot pay Bob by transferring funds directly to Bob's card. Bob must deposit the funds before respending them. His deposit of the funds presents a claim (via the interbank clearing system) to Alice's bank for reconciliation and settlement. The balance on Alice's card (or in an internet-transferable electronic purse that shares this feature) is consequently more like a digital cashier's cheque than like a bank note that can circulate indefinitely before redemption.

MasterCard's Mondex system (which has undergone prototype testing in several English and American cities, but has not yet proven popular with consumers), by contrast, allows repeated card-to-card transfers. Like analogue currency, Mondex card balances are bearer media, not linked to personal bank accounts. The balance-issuing institution need only know the total of its outstanding currency-card liabilities, not who holds them at any moment.

For reasons we don't fully understand, Mondex is currently structured so that only one bank is the 'originator' of card balances in any given currency unit. All Mondex card balances denominated in US dollars, for example, are to be liabilities of the Chase Manhattan Bank. MasterCard might do better to allow competition among its members in issuing card balances, as the GeldKarte system does. At present, the system will not spread if Chase Manhattan lacks courage or imagination in marketing the card. MasterCard could instead give all its members the incentive to launch their own promotional schemes by letting them all originate card balances.

Because of the shadow-account system, the cards that perform both EuroCheque and GeldKarte functions do not – unlike analogue currency – preserve the user's financial privacy. The lack of privacy may be a serious disadvantage to attracting users away from analogue currency. There is reportedly an 'account-free' version of the GeldKarte that does preserve privacy, a card that can be purchased with cash and that is not linked to a personal bank account.[12] But such cards are inconvenient to acquire and reload. Privacy is technically feasible in downloadable currency cards. It could be provided by clearing card payments only against the issuing institution's general account. If personal information is omitted from the balance transfer message (unlike current practice in debit- and credit-card transactions), the bearer can remain as anonymous as if paying in paper bank notes.

The incentive for banks to issue electronic money is clear: float. If electronic money balances pay zero interest, as analogue currency traditionally has, the bank receives an interest-free loan from customers holding its card balances. Conceivably, personal computers and smartcard devices could be programmed to pay interest on electronic money balances, augmenting the balance by a specified percentage of each day's recorded remaining balance since the last transaction.[13] If such programming can be developed and cheaply copied to PCs and smartcard readers or loaders, and no regulation or effective cartel agreement blocks it, competition will force the banks that issue electronic money to pay interest on electronic money. The rate will presumably be close to the rate on transferable deposits, leaving the bank with a spread just sufficient to cover its administration costs. Small-denomination currency would then bear interest for the first time in history.

The payment of interest on electronic money, combined with convenience and the desired degree of anonymity, would enhance the prospect of the public's turning away from government-issued analogue currency. If interest remains too costly to deliver, however, the banks issuing electronic money will find it efficient to compete entirely on non-interest dimensions, the most important of which is presumably providing convenience in loading and spending.

Paper bank notes might be more efficient (have lower unit costs for providing the same services) than smartcard currency today (Lacker, 1996). We won't know unless governments allow competitive banks to issue paper notes as well as currency cards. Where legal barriers against private paper bank notes exist, electronic money media provide an 'end run' around the barrier. If nominal interest rates are high enough, float profits can enable private firms to issue electronic money and displace some analogue government currency despite the higher unit costs of electronic money media. Absent actual or anticipated legal restrictions against paper bank notes, however, there is no reason for less efficient media of exchange to prevail (White and Boudreaux, 2000).

Should technical progress progressively lower the relative price of the hardware needed to accept currency smartcard payments, smartcard acceptance will become more common. It is already common for photocopy machines to be equipped with card readers in addition to, or instead of, slots for coins and paper notes. (Smartcards differ from existing prepaid photocopy cards in that a microchip can carry more information than a magnetic stripe, and in that they aim to be accepted much more generally.) The set of sellers who do not accept electronic money, because their transaction volume is too small to justify an investment in the hardware, will shrink. If the set of analogue currency transactions falls below critical mass, and consumers no longer routinely carry analogue currency, the use of bills and coins could practically disappear, much as the use of the smallest-denomination coins has practically disappeared in many countries.

If the public does come to replace its holdings of central bank notes almost entirely with electronic money balances, there are fiscal implications: the central bank will be losing the float (or seigniorage) that it currently enjoys from holders of its non-interest-bearing currency. The competing commercial banks are not the recipients of a corresponding windfall, however; the public is. If the banks pay interest to holders of electronic money, the public's gain is obvious. If the banks do not pay explicit interest, but instead focus entirely on providing customers with desired in-kind benefits (which we could call 'in-kind interest'), the public's gain is equally real. Where interest competition is legally permitted, non-interest competition will prevail only to the extent that, per unit of bank expenditure, it delivers in-kind benefits that customers find at least as attractive as explicit interest net of the cost of collecting interest. With either price (explicit interest) or non-price (in-kind interest) competition, banks' potential float profits are distributed to the public (White and Boudreaux, 2000).

Suppose that analogue currency does disappear from common circulation. This does not usher in 'the end of money', as some enthusiasts (for example Rahn, 1999) have suggested. Rather, it merely undoes the current government monopoly of currency. It returns us to a world where not only cheque payments but also the money used in small transactions is privately issued, as it was before the monopolization of note-issue by central banks. Electronic money payments and electronic deposit transfers are no less *money* payments than are analogue currency payments and paper cheque transfers. Bank-issued payment media continue to be claims to an ultimate money of redemption or base money.

Base money today consists of irredeemable (fiat) 'liabilities' of the central bank and Treasury. They come in two forms: currency notes and coins, and deposit balances on the books of the central bank (which commercial banks own and use for paying one another). Eliminating coins and central bank notes – by the public voluntarily swapping its holdings with banks in exchange for bank-issued card balances or deposits – would not eliminate banks' deposit balances. In fact the nominal stock of base money would not change, as banks would swap the central bank notes turned in by the public for central bank deposit balances that are still useful for settling net flows of funds between banks. Settlement balances at the central bank would then constitute the entire stock of base money.

The transition from analogue government currency to digital (or analogue) private currency therefore does not change the monetary standard. The base money remains a fiat money, and bank-issued money remains a redeemable claim to that fiat money. The disappearance of central bank notes could make the unanchored nature of fiat money more obvious to the public, but a change in the standard will not automatically follow. Despite the optimism of some visionaries and promoters (e.g. <http://www.e-gold.com>) that internet payments could mean the spontaneous re-emergence of a gold standard or the emergence of some novel commodity standard, internet sellers will still want to be paid in fiat-money-denominated balances that most of their trading partners currently accept.

## 3. BANK RESERVES, INTERBANK SETTLEMENT AND WHOLESALE PAYMENTS

As we have seen, the general course of payments system evolution is one in which private financial firms seek to encourage transactors to employ their IOUs (whether paper, plastic, or electronic) in place of base money. We can imagine the limiting case where the non-bank public holds zero base money. Even in that case, however, total demand for base money would not go to zero because banks and other issuers would continue to hold base money as a reserve medium.

Today banks hold base-money reserves partly to meet minimum statutory requirements. Economists have come to understand that reserve requirements are not needed either to ensure banking-system liquidity or to avoid over-supply of private money. Instead, they now view statutory reserve requirements primarily as a distortionary tax on banks. Monetary authorities, responding to this perspective (and to international competition), have become increasingly willing to abandon statutory reserve requirements altogether (for example the Bank of Canada), or to render them practically irrelevant.[14] Some (such as the European Central Bank) have begun paying interest on reserves to reduce the distortion, or are considering doing so. So long as central banks are self-financing, such interest payments must fall short of interest earnings on underlying central bank assets, so that an opportunity cost of holding reserves will remain. Global competitive pressures will therefore promote the abolition of statutory reserve requirements, even if central banks attempt to mitigate the pressures by paying positive (but subcompetitive) interest on reserves.

Even if holding reserves continues to be costly, the abolition of reserve requirements does not imply that banks will reduce their reserves to zero. Banks will continue to have a prudential demand to hold base-money reserves so long as base money remains the preferred medium of redemption and interbank settlement, that is, the asset banks typically use to pay off their claims to depositors and to one another. Bank B acquires a claim on Bank A whenever a customer transfers money (by cheque, wire, debit card, or other device) from his Bank A account in favour of a recipient's account at Bank B. Bank A makes good on the claim by transferring base money to Bank B.

Banks prefer to receive settlement in base money rather than financial claims, and are likely to continue to do so, for two main reasons. First, base money never confronts its recipient with a bid-ask spread or turnaround cost in acquiring and then spending it. It does not have bid and ask prices in terms of, but instead defines, the unit of account. Second, a base-money payment is 'final': its recipient faces no credit risk. Banks will continue to want an asset with those properties for interbank settlements.

Banks will of course continue (as in the past) to seek ways to economize on their costly holdings of settlement media. The most important historical innovation in this respect was the development of multilateral clearing and settlement. Individual payment orders (whether paper cheques or electronic transfers) are processed through a central clearinghouse, which calculates net credits and debits resulting from all gross transactions, typically on a daily basis. A bank then makes or receives one payment, via the clearinghouse, to settle with all its clearing partners simultaneously. Multilateral clearing (or 'netting') allows a huge volume of transactions in bank-issued money to be settled with a small quantity of base money. It has therefore long been the preferred settlement method of private banks. In our earlier paper (Selgin and White, 1987), we discussed the spontaneous origins of private clearinghouses – institutions to facilitate economical clearing and settlement – during the 19th century.

Multilateral clearing and settlement was first organized by private market institutions, and private clearinghouses are still responsible for the clearing and settlement of a substantial volume of payments in many nations. But governments substantially increased their role in the organization of interbank payments during the 20th century. With the rise of central banks, enjoying a government guarantee against failure and a legal monopoly in issuing paper currency, private banks began to use central bank liabilities instead of base money (gold or silver) as a reserve and settlement medium. This practice was voluntary and convenient so long as central banks honoured their pledges to redeem their notes and deposits in the precious metals. It was rendered obligatory when those pledges were dishonoured. The advent of fiat money elevated central bank liabilities to the status of final settlement media, but did not by itself imply nationalization of the clearing and settlement process. In some countries (for example the United States) central banks did take over the clearing and settlement functions formerly run by private clearinghouses, but elsewhere (for example Canada) private clearinghouses continued to operate. Even where they were nationalized, clearinghouses continued to practice multilateral clearing and settlement, and to allow the reserve economies associated with that practice, at least with regard to small cheque payments.

Today central banks that provide clearing and settlement of retail payments are finding it increasingly difficult to compete on a level playing field with private clearinghouses. They are also finding it difficult to maintain the legal restrictions and subsidies (often implicit) that used to give them an advantage. The Federal Reserve, for one, recently explored (but ultimately decided against) the option of getting out of the cheque-clearing business.[15] We imagine that, in the not-too-distant future, the processing of retail payments will once again be fully privatized in all countries with well-developed banking systems. Privatization will end the implicit taxes and subsidies typically associated with state-administered clearings, and will thereby encourage greater efficiency in retail payments. For example, users of paper cheques will have to bear the full costs of paper transactions, which will encourage them to embrace electronic alternatives like cheque imaging and electronic debit-card transfers.

Wholesale payments via wire transfer present a much more complex story. Here the role of government has been increasing, especially during the last decade. While private clearinghouses (like the New York Clearinghouse Association) continue to administer significant volumes of large payments in some nations, governments have imposed increasingly severe legal restrictions on them. Central banks have taken steps to protect or enhance their own involvement in wholesale payments. In place of the private marketplace practice of multilateral clearing with end-of-day net settlement, central banks (for example the European Central Bank in its TARGET system) have sought and largely succeeded in imposing 'real-time gross settlement'. In a strict real-time gross settlement system, payments are settled continuously by immediate transfer of central bank money representing their full or gross value. This procedure is supposed to avoid the 'systemic risk' problem that arises when banks extend credit to their customers in response to payment orders that have yet to be settled.

Because it forgoes opportunities for netting, strict real-time gross settlement offers none of the reserve economies available though multilateral clearing and settlement. Consequently it has never been embraced voluntarily by the private sector. Strict real-time gross settlement is costly to banks, compelling them to maintain high start-of-day reserve ratios to avoid a high risk of settlement default, and thereby handicaps them in international competition. To reduce the cost, central banks in most nations (Switzerland is a prominent exception) have granted intraday credits to private banks. Some require that intraday loans be fully collateralized; others do not. In general, real-time gross settlement has gained ground, despite its relative inefficiency, because the more efficient alternative of deferred net settlement has been legally restricted or because the true costs of real-time gross settlement have been externalized via subsidized intraday central-bank loans.

Wholesale payments represent an exceptional case in which market institutions have been yielding ground to state institutions. Will that trend continue, or will market forces regain the upper hand, allowing banks to take fuller advantage of opportunities to economize on holdings of base money?

To answer this question, we must first consider why governments have been able to expand their role in wholesale payments, despite being compelled by market forces to reduce their involvement in most other areas of the payments system. We have mentioned banks' desire for settlement finality. Finality is typically achieved today by settling on the books of a central bank whose deposit liabilities are (along with paper currency) base money. For a private clearinghouse to settle on the books of a central bank, it must maintain an account with that central bank. The central bank can therefore effectively thwart settlement on its books by any competing private clearing system simply by refusing to grant the clearinghouse an account.

In principle, a competing private clearinghouse could achieve finality without having an account at a central bank. It could have its members settle by physical transfer of fiat currency or, to avoid the costs of moving bundles of paper currency around, by transfer of claims on the clearinghouse itself that are absolutely secure (100 percent backed by currency). Private commercial-bank clearinghouses in the late-19th century US normally used the latter system, holding 100 percent gold reserves (Cannon, 1910).

Clearinghouse members might be willing to sacrifice some degree of payments finality for an interest return. A private clearinghouse could pay interest on settlement accounts by holding fractional reserves of currency and investing the balance of clearinghouse assets in low-risk securities. A central bank that wants to compete for clearing and settlement business could, of course, respond by paying interest on its deposit liabilities (but not on its currency). It would thereby increase the return on its accounts relative to the return on private settlement accounts.

A commercial bank's incentive to use a central bank for clearing and settlement will still depend on the extent to which the central bank allows its clients to take advantage of economies from multilateral netting. Suppose that a central bank pays an interest rate of $y$ on its deposits, lower than the rate $r$ the commercial bank can earn on non-reserve assets (bank loans), but greater than the rate $z$ that a private clearinghouse pays on settlement balances. At the same time suppose that the central bank's gross settlement system requires a commercial bank to hold $N$ times as much settlement media as a private net settlement alternative. In that case, the opportunity cost of participating in the central bank's system is greater so long as $N(r-y) > (r-z)$. As Jeffrey Marquardt (1994, p. 47) has argued, the reduction or abandonment of statutory reserve requirements (in effect) increases the value of $N$, by reducing the amount of settlement media a commercial bank has to hold when using private clearing, and thus unintentionally tends to favour net settlement systems.

Some writers (for example Eisenbeis, 1995, p. 343) argue that ongoing technological trends favour real-time gross settlement. Declining computation costs, in particular, lower the costs of continuously processing transactions. But these same trends also lower the costs associated with multilateral netting, so they are unlikely to decide which system prevails.

One factor that *has* favoured government involvement in wholesale payments has been central banks' ability to externalize the costs of intervention. By extending intraday credits at insufficiently risk-adjusted prices, as for example the US Federal Reserve System does, some central banks (and thus, indirectly, the taxpayers) take on credit risk that should be either avoided or borne by private transactors (including banks). This problem is only part of a more general problem of implicit and explicit central-bank guarantees and related moral hazards. In the case of deposit insurance, at least in the United States, taxpayer losses from morally hazardous banking eventually pushed regulators into limiting the extent of guarantees and instituting some semblance of risk-based pricing. The long run for intraday settlement credits lies in the same direction.

Just how quickly governments disengage from wholesale payments will depend in part on how quickly economists' attitudes change. Economists have generally supported government involvement, at least in principle, believing that a free-market wholesale payments system would present serious externality problems (Folkerts-Landau et al., 1997). With governments around the globe intervening in wholesale payments, there is no free-market benchmark for measuring the inefficiencies of intervention. Although the market-failure arguments against deferred net settlement in wholesale payments are far from convincing (see Selgin, 2000), prevailing opinion has yet to change. The private costs of gross settlement are relatively small when the central bank provides intraday credit, and large social costs (losses to taxpayers from subsidized risk-taking) are yet to appear. We therefore expect that government involvement in wholesale payments will not disappear soon.

Yet we should note developments pointing in the other direction. First, the spread of branch banking, not only nationwide (as in the US) but worldwide, will generate an increase in the share of intrabank ('on-us') transactions. That is, the volume of transfers from one customer to another customer of the same bank will increase relative to that of interbank transactions that require clearing. At the same time, the number of clearing banks will decline, making it easier for the banks to arrive at prior arrangements for internalizing settlement risks. The associated declines in the gross value of interbank payments and in the (supposed) externalities associated with such payments should lead to a corresponding reduction in the perceived urgency of wholesale payments regulation. Second, the consolidation of international currencies will lead to a reduction in the volume of foreign exchange transactions. The corresponding reduction in 'Herstatt' risk will alleviate another concern that has motivated government involvement in large-value payments, and the push toward real-time gross settlement in particular. The advent of round-the-clock clearinghouses, with special facilities for co-ordinating payments between clearinghouses, will also serve to minimize Herstatt risk while preserving the economic advantages of multilateral deferred net settlement.

# 4. IMPLICATIONS FOR MONETARY POLICY

Many writers have misconceived the implications of future payments evolution for conventional monetary policies.

As we have noted, market forces promote the substitution of privately-issued monies for central-bank-issued money, particularly where the former are interest-bearing and the latter are not, in the portfolios of the non-bank public. Market forces also tend to reduce reliance upon central bank money as a medium for settling interbank balances. The real demand for central bank monies, and hence the real monetary base, will consequently shrink both in absolute terms and relative to broader monetary aggregates.[16] Some writers imagine that such absolute and relative shrinkage in the real quantity of central-bank monies implies that central bankers will have less control over nominal magnitudes expressed in their currency units. Critics of central banking welcome a new economic era in which central bankers will no longer be capable of creating monetary disturbances. Central bankers themselves fret that they will no longer be able to succeed at macroeconomic stabilization. Both sides share the basic premise that central banks' power to influence nominal and real variables is proportional to the real size of their balance sheets, measured either in absolute terms or relative to the size of broader monetary aggregates.

Thus Kevin Dowd (1998, p. 327), a critic of central banking, envisions a 'gradual erosion of central bank power by market forces', and predicts that

> as base money becomes less significant, it will gradually lose its effectiveness as a channel through which the central bank can influence the broader monetary system. The fulcrum on which the monetary policy lever operates will erode away and make monetary policy less and less effective as time goes on.

Benjamin Friedman (1999), a supporter of central banking, makes essentially the same prediction in more pessimistic language. He worries that ongoing financial market developments 'threaten to weaken or undermine ... the efficacy of monetary policy'. Unlike Dowd, who would like to see the weakening continue, Friedman (1999, p. 338) wonders whether 'aggressive regulatory changes' may be needed 'to preserve the economic relevance of the central bank's monopoly over the supply of reserves' and thereby prevent unpredictable and undesirable fluctuations in nominal magnitudes.

A recent BIS report (BIS, 1996, p. 7) shares Friedman's view, worrying that the spread of private electronic monies 'could shrink central bank balance sheets significantly' and that such shrinkage will eventually 'begin to adversely affect monetary policy implementation'. In particular, a substantial enough shrinkage in central bank balance sheets will supposedly undermine central banks' ability to achieve needed reductions in outstanding stocks of base money by means of open-market sales and other conventional procedures:

> The relatively modest size of open market operations on normal days suggests that a relatively small balance sheet might be sufficient. However, special circumstances could arise in which the central bank might not be able to implement reserve-absorbing operations on a large enough scale ... because it lacked sufficient assets.

Such concerns are misplaced. It is of course true that a decline in the real demand for central bank money must be matched by a corresponding reduction in its nominal quantity if inflation is to be avoided. It is generally incorrect, however, to think that a central bank's power to change monetary magnitudes, including the size of its own balance sheet, declines as that balance sheet shrinks. A central bank becomes impotent only in the limiting case (considered below) where the demand for its money falls to zero. To see why, consider the simple money multiplier relationship, $M = mB$, where $B$ is the nominal quantity of central-bank-issued base money (which is typically the lion's share of the liabilities on the central bank's balance sheet). $M$ is some broader money aggregate that includes private exchange media denominated in central bank money, and $m>1$ is the base-money multiplier. As the demand for base money declines relative to the demand for private substitutes, the money multiplier becomes larger. Any decline in the relative importance of base money is thus matched by a corresponding increase in the *power* possessed by each unit, that is, in the number of units of broad money that will be pyramided upon each outstanding unit of base money. The 'fulcrum on which the monetary policy lever operates' becomes *more* rather than *less* effective. The absolute nominal magnitude of open-market operations needed to achieve any desired change in the broad money stock, the price level, or nominal income is scaled down accordingly.

The fear that a central bank's balance sheet might become 'too small' to allow it to 'implement reserve-absorbing operations on a large enough scale' to achieve a desired policy target is no less groundless. No matter how small the starting value of $B$, for any given money multiplier, any $x$ percent reduction in $B$ will result in an $x$ percent reduction in $M$ and in other nominal magnitudes, *ceteris paribus*. Unless policy requires that the monetary base be reduced by more than 100 percent (a *negative* price-level target, perhaps?), it is clearly wrong to claim that central banks might one day be unable to achieve large enough reductions in $B$.

To insist that any positive demand for central bank money makes it possible for central banks to achieve price-level, inflation, or nominal-income goals using conventional policy tools is not to deny that certain interest-rate targets may become more difficult to achieve as the demand for base money declines. Some innovations that reduce the real demand for base money may also render that demand more volatile. For example, statutory reserve requirements generate a relatively stable demand for bank reserves, above and beyond the precautionary demand. When reserve requirements are lifted, a bank's demand for reserves becomes a precautionary demand pure and simple, varying not only with the mean quantity of its liabilities, but also with less predictable changes in their variance. A reduced demand for base money may then be associated with greater difficulty in targeting the interbank lending rate, which moves with the demand for bank reserves. The Federal Reserve has long opposed repealing statutory reserve requirements on the grounds that reserve requirements make it easier to target the Federal Funds rate.[17]

Other innovations that reduce the demand for base money may actually assist the achievement of monetary policy objectives. If electronic money and other private exchange media come to completely displace base money from the public's currency holdings, and statutory reserve requirements are eliminated, then base money will then be demanded solely for the purpose of interbank settlement. For any given settlement technology and real interest rate, the precautionary demand for settlement balances will be positively related to the volume of transactions, which is equal to the quantity of bank-issued money multiplied by its transactions velocity. With the demand for base money independent of the public's desired ratio of currency to deposits, a frozen stock of base money can achieve near-constancy of aggregate demand. A simple monetary base growth rule can correspondingly achieve a stable growth rate for nominal spending, a goal that many monetary policy theorists favour (see McCallum, 1989; Bean, 1983; Bradley and Jansen, 1989). Suppose, for example, that the market for bank reserves is initially in equilibrium with a given stock of base money. An increase in the quantity or velocity of bank-issued money will mean an increased demand for reserves, which will bid up the interbank lending rate. The consequently higher cost of reserve shortfalls will in turn encourage banks to restrict their issues. Aggregate demand – the total volume of spending on goods and services – will thus tend to be a relatively stable multiple of the stock of base money (Selgin, 1994). Financial deregulation and monetary privatization can help to reduce the size and frequency of fluctuations in aggregate demand and thus of business cycles.

In a future world of globalized currencies, the stabilizing tendency just described will not act on *national* income, but on *worldwide* income in dollars, euros, or yen. International dollar flows will mean that changes in the volume of dollar income within the US will tend to be offset by opposite changes in dollar income elsewhere. The invisible hand's potential contribution to macroeconomic stability must be understood in terms of *global* stability rather than stability of traditional national targets. Fluctuations in national indicators will tend to reflect underlying changes in the worldwide distribution of demand for money and goods. Like fluctuations in the relative fortunes of subnational regions today, they should not be taken as evidence of any monetary policy failure.

Future payment-system innovations that privatize and globalize currency do not threaten macroeconomic stability, but they do threaten the seigniorage profits central banks derive from issuing fiat currency. Market forces for currency privatization and globalization will act most strongly on the worst (highest inflation) currencies, which are not coincidentally issued by those governments that use seigniorage to finance the largest shares of their budgets (see Click, 1998). Reduced seigniorage will force them to undertake some combination of expenditure reductions and increases in other tax revenues. The market forces that reduce governments' role in money may thereby also promote a more general reduction in the scope of government.

Where the real domestic monetary base shrinks far enough (the limiting case being where it shrinks to zero with complete privatization or dollarization), seigniorage will become too small to cover the central bank's budget. The central bank will become a fiscal drain rather than a source of profit. An explicit budget appropriation will make the expense of its operations more transparent. Political pressure will then arise for reducing the size and scope of central bank operations. Governments whose profits from central banking have turned small or even negative will become more favourable toward alternatives, such as currency boards or official dollarization. The process of monetary denationalization may thus become self-reinforcing in a manner reminiscent of the Mengerian monetary selection process.

## 5. WHITHER FIAT MONEY?

So far we have assumed that the demand for central bank money – or at least the demand for the money of a few central banks – remains positive. Private monetary innovations and deregulation will reduce the demand for central bank money, but are unlikely to eliminate that demand entirely. Private monies will continue to take the form of redeemable claims to central bank money. Whatever their practical advantages, such claims necessarily pose a positive default risk and positive information costs (about the current size of that risk, if nothing else), making central bank money uniquely default-risk-free and liquid. These risk and liquidity advantages will likely preserve some demand for central bank money even if cryptographic and clearing innovations (as discussed above) make private monies equally anonymous.

As noted above, central bank money is especially likely to continue to serve as a medium of settlement among private money issuers, both because of its freedom from default risk and because of the low transactions costs involved in settling on the books of a central bank. Settlement of the books of a private clearinghouse association bank would lack the same finality. Banks with positive clearings would find themselves holding less-than-perfectly-secure clearinghouse-issued claims to base money, rather than base money itself, an asset of unambiguous nominal value. The desire for payments finality is perhaps the most fundamental reason that a demand for central bank money is likely to persist.

Even so, a complete substitution of private for central bank liabilities remains a distinct (if remote) possibility with interesting economic implications. Network effects, as we have noted, give private issuers the incentive to continue to denominate and redeem their monies in units of central-bank-issued base money. Such private monies will remain valuable only so long as base money remains valuable. As the real demand for base money declines, the central bank must correspondingly reduce its nominal quantity to preserve its value. As the demand for central bank money approaches zero, its quantity must also approach zero to keep nominal prices from rising toward infinity.

But what happens if the demand for base money actually reaches zero? What happens if banks no longer maintain accounts with the central bank (preferring instead to settle using private clearinghouse balances backed by interest-earning government debt), and if other firms and consumers no longer hold central bank notes? In that case, every outstanding unit of central bank money would be a 'hot potato', not wanted in anyone's portfolio. Even the tiniest nominal quantity of base money would generate an infinite price level, rendering both base money and the private money denominated in it worthless. In such a world monetary privatization would be a victim of its own success, ushering in nominal indeterminacy and presumably opening the door to financial and economic chaos.

Thus, although he is wrong to suggest that a central bank's ability to control nominal magnitudes declines continuously with the size of its balance sheet, Benjamin Friedman (1999, pp. 337–8) is essentially correct in making the following observation, which assumes fiat money:

> At its most basic level, economic theory provides no clear answer to what would determine an economy's price level if what its inhabitants used as money depended entirely on their own ability and willingness to innovate, without effective restraint from the central bank or some other monetary authority.

Some economists reject Friedman's statement, and similar earlier statements (for example Milton Friedman and Anna Schwartz, 1986, p. 5), even while accepting (at least for the sake of argument) the premise of a zero demand for central bank money. Some base their rejection on an improper appeal to the mathematics of limits. Thus Stacey Schreft and Bruce D. Smith (2000), supposing (dubiously) that 'the demand for base money may virtually or entirely vanish in the not-too-distant future', argue that a zero demand for base money would 'pose no threat to the traditional methods employed for conducting monetary policy'. Their claim rests, however, upon their having confused what happens 'if the demand for base money asymptotically goes to zero' (p. 3) with what happens when it actually *reaches* zero, which is another thing altogether.

To see why, consider an economy with a positive demand for base money and an initial price level $P$. Following the standard equation of exchange, let $P = M/(y/V) = M/m^D$, where $M$ is the nominal stock of base money, $y$ is real output, $V$ is the velocity of base money, and $m^D$ measures the real demand for base money. It is true that, as $m^D$ approaches zero, some percentage reduction in $M$ (a 'traditional...monetary policy') will suffice to keep the price level constant. But once $m^D$ actually reaches zero, $P$ becomes undefined, a ratio with zero as its denominator. No reduction in the nominal quantity of base money will suffice to maintain money's purchasing power once it ceases to be wanted by anyone.

Other economists conclude that conventional monetary policy can be carried out, despite assuming a zero demand for base money, only by failing to think through the implications of the assumption. Thus Charles Goodhart (2000, p. 24) writes that 'neither currency, nor banks, are essential to the ability of a Central Bank to set the interest rate in its own country' because the Central Bank, being a non-profit-maximizing entity, 'is always in a position to dictate the finest terms on either the bid, or the ask, side of the money market' (ibid., p. 27). In identifying monetary policy with the manipulation of money-market interest rates, Goodhart neglects fundamental questions having to do with the supply and demand for base money. What 'money market' does he have in mind, in which the central bank can meet any excess demand or absorb any excess supply at the going interest rate, if not the market for final settlement media taking the form of deposit credits on the books of the Central Bank? Who are the demanders in this market, if there are no banks, and what use do they have for central bank liabilities? Finally, granting as Goodhart does (p. 25) that 'real factors [will still] determine ... the real interest rate' in the long run, what will determine *nominal* rates when there is no limit to the velocity of base money and (therefore) no anchor to prices expressed in the traditional unit of account?[18]

Knut Wicksell (1935), addressing the question in a gold-standard context, believed that monetary evolution and financial stability were ultimately incompatible. He argued that unimpeded market forces would lead to the development of a 'pure credit' system of exchange that would eliminate any need for gold as an exchange or settlement medium. In such a system, the existence of an industrial (non-monetary) demand for gold would prevent gold from becoming utterly worthless, thus allowing it to continue to serve as the economy's medium of account. But the relatively volatile nature of the industrial demand for gold, he thought, would render a 'pure credit' gold standard highly unstable. As a way out of this imagined future predicament Wicksell proposed – ironically enough – a switch to fiat money. He apparently overlooked the possibility that a fiat-money system might also become a 'pure credit' system, with private IOUs displacing central bank money, thereby making fiat money (which by definition has no industrial use) utterly worthless.

The forces that favour the future substitution of commercial-bank-issued for central-bank-issued money appear less powerful than those that historically favoured the substitution of banknotes and checkable deposits for gold and silver coins. Coins were a relatively clumsy medium of exchange. Users of banknotes and deposits found them much more convenient. (And they lost little in the way of security: bank defaults were minimal in countries without perverse legal restrictions on banks, and some bank liabilities were presumably *more* secure from theft.) E-money and redeemable banknotes have yet to demonstrate any similarly great convenience advantage over fiat central bank notes. Should technical innovations promise to give private monies a decided edge, central banks might respond to the potential competition by embodying similar innovations in their own liabilities.

With respect to retaining the demand for base money as a settlement medium, nothing prevents central banks from paying interest on the deposit portion of the monetary base that commercial banks hold for interbank settlements. Such a reform could offset private innovations, such as interest-bearing private settlement accounts, that might otherwise erode the demand for base money. The Federal Reserve views such interest payments as means for enhancing the efficiency of the US banking system without scrapping statutory reserve requirements. International competitive pressures and a dwindling demand for central bank money may eventually force central banks to pay interest on reserves, at a rate equal to the rate earned on central bank assets minus intermediation expenses, even where reserve holdings are entirely voluntary. The possibility that the demand for base money will fall to zero even when it bears interest seems to us remote enough to conclude that fiat money is, after all, likely to survive foreseeable financial innovations.

## NOTES

\*   We thank Michael Latzer, Stefan Schmitz, and Erich Streissler for comments.
1.   We borrow the term 'monetary nationalism' from Hayek (1937).
2.   Edward J. Kane (1987) provides an early analysis of 'the regulatory dialectic' between technology and financial regulation in a competitive international arena.
3.   For a brief account of Ecuador's experience see 'Ecuador Drifts Between Opportunity and Deadlock', *The Economist*, 21 Dec. 2000. On the rationale for dollarization see LeBaron and McCulloch (2000).
4.   A private entrepreneur is currently marketing a silver-backed currency in the United States. Chief among the obstacles to its widespread acceptance is that banks won't take it (White, 2000).
5.   For a discussion of network effects, redeemability and the unit of account see Schmitz's contribution to this volume and the literature cited therein.
6.   For the historical developments in several nations, see Smith (1990). In the United States commercial banks today can supposedly issue notes, owing to the elimination of legal restrictions in 1976 and 1994. But it is doubtful whether the Federal Reserve would tolerate any attempt by a commercial bank to take advantage of this regulatory loophole.
7.   A 'cheque card' (for example EuroCheque or Visa Check) skips the phone call, and substitutes the bank's guarantee (vouched for by the card) that the payment will be good at the end of the day.
8.   Here we wish to distinguish currency-like electronic money (spending of which transfers monetary value from holder to holder without bank involvement) from deposit-like electronic money (spending of which triggers account-balance transfers on the books of one or more banks). This distinction relates to the 'back end' of the transaction, i.e. to whether it requires clearing. If permitted, we would use the term 'electronic currency' or 'digital currency' for the first type of money. The electronic payments literature, however, typically distinguishes among

varieties of electronic money only by their 'front end' characteristics, i.e. whether the money is carried on a chip card or a mobile phone or a computer hard drive.

9. Relatively expensive hardware is necessary to address bank concerns about security and consumer concerns about anonymity. Cheaper hardware would exacerbate these other obstacles.

10. See the press accounts linked at http://csecmc1.vub.ac.be/cfec/geldkarte.htm.

11. On the integration of the GeldKarte with the Internet see <http://www.kuk.net/geldkarte/produkte/projekt.htm>.

12. Internet literature on GeldKarte mentions such a card, but its actual use in Germany appears to be practically unknown.

13. A very cleverly programmed card would hold electronic money balances from multiple issuers, but would spend balances issued by other banks ahead of the card issuer's, so as to maximize the issuer's float.

14. On the distortionary effects of reserve requirements, and Canada's recent phasing out of its reserve requirements, see Clinton (1997). On the historical use of reserve requirements as a tax in the United States see McCarthy (1984).

15. Federal Reserve System (1998).

16. Currency substitution may increase the real monetary base of a particular favoured currency, for example official or unofficial dollarization may increase the real US dollar base, for some time despite an overall trend toward privatization of money balances.

17. The Fed concedes that statutory reserve requirements are not necessary for controlling inflation or for maintaining the liquidity of the banking system. Other central banks attach less importance to the goal of smoothing interbank lending rates, and have therefore been less opposed to ending statutory reserve requirements. Recognizing the competitive disadvantage to US banks, Fed officials have proposed to pay interest on reserves in lieu of abolishing reserve requirements.

18. Of course, the central bank could in principle re-establish a nominal anchor by redefining the monetary unit in terms of some other still-scarce asset and by making its liabilities genuine claims to that asset, and, hence, no longer fiat money in the usual sense of the term.

Goodhart (2000, p. 25) claims that Michael Woodford (2000) reaches conclusions closely resembling his own. In fact Woodford's analysis takes for granted a continuing positive demand for base money as a bank reserve medium, albeit a demand that may only be sustained by means of interest payments on reserves.

# REFERENCES

Bank for International Settlements (1996), *Implications for Central Banks of the Development of Electronic Money* (<http://www.bis.org/publ/bisp01.pdf>).

Bean, C. (1983), 'Targeting Nominal Income: An Appraisal', *Economic Journal,* **93**, pp. 806-19.

Benston, G. J. (1991), 'Does Bank Regulation Produce Stability? Lessons from the United States', in: F. Capie and G. E. Wood (eds), *Unregulated Banking: Chaos or Order?*, London: Macmillan.

Bradley, M. D. and D. W. Jansen (1989), 'Understanding Nominal GNP Targeting', Federal Reserve Bank of St Louis *Economic Review,* **7** (6), pp. 31-40.

Browne, F. X. and D. Cronin (1995), 'Payment Technologies, Financial Innovation, and Laissez-Faire Banking', *Cato Journal,* **15**, pp. 101-16.

Cannon, J. G. (1910), *Clearing Houses*, Washington: Government Printing Office.

Click, R. W. (1998), 'Seigniorage in a Cross-section of Countries', *Journal of Money, Credit, and Banking*, **30**, pp. 154-71.

Clinton, K. (1997), 'Implementation of Monetary Policy in a Regime with Zero Reserve Requirements', Bank of Canada Working Paper, pp. 97-98.

Cohen, B. J. (1998), *The Geography of Money*, Cornell: Cornell University Press.

Dowd, K. (1998), 'Monetary Policy in the 21st Century: An Impossible Task?' *The Cato Journal,* **17**, pp. 327-31.

*The Economist*, 'Ecuador Drifts Between Opportunity and Deadlock' (21 December 2000).

Eisenbeis, R. (1995), 'Private Sector Solutions to Payments System Stability', *Journal of Financial Services Research,* **9**, pp. 327-49.

Fama, E. (1980), 'Banking in a Theory of Finance', *Journal of Monetary Economics,* **6**, pp. 39-57.

Federal Reserve System (1998), Committee on the Federal Reserve in the Payments Mechanism, *The Federal Reserve in the Payments System*, Washington.

Folkerts-Landau, D., P. Garber and D. Schoenmaker (1997), 'The Reform of Wholesale Payments Systems', *Finance and Development,* **34**, pp. 25-28.

Friedman, B. (1999), 'The Future of Monetary Policy', *International Finance,* **2**, pp. 321-38.

Friedman, M. and A. J. Schwartz (1986), 'Has Government Any Role in Money?', *Journal of Monetary Economics,* **17**, pp. 37-62.

Fry, M. J. (1988), *Money, Interest, and Banking in Economic Development*, Baltimore: The Johns Hopkins University Press.

Goodhart, C. (2000), 'Can Central Banking Survive the IT Revolution?', *International Finance*, **3**, pp. 189-209.

Hayek, F. A. (1937), *Monetary Nationalism and International Stability*, London: Longmans, Green.

Hayek, F. A. (1978), *Denationalisation of Money*, 2nd edn, London: Institute of Economic Affairs.

Kane, E. J. (1987), 'Competitive Financial Reregulation: An International Perspective', in R. Portes and A. Swoboda (eds), *Threats to International Financial Stability*, Cambridge: Cambridge University Press.

Krueger, M. (2000), 'Towards a Moneyless World?', unpublished manuscript, Institute for Prospective Technological Studies, Sevilla, University of Durham.

Lacker, J. M. (1996), 'Stored Value Cards: Costly Substitutes for Government Currency', Federal Reserve Bank of Richmond, *Economic Quarterly*, **83**, pp. 1–25.

LeBaron, B. and R. McCulloch (2000), 'Floating, Fixed, or Super-Fixed? Dollarization Joins the Menu of Exchange-Rate Options', *American Economic Review, Papers and Proceedings*, **90**, pp. 32-37.

Macintosh, K. L. (1998), 'How to Encourage Global Electronic Commerce: The Case for Private Currencies on the Internet', *Harvard Journal of Law and Technology*, **11**, pp. 733-96.

McCallum, B. T. (1989), *Monetary Economics: Theory and Policy*, New York: Macmillan.

Marquardt, J. (1994), 'Monetary Issues and Payment System Design', in: B. J. Summers (ed.), *The Payment System. Design, Management, and Supervision*, Washington, DC: International Monetary Fund, pp. 41-52.

Menger, C. (1909), 'Money', chapter 2 in this volume.

McCarthy, F. W. (1984), 'The Evolution of the Bank Regulatory Structure: A Reappraisal', Federal Reserve Bank of Richmond, *Economic Review*, pp. 3-21.

Rahn, R. (1999), *The End of Money and the Struggle for Financial Privacy*, Seattle: Discovery Institute Press.

Schreft, S. and B. D. Smith (2000), 'The Evolution of Cash Transactions: Some Implications for Monetary Policy', Working Paper, Federal Reserve Bank of Kansas City.

Selgin, G. (1994), 'E-Money: Friend or Foe of Monetarism?', in: J. A. Dorn (ed.), *The Future of Money in the Information Age*, Washington, DC: The Cato Institute, pp. 97-100.

Selgin, G. (2000), 'Wholesale Payments: Questioning the Market-Failure Hypothesis', Unpublished working paper, University of Georgia.

Selgin, G. and L. H. White (1987), 'The Evolution of a Free Banking System,' *Economic Inquiry,* **25**, pp. 439-57.

Selgin, G. and L. H. White (1994), 'How Would the Invisible Hand Handle Money?', *Journal of Economic Literature*, **32**, pp. 1718-49.

Selgin, G. and L. H. White (1999), 'A Fiscal Theory of Government's Role in Money', *Economic Inquiry*, **37**, pp. 154-65.

Smith, V. C. (1990), *The Rationale of Central Banking*, Indianapolis: Liberty Press.

White, L. H. (1984), 'Competitive Payments Systems and the Unit of Account', *American Economic Review*, **74**, pp. 669-712.

White, L. H. (2000), 'A Competitor for the Fed?', *Ideas on Liberty* (July).

White, L. H. and D. J. Boudreaux (2000), 'Is Nonprice Competition in Currency Inefficient? A Reply to Sumner', *Journal of Money, Credit, and Banking*, **32**, pp. 150-53.

Wicksell, K. (1935), *Lectures on Political Economy*, vol. 2., 'Money', London: Routledge.
Woodford, M. (2000), 'Monetary Policy in a World without Money', *International Finance*, 3, pp. 229-60.

# 5. The institutional character of electronic money schemes: redeemability and the unit of account

## Stefan W. Schmitz[*]

---

While the idea that currency competition[1] would result in the provision of preferable (for example more stable) units of account is neither recent nor tied to the emergence of new electronic payments systems it has become quite popular among commentators on e-cash. The reasons for the revival are mostly to be found in new technology:[2] (*i*) Due to advances in encryption technology and the diffusion of internet usage, the issue and circulation of newly introduced media of exchange is cheaper than the production and distribution of physical cash and coins. (*ii*) Current legal restrictions prohibiting the private issue of bank notes do not apply to electronic money.[3] (*iii*) Transaction costs of calculating relative prices of different units of account are lower due to continuous trading of an increasing number of assets on financial markets and inexpensive online price information. (*iv*) The transaction costs of exchanging different units of account on online markets are lower than on traditional retail markets for foreign exchange. The following citation serves an illustration for this point of view: 'For the first time ever, each individual has the power to create a new value standard with an immediate worldwide audience' (Matonis, 1995, p. 1).

The consequences that the dispersion of electronic money will have on the role of national currencies as units of account are not fully understood within the economics profession:

> Whether the declining demand for central bank money might influence the role of national currencies as primary standards of value is not yet known. We are encouraged, however, that theoretical and empirical economic research are focusing energies on this topic. The possibility of a stable, privately issued currency that is not convertible into a national currency is subject of a growing literature. (Jordan and Stevens, 1996, p. 2)

While assets that dominate money in their rate of return are available, they are (in most circumstances in retail payments) less liquid than cash and coins. The emergence of new electronic payments systems – it is argued – would enable private entities (banks, online shopping sites and so on) to issue media of exchange that are at least as liquid as cash and coins while dominating them in their rate of return.[4] A competitive environment would guarantee the emergence of units of account that exhibit a higher degree of price stability (or even deflation) than current units of account administered by national central banks, that is they would appreciate *vis-à-vis* high powered money (or in its absence a basket of goods) and, thereby, yield a positive return.

According to this point of view, issuers of electronic money would compete on the basis of three core functions: (*i*) the management of the portfolio of assets backing the issue of electronic money (if the electronic money is redeemable), (*ii*) the management of the payments system (including marketing, non-pecuniary benefits, and security), and (*iii*) with respect to the regulatory regime they are subject to (if there is any prudential supervision at all).[5]

Although new electronic payments systems are not widely accepted and used in the euro zone at the moment,[6] the ECB has also expressed worries about the potential threat to the unit of account function of the national currencies (and later of the euro) due to the emergence of electronic money.[7] The ECB has therefore proposed an amendment to the Council directive on the taking up, the pursuit and the prudential supervision of the business of electronic money institutions.[8] In particular the ECB demands that electronic money institutions should be obliged to redeem their electronic money liabilities in central bank money at par value. Similarly, Rolnick (1999) argues – based on historical evidence concerning the Free Banking Area[9] – that bank issued e-cash may not exchange at par without public intervention.

In this chapter it is argued that such a requirement is not necessary. The dynamics of institutional change within the payments system would lead to a preservation of the unit of account function without explicit regulatory intervention requiring redeemability in central bank money (or a cash balance on a deposit account).

The following section will review the literature on currency competition in order to show that the competitive, parallel use of multiple units of account is not desirable[10] and, due to the time inconsistency problem, indeed is not feasible. In the second section, the potential emergence of new electronic payments systems based on alternative units of accounts is analysed from an evolutionary point of view. As institutional change is path dependent, the decisions of individuals have to be analysed within the current institutional structure of the payments system – the dominance of a single unit of account in a relevant market. The final section concludes and summarizes the chapter.

# 1. CURRENCY COMPETITION: THE LITERATURE

Klein (1974) lists a number of arguments for the current shape of monetary arrangements in industrial countries. These are characterized by a fractional reserve banking system providing inside money based on a government monopoly of the issue of fiat money (outside money). The banking system is usually subject to prudential supervision and, in many cases, minimum reserve requirements.

Based on the assumption that *monetary policy* can have stabilizing effects in the shortrun, government economic policy might call for the control of the necessary means of conducting monetary policy, that is the control over the supply of money or the money market (short-term) interest rate.[11] However, Klein concludes that, even if the government were only one of a number of suppliers of competing inside monies while the dominant outside money were issued by a private entity, the government could still engage in a short-run stabilization policy by inflating at a higher rate than the dominant money. The government would lose reserves of outside money due to the redeemability of the inside monies in the dominant outside money. Although the government would incur additional costs by holding those reserves, it could still conduct stabilization policy by manipulating the supply of its own inside money.

An alternative class of arguments mentioned by Klein states that the supply of information and, thereby, the creation of consumer confidence might be interpreted as a *natural monopoly*. Due to positive real costs associated with the detection of and reaction to unanticipated changes in the quantity of money, reputation is '... of exceptional value relative to other inputs in the money industry' (Klein, 1974, p. 447). In a competitive environment, each issuer has to incur costs associated with establishing a reputation while in the case of a monopoly only one issuer would have to establish a reputation. Given declining costs of establishing a reputation, a single issuer would supply a correspondingly higher (nominal and real) quantity of money than each individual issuer in a competitive environment and the costs of establishing a reputation would not increase proportionally, i.e. a 'non-rivalry in production' is associated with the input reputation.[12] Thus, '... a single firm or private trade association would be efficient in producing confidence for a group of monies' (Klein, 1974, p. 447). Nevertheless, the existence of a natural monopoly in the supply of money does not necessarily imply a governmental monopoly but might also be subject to publicly regulated private production. A natural monopoly requires decreasing incremental average costs at all levels up to market output, a criterion that is almost impossible to assess empirically.

Vaubel (1984, p. 45) discusses further arguments in favour of the interpretation of the unit of account as a natural monopoly. As the number of different means of payment in an economy is usually larger than one, he concludes that only the unit of account function might exhibit characteristics of a natural monopoly. In that case monopoly provision of the unique standard of value in the economy would be justified but, however, this does not necessarily imply government monopolization of the production of money and restrictions on free entry. Since the characteristics of the optimal unit of account are not known with certainty (for example deflation at the real rate of interest or stable purchasing power?), and government bureaucrats might face a non-optimal incentive structure relative to private entities, Vaubel suggests that the restrictions of free entry should be abolished. 'Only if a governmental producer of money can prevail in conditions of free entry and without discriminatory subsidies is he an efficient natural monopolist' (Vaubel, 1984, p. 47). The optimal unit of account, its properties, and the most efficient mode of production should be the outcome of *'competition as a discovery procedure'*.

Issing (2000) criticizes this Hayekian argument on grounds of the uncertainty associated with the adjustment process itself and the regulatory issues once a single issuer has emerged from the process.[13] Until all issuers of low quality currencies are driven out of the market, individuals would have to bear *high transaction costs* (including information costs). Furthermore, the process itself would be characterized by different rates of inflation and fluctuating exchange rates of different currencies. Thus, the co-ordination of individual plans based on relative prices of goods as well as currencies would be inhibited by higher transaction costs (including information costs). The optimal choice of a store of value would be subject to uncertainty about the future unit(s) of account.

Hellwig (1985) denies the validity of a fundamental assumption in the Hayekian argument, namely, that the banks issuing outside money could control the rate of inflation of their currencies (for example by manipulating supply or a short-term interest rate). His argument applies to currencies with a stable relative price that is expected to remain stable by all individuals, and to currencies that cannot be distinguished from each other. At exchange rate $x$, therefore, one unit of one currency would be considered a perfect substitute for $x$ units of the other. Under the assumption of a stable exchange rate, the inflation of one currency might be interpreted as inflation of a composite currency. Thus, the price level is treated as a *public good*, that is the price level is subject to a negative not individually attributable, non-exhaustive externality. Since there is no market solution to this externality, a decentralized decision process will produce too little of the good price level stability. At a stable exchange rate, a positive value of the aggregate money supply, and in the absence of production costs of money balances, the profit maximizing rate of monetary expansion is infinite. Consequently, the value of the aggregate quantity of money is reduced to zero, that is the price level is infinite and outside money is no longer accepted in transactions. The treatment of the aggregate quantity of money as a composite good of the different outside monies is a presumption that Klein (1974) takes into consideration explicitly. He assumes that currencies are distinguishable such that the term price level is unambiguous only with respect to each individual currency but not with respect to the aggregate quantity of money.

The presence of *network effects* and/or *switching costs* might lead to excess inertia,[14] that is even if some competitors offer a preferable currency it might be hard to drive an incumbent issuer out of the market. Competition might be ineffective at the margin. Dowd and Greenaway (1993) show that for an individual, switching – regardless of others switching as well – only pays if the discounted network independent benefits[15] outweigh the forgone network dependent benefits of the old currency plus the switching costs (for example psychological costs of getting used to the new unit of account). Even if individuals are willing to switch to a new currency, provided that others would do so, a co-ordination problem arises: that is the individual's expectations concerning the decisions of others are crucial. Switching is only welfare improving if the aggregated discounted network independent and network dependent benefits of switching outweigh the aggregated switching costs. Furthermore, Dowd and Greenaway (1993, p. 1184) cite a 'stylized fact' that even limited currency substitution occurs only during episodes of hyperinflation and conclude '... that monetary authorities can "get away" with a great deal of monetary "misbehavior" before loss of market share to competing currencies poses any significant problem'. [16]

If the adjustment process leads to the emergence of a single monopoly issuer the familiar issue of a *non-optimal incentive structure* arises anew.[17] The threat of entry would serve to discipline the issuer if the assumptions of the contestable markets theory were met:[18] (*i*) All costs associated with market entry are reversible, that is there are no sunk costs. (*ii*) An entrant can build capacity and gain access to distribution networks before the incumbent is able to react. (*iii*) The incumbent does not have a comparative advantage due to his own experience in the market. The financial services industry, it might be argued, has already built capacity and has established or gained access to distribution networks in order to market a large variety of financial products. Furthermore, some private financial institutions do already operate payments systems such that they should not suffer a competitive disadvantage in providing the specific payments system 'currency'. But, as mentioned above, this reputation and consumer confidence are of critical importance in the market for fiat-type money. Since costs associated with their production are sunk costs and their production might take considerable time, some of the major assumptions of contestable markets theory might not be met.

Government monopoly provision of currency might also be justified by the existence of 'economies of scale' in consumption, that is a payments system might never reach *critical mass* due to high network effects as long as the network is still in its infancy. Vaubel (1984) discusses the role of government in the context of network effects in detail and concludes that it might be necessary for early adopters to subsidize late adopters until the network reaches critical mass. The subsidy reflects the positive externality conveyed by the marginal late adopter in equilibrium (Pareto-efficient network size) on early adopters. However, the existence of network effects does not imply government subsidies let alone government monopoly provision of currency.

A government monopoly would be efficient if the government had a *comparative advantage* in producing confidence.[19] This could be based either on the ability of the government to declare its own money legal tender or on the existence of economies of scope between the production of confidence and other goods supplied by the government (for example national defence). However, the government is also faced with comparative disadvantages. Government officials do not own the reputation they are supposed to establish or conserve and, thus, are subject to a non-optimal incentive structure. Finally, Klein (1974) concludes that the arguments based on a comparative advantage are at least ambiguous and do not justify governmental monopoly production of outside money.

Vaubel (1984, p. 28) discusses several arguments for governmental monopoly provision of money based on *public good* characteristics associated with money. An individual holding money balances is less likely to become illiquid. Thus, potential trading partners are more likely to be able to trade with the individual. Vaubel argues that money balances possess neither of the public good characteristics of non-rivalry in and non-excludability from consumption. But the increased likelihood of an exchange satisfies both criteria. However, the positive externality might be compensated for by a negative externality, that is the decreased likelihood of an exchange with someone else who holds money balances. More importantly, the existence of a unit of account facilitates co-ordination of individual plans based on relative prices. Neither can individuals who do not hold money balances be excluded from basing their plans on information conveyed by relative prices (non-excludability) nor will this reduce the benefits of a unit of account for money holders (non-rivalry). Vaubel concludes that this might be a rationale for the government to define a unit of account and publish a price index for it. Since the government does not know what the optimal unit of account and its characteristics are, it should not impose but merely propose a specific unit of account. However, it would not necessarily imply the governmental monopoly production of money. White (2000), on the other hand, argues that a standard such as the unit of account, once established, does not require any further policy intervention – it is self-sustaining.

The use of different currencies by parties to a transaction implies that the costs of conversion and, possibly, of hedging against currency mismatches between actual and desired holdings have to be incurred. Who actually bears these transaction costs depends on the market structure, elasticities of supply and demand, and may be the result of a negotiation process. If both the seller and buyer share the costs of conversion, their choices of currencies might cause *external effects*. Vaubel (1984, p. 42) distinguishes three limiting cases: (*i*) The seller faces the same (weighted) price elasticities of demand and the same conversion costs in each currency domain such that he will choose the currency in which his sales reach the highest volume. Due to the fact that the elasticities of demand are the same in all currency domains, the seller's private costs of conversion are proportional to the social costs of conversion. Thus, by minimizing his own share he also minimizes the social costs. The decentralized solution does not lead to an allocation that is different from the one chosen by a central planner. (*ii*) Again, the seller faces the same (weighted) price elasticities of demand in all currency domains. But it is assumed that he would conduct the same number of transactions with the same volume in all domains if there were no currency conversion costs. In this case, the seller chooses the currency with the lowest fixed and variable conversion costs such that his total currency conversion costs are minimized. Again, his conversion costs are proportional to the social conversion costs. Thus, the decentralized solution does not deviate from the allocation chosen by a central planner. (*iii*) In the third case, it is assumed that all currencies have the same fixed and variable conversion costs and – in the absence of conversion costs – the seller would conduct the same number and volume of transactions in all domains. But the (weighted) price elasticities of demand are different in different domains. In this case, the seller will choose the currency that is associated with the highest price elasticity of demand. In a partial equilibrium analysis, the buyers, having a perfectly price inelastic demand, will also have to bear the seller's share of the conversion costs and the seller's currency choice indeed deviates from the allocation chosen by a central planner. If, however, the demand is perfectly elastic in all currency domains the seller has to bear the entire conversion costs and minimizes social costs by minimizing his private conversion costs. The decentralized allocation is, again, identical to the one chosen by a central planner. Vaubel (1984, p. 44) concludes that '... if perfect or imperfect competition prevails, transaction cost externalities do not lead to suboptimal currency choices'. However, the use of a common currency enables the trading partners to avoid these costs in the first place, though at the cost of disregarding effects on individual portfolio balance and preference concerning the unit of account.

Hellwig (1985) argues that the displacement of outside (fiat) money by redeemable inside money might lead to the *over accumulation of real assets*, that is the real rate of return on capital would be less than the rate of time preference in the society.[20] Abstracting from default risk of issuers and fraud (counterfeit), the inside money will have a return structure equivalent to that of the underlying asset(s). In an economy with collective and individual risk, individuals want to insure against endowment fluctuations. One way to do so is to adjust money balances to changes in subjective expectations concerning the marginal utility of endowments in future periods. If the marginal utility of future endowments is sufficiently volatile and inventory costs of the underlying real asset(s) are low relative to the real rate of return – and abstracting from network effects and excess inertia – then inside money will displace non-interest-bearing outside money. The portfolio choice between inside and outside money is biased against the latter due to the assumption of non-interest-bearing outside money. The government could raise taxes in order to ensure a real rate of return sufficient to prevent inside money from displacing outside money. The stock of real capital held permanently as reserves to back the inside money could then be invested or consumed without decreasing the level of insurance as outside money – according to Hellwig – provides the same insurance service as inside money, albeit without incurring the opportunity costs associated with reserve holdings of real capital. However, the fact that an outside (fiat) money is preferable to inside money is not necessarily an argument in favour of governmental monopoly provision of the former.

The overview of the literature shows that the parallel use of multiple units of account is generally not considered to be desirable due to natural monopoly and public good considerations regarding the unit of account. The efficiency-enhancing effects of the existence of a unit of account rest upon its uniformity, as this minimizes the transaction and information costs associated with price comparisons.[21] Competition in the unit of account would lead to the emergence of a single issuer who would face a similar incentive structure to a government monopoly. Furthermore, the adjustment process would lead to fluctuations in the exchange rates between different currencies and make the co-ordination of individual plans based on relative prices more difficult. However, the arguments do not provide a clear rationale against free entrance. The presence of network effects and switching costs might make it very hard to drive an incumbent issuer of a dominant currency out of the market.

### Time Inconsistency and Redeemability

The importance of the problem of time inconsistency in the provision of fiat-type or outside money has been discussed by a number of authors and is not constrained to the competitive supply of fiat-type money.[22] Individuals choose to accept outside money on the basis of its expected future value in exchange. That value, though, is not independent of the issuer's future actions, that is the future supply of outside money. Initially, the issuer has to commit to some future path of money supply (for example one that will keep the purchasing power of the currency constant) in order to create demand for money balances in his currency. At a certain point of time this commitment is profit maximizing, that is it is a part of an optimal plan. Once the public has decided to hold and accept the currency, maintaining the commitment may no longer be optimal. Assuming that the marginal costs of producing an additional unit of the currency is zero it will be optimal for the issuer to increase the supply of money until his marginal revenue is also zero. If it remains impossible for the same issuer to rebuild his reputation afterwards he will go out of business. The expected cost of inflating the currency is the discounted expected value of forgone future profits from the provision of outside money. The related (discounted) expected profit is equal to the sum of revenues from the issuance of additional outside money over time until the marginal revenue of an additional unit of outside money is indeed zero.[23]

Whether keeping the commitment in later periods is profit maximizing depends on the relation between the expected cost and revenue of inflating in each period.

The lower the discounted expected value of forgone future profits from the provision of outside money, the higher is the incentive for the issuer to inflate. It depends on his subjective discount rate, the real demand for the currency in each period, as well as the time the issuer plans to stay in business. The more heavily the issuer discounts future profits and the lower the real demand for money in each period, the lower his discounted expected value of forgone profits will be.

The higher the related (discounted) expected profit of inflating, the higher is the issuer's incentive to inflate. It depends on the real demand for the currency in each period, as well as the time that elapses between the issuer's decision to inflate and the public's refusal to accept the currency any longer, that is real demand reduces to zero.[24] The faster the public learns about the issuer's reluctance to keep his commitment, and therefore adjusts the real demand for the currency, the lower the profits of inflating.

Klein (1974) models the maximization problem of the issuer of fiat-type money explicitly and argues that it is not wealth maximizing for an issuer of fiat-type money to inflate infinitely. He assumes that currencies of different issuers can be identified costlessly and that all issuers are price takers and are confronted with an infinitely elastic demand for monetary services curve. The real demand for money is modelled as a decreasing function of the opportunity costs associated with real money balances (the difference between nominal interest paid on bonds denominated in that currency and nominal interest paid on money holdings) and an increasing function of consumer confidence (embodied in 'brand-name capital'). An unanticipated increase in the nominal quantity of money affects real profits in three ways: (*i*) As the marginal costs of producing nominal balances are assumed to be zero, the issuer accrues the real revenue equal to the additional quantity of nominal money issued. (*ii*) The unanticipated increase of the nominal quantity of money will change the inflation expectations of the individuals holding balances in the currency under consideration. In order to compensate them for this increase in anticipated inflation the issuer has to redistribute a portion of his proceeds to them. Otherwise their demand for real balances would shrink. Assuming that individuals cannot perfectly observe the contemporaneous increase in the quantity of nominal balances and the exact increase in the nominal price level, their share of real revenues of unanticipated inflation is smaller than 100 percent. The share accruing to the issuer is therefore always positive. The real revenue from inflating increases without bound with the growth of the nominal quantity of money. Consequently, the issuer would have an incentive to inflate infinitely, that is until the marginal revenue from inflating is zero. 'The only constraint on the extent of the firm's profit rate is the existence of some rising costs of increasing [the nominal quantity of money] which places a limit on the rate at which a firm can profitably increase the supply of its money in circulation' (Klein, 1974, p. 436).

Klein, then, argues that (*iii*) brand-name capital is the constraint that solves the time inconsistency problem. The holders of the currency are compensated for any reduction in the *stability* of the future price level caused by an unanticipated increase in its nominal quality inasmuch as a share of the resulting *profits* is redistributed to them. In order to keep real money demand constant, the issuer also has to compensate the holders of money for the reduced *predictability* of the price level. The deviation of the actual from the anticipated increase reduces the real market value of the firm's brand-name capital (that is consumer confidence). The larger the deviation, the higher is the *nominal interest* demanded by the holders of the currency in compensation for the reduced *predictability* of the future price level.[25] Thus the real value of brand-name capital decreases. Assuming consumers and producers have the same expectations concerning the short-term gains from unanticipated increases in the nominal quantity of money, Klein concludes that an equilibrium exists in which a wealth-maximizing firm will not inflate infinitely. In equilibrium, the firm's share of the real revenues from unanticipated increases in the nominal quantity of money (after compensation for changes in anticipated inflation) equals the firm's real loss in terms of increased nominal interest payments to money holders in order to compensate them for the reduced *predictability* of the future price level.

White (1999) discusses Klein's model in detail and denies that it presents a satisfactory solution for the time inconsistency problem.[26] As mentioned above, under Klein's assumptions the share of the real revenue from an unanticipated increase in the nominal quantity of money accrued by the issuer increases without bound in the growth of the nominal quantity of money (even after compensating the holders of money for the decrease in the *stability* of the price level). Consequently, the compensation demanded by holders of money for the decreased *predictability* of the future price level (that is the increased nominal interest rate paid on nominal balances) also has to increase without bound along with the growth rate of the nominal quantity of money as well as relative to the nominal interest rate on bonds denominated in the currency. This would imply that the real value of brand-name capital would have to become infinitely negative. Otherwise it would pay for the issuer to inflate infinitely. If the nominal interest rate on money holdings is bound above, the first-order condition for profit maximization derived by Klein will not suffice to prohibit infinite inflation. White, then, argues that the difference between the nominal interest rate paid on money holdings and the nominal interest rate paid on bonds denominated in the currency is bound below by zero. In terms of Klein's formulation, this implies that the real value of brand-name capital is bound below by zero, too. At this point, individuals would demand a nominal interest rate for money holdings equal to that paid on bonds. Any further increase in the nominal interest rate paid on money holdings implies that the yield on money increases above that of bonds. The issuer would have to resort to further inflationary over-issue in order to be able to meet his obligation to the holders of money. As long as individuals cannot perfectly foresee the future amount of unanticipated inflation, they cannot adjust their ex-ante demanded interest receipts to prevent the issuer from over-issue. Instead of assuming that the public would be able to foresee the currency's future deviations from *stability* (that is correctly perceive the actual increase in the nominal quantity of money) Klein assumes perfect foresight with respect to future deviations from the *predictability* of the future price level. Otherwise, holders of money are unable to adjust their demanded ex-ante interest rate in a way that would prevent the issuer from inflating further. In order to anticipate correctly the deviations from *predictability,* individuals would have to be able to observe the contemporaneous change in the nominal quantity of money and, consequently, also the deviations from the *stability* of the price level. 'Solving the problem of cheating, in this way, amounts to re-introducing perfect foresight through the back door' (White, 1999, p. 238).

Taub (1985) analyses the time inconsistency problem in an overlapping generations framework. Money demand is endogenous and individuals have rational expectations. Currencies can be distinguished without cost, and optimal supply by firms is determined in a Nash equilibrium. Taub distinguishes two dynamic structures – open loop control and feedback control. In the former, firms can commit to an infinite sequence of future money growth rates while in the latter the enforcement mechanism is weaker and firms can optimize their decisions concerning current and future money growth rates anew each period. If commitment is possible, time inconsistency problems do not arise and the competitive outcome implies that the rate of return on money holdings is equal to the inverse of the discount factor. The solution is efficient.

Under feedback control, the assumption of complete impossibility of commitment reduces real money demand to zero. If firms can manipulate contemporaneous money growth after individuals have decided how much real balance to hold for the period, it is optimal for the issuers in the model to inflate infinitely within the current period. As individuals anticipate this solution they will decide not to hold real balances in the first place. Taub therefore considers a structure that allows firms to commit for exactly one period, that is firms take the contemporaneous growth rate of money as given. The analysis is restricted to stationary equilibria in which the relative shares of real balances for each firm remain constant over time. In equilibrium the demand for real balances is below the efficient level since – even under competitive supply of fiat-type money – inflation is always positive in the model. However, the stationary equilibrium is not consistent with free entry. A firm entering the market cannot take its contemporaneous growth rate of money supply as given, since it did not exist in the previous period. Taub shows that – for large numbers of issuers – firms initially choose to deflate their currencies. As this is inconsistent with stationary equilibrium, the competitive solution with inflation has to be reached asymptotically. Due to the fact that the stationary equilibrium is dynamically unstable, the economy will reach the only dynamically consistent long-run equilibrium in which money demand is zero. Thus, Taub concludes, the competitive issue of fiat-type currency is not possible.

In Klein's model, the wealth of the issuer of the currency increases without bound in the growth of the nominal quantity of money. Thus, individuals could be compensated ex-post for unanticipated increases in the nominal quantity of money. Klein draws conclusions from US monetary history where convertibility of privately issued bank notes into dominant outside money emerged under conditions of a competitive market structure.[27] Selgin (1997) argues that institutional change within the monetary system was historically the driving force behind the emergence of convertible money replacing commodity money. Fiat money, on the other hand, was the result of government intervention (for example nationalization of the note-issuing banks).[28] Also Vaubel concedes that '... if there is a danger of "profit snatching", money holders will prefer currencies that offer value guarantees' (Vaubel, 1985, p. 554). Concluding the discussion of Klein's model White (1999) argues that the problem of time inconsistency has traditionally been approached by offering such value guarantees, that is redemption contracts. In a competitive environment, different inside monies redeemable in the dominant currency would emerge, but competition in privately issued fiat-type currencies is widely considered to be infeasible. Neither the advantages nor the spontaneous emergence of a single unit of account in a relevant market justify barriers to entry in order to avoid potential competition in the provision of a unit of account.

## 2. INSTITUTIONAL CHANGE IN THE PAYMENTS SYSTEM: REDEEMABILITY AND THE UNIT OF ACCOUNT

An evolutionary analysis of new electronic payments systems has to start from the current institutional setting, taking into consideration that institutional change in the monetary system is path dependent. The question one therefore has to address is whether individuals (for example sponsors of new electronic payments systems, users and so on) are likely to switch to a new unit of account given the dominance of an established unit of account in the respective market.

### Network Effects, Compatibility and the Redeemability of Electronic Money

An electronic money scheme can be interpreted as a network exhibiting network effects.[29] The willingness to pay for joining depends on the expected number of future participants (that is merchants who accept a specific currency or electronic money and consumers in schemes that permit peer-to-peer transfers). An additional individual joining a certain new electronic payments system affects those already using it in two ways: first, the number of potential partners in exchange increases (direct network effect). Second, the greater the number of market participants accepting the specific currency or electronic money, the more competitive and liquid the market becomes. If there is price discovery in the market, the market price becomes more accurate (indirect network effect). Menger stresses the effect of the emergence of a generally accepted medium of exchange on price formation:

> [Before the emergence of a generally accepted medium of exchange] haphazard prices and other kinds of uneconomic price formations were easily the rule, but from now on price formation takes place with all those participating who offer a commodity on the market in question and at the same time all those who seek to acquire this commodity. Price formation will become more concentrated on and be adapted to the general market situation or, at least, will correspond to it far better than could be the case on barter markets. Current market prices are formed; and from now on the valuation of goods in money terms is incomparably more exact and economic than on barter markets, with their fragmented trading in goods and with price formation influenced by chance occurrences of all kinds or by rigid customary exchange ratios and statutory prices. (Menger, 1909, p. 11)

Streissler (in his contribution to this volume, p. 19; original emphasis) interprets Menger's view of the emergence of a general medium of exchange on price formation as creating an '*information network* between all participants in the market'.

However, not all markets engage in price discovery. Non-participants can often observe the equilibrium market price established in a particular market. This information can be used in another market in which exchange takes place at the equilibrium market price established in the former (price matching). The opportunity to free-ride could provide incentives for the market engaged in price discovery to reduce the availability of information on prices (for example through proprietary information systems) or the value of the information contained in the observable equilibrium market prices (for example by reporting large bid-ask spreads).[30]

A supplier of a new electronic payments system faces the strategic decision concerning the compatibility of his new network with the existing payments system. Payments that involve transactions via both the new electronic payments system and the existing dominant payments system can be interpreted as composite goods. Its components are the transactions via the two different payments systems. Complete compatibility is reached when the two components are combined to a composite good without increasing the cost of the combined transaction – against the sum of the costs of each component such that the completely compatible networks can be treated as one single network.[31] This strategic decision has two dimensions. First, the technological dimension concerns the interoperability of the components of an electronic payments system (for example protocols, hard- and software). Second, an economic dimension concerning the unit of account underlying the new electronic payments system (such as a mutual fund index or the unit of account of the dominating payments system in the relevant market – for example US$, ¥ or euro). There are two different strategies through which technological compatibility can be reached: first, the adoption of a common standard and, second, the adoption of an adapter. While the former can only be based on a unanimous decision of all network operators (sponsors) concerned, the latter can be enacted unilaterally.[32] So far no single technological standard has emerged out of the vast number of innovative solutions for new electronic payments systems (for example DigiCash, CyberCash, Netbill and Proton, Mondex). Most of the prevailing technologies are not compatible, that is a consumer cannot pay a merchant if they are subscribers of two different network-based electronic payments systems. However, the focus of this chapter is on the economic dimension of compatibility.

Economides (1991) analyses the strategic decision of network operators (sponsors) to achieve compatibility in a non-co-operative setting – for smaller networks it pays to be compatible, while for the large, dominant network incompatibility is advantageous. Katz and Shapiro (1985) find that the joint incentives of the large and the small network operators are lower than the social incentives – but those of the small network operator are still considerable. The potential inadequacy of the social incentives is a consequence of the fact that the incentives of the large network's sponsor are too low. The analysis suggests that the sponsors of the dominant payments system in retail transactions (the Central Banks) might rationally oppose compatibility with new electronic payments systems if they were profit-maximizing entities, since they cannot appropriate the entire benefits of compatibility. However, the CBs are not-for-profit public institutions which aim, ideally, to preserve the stability and enhance the efficiency of the economic payments system. However, for sponsors of new electronic payments systems there are strong incentives to adopt the unit of account of the dominating retail payments system in the relevant market. The network effect implies that operators of new electronic payments systems can increase their demand by credibly committing to a one-for-one fixed exchange rate of electronic money against the dominant currency. In order to ensure the stability of the exchange rate (and the related expectations) the operator of the new electronic payments system would have to offer redeemability on demand.

## Switching costs

The Dowd and Greenaway (1993) analysis also offers strategic implications for providers of new electronic payment systems. They conclude that – if no-one else is expected to switch – switching to a new currency is only individually optimal if the discounted network independent benefits of switching outweigh the switching costs and the discounted forgone network dependent benefits of the abandoned currency. In the other extreme case – if everyone else is expected to switch – it would be individually optimal not to switch if the switching costs outweigh the discounted network independent and network dependent benefits of switching. It can therefore be optimal for a society to stick to an inferior (electronic) payments system if the switching costs are substantial. Switching costs include for example the psychological cost associated with the use (such as calculating and quoting prices) of a new unit of account and the necessary changes in accounts denominated in it. Therefore, fixing the exchange rate at one-to-one with respect to the existing unit of account once and for all can also increase the probability of adoption of a new electronic payments system by, at least partly, avoiding the switching costs associated with the adoption of a new unit of account. Brunner and Meltzer (1971) also argue that it is optimal for issuers of private money to maintain a fixed exchange rate against a dominant money and to offer redeemability on demand as this reduces the information costs (for example with regard to the quality of the privately issued currency) incurred by users of private money.

## Sunk costs

Individuals joining a new electronic payments system invest in the new technology in various ways (including software, acquiring the necessary technological competence and buying an initial balance of electronic funds). Some of these fixed costs are irreversible (that is sunk costs) such as the time and effort invested in learning how to operate the system. The decision to incur these sunk costs can be interpreted as an investment decision based on the expected value of joining the system for the consumer, which in turn is based on expected number of users. Individuals who join a new electronic payments system have to acquire an initial balance through a transfer of wealth to its operator. Unless the operator offers redeemability on demand, this initial balance is also, at least partly, lost if the payments system does not reach critical mass. By reducing the real value of the amount at risk for the consumer, for example through redeemability on demand, the operator can reduce the barriers to adoption.

### Network Effects, the Unit of Account and Market Prices

Two distinct approaches towards market prices in new electronic payments systems can be distinguished: Market prices are either assumed to be given by exchange in the dominant currency (price matching) or a new electronic payments system engages in price discovery.

Market exchange in the dominant currency determines market prices that are often public information. The price in a new electronic payments system – based on a unit of account different from the dominant one – is determined in two steps. The market price of a certain good quoted in the dominant unit of account ($P_G$) is multiplied by the relative price of the unit of account of the new electronic payments system in terms of the dominant unit of account (the nominal exchange rate at the ask-price $E_{ASK}$) – the price of the good in terms of eMoney is given by $P_{EM} = P_G * E_{ASK}$. That implies that the new unit of account must also be continuously traded on a market denominated in the dominant unit of account. The necessary calculations used to be time consuming and timely information on market prices expensive. It is argued that technological progress makes new electronic payments systems based on alternative units of account feasible.[33] Participants in the new electronic payments system, therefore, free-ride on price information established in two different markets – for the good exchanged and for the unit of account – denominated in the dominant unit of account. Furthermore, the accuracy and information content of the prices established on the market denominated in the dominant unit of account might be reduced as trade shifts partly from that market towards one which follows a price matching strategy.[34]

Even if a price in the alternative unit of account can be calculated, the alternative unit of account is only accepted at precisely that price if – at a relative price of the two currencies of $x - x$ units of the alternative unit of account are considered to be a perfect substitute for one unit of the dominant unit of account. This in turn implies that the expected future relative price must also be expected to be $x$. The relative price of the two units of account is expected to remain perfectly stable in the future and, furthermore, these expectations have to be shared by all individuals.[35]

But if the exchange rate between the alternative unit of account and the dominant one is subject to fluctuations and uncertainty, the alternative unit of account will only be traded at a spread between bid- and ask-prices. The spread is determined by the degree of uncertainty, the risk preferences of individuals, resource costs of holding inventory positions in different risky assets and the related uncertainty, the market structure, potential asymmetries of information amongst traders, and transaction and information costs.[36] Consequently the price of the good exchanged in terms of eMoney is higher than the corresponding price in terms of the dominant unit of account times the nominal market clearing exchange rate $E$ which lies between the bid- and the ask-prices $P_{EM} > E*P_G$. According to Menger the dominant unit of account involves the smallest spread in trade – it is the most saleable, that is the most liquid good available.[37] Individuals holding a stock denominated in an alternative unit of account might have to exchange part of their holdings for the dominant currency. This again implies transaction costs. In order to complete a transaction in another unit of account individuals would have to exchange currencies on markets and bear the related costs (for example bidask spread, transaction and information costs).[38] This point was already emphasized by Menger (1909, p. 30): 'Whoever hoards trade goods of another kind [than the generally accepted medium of exchange] must, when he has resort to the accumulated stock, commonly first exchange them for the general medium of exchange, while he who has hoarded the latter avoids (or is already past) the trouble, uncertainty, and economic sacrifices of this transaction.' Individuals willing to minimize the transaction costs associated with trade therefore prefer to trade in the dominant unit of account rather than in an alternative one.

The unit of account function of money, and all other functions such as the store of value function, are consequences of its use as the general medium of exchange.[39] Only in a world where all goods are equally saleable and are expected to remain so in the future, can all goods (and combinations thereof) be employed as the unit of account. Relative prices are not determined in exchange but by a Walrasian auctioneer without involving any transaction and information costs regardless of the existence of a generally accepted medium of exchange.[40] In a less perfect world, relative prices are determined in exchange of goods for the medium of exchange, and assets providing a positive expected return against the dominant unit of account are not generally accepted in exchange without spread.

As an alternative to following a price matching strategy, a new electronic payments system can engage in price discovery. As the alternative unit of account is less marketable than the dominant one, the market structure may not be as competitive as in the market denominated in the latter. The information network created by the new electronic payments system involves a smaller number of participants than the dominant unit of account. Exchange would take place less frequently and – in a market characterized by random order arrival rates – timely information on market prices would be less accurate and spreads between bid- and ask-prices would be higher to reflect the increased risks associated with larger fluctuations of the market price.[41] The larger fluctuations are a consequence of the lower frequency of trades, as random fluctuations in order arrival rates and the related uncertainty increase with the time interval between subsequent trades. Consequently, individuals would prefer to exchange their goods on markets that provide the most precise pricing information available owing to lower associated spreads and an increased frequency of trades.

The analysis so far has assumed exclusive trading on the market denominated in the alternative unit of account. Hence, price discovery would take place on a single market only. If the good is traded on multiple markets denominated in different units of account simultaneously and if more than one market follows a price discovery strategy, the relation between the market established in different markets has to be analysed. In the limit, arbitrage will reduce the difference between these prices towards the marginal costs of arbitrage. Lack of complete compatibility adds to these costs, in such a way that the market denominated in the alternative unit of account will generate lower bid-prices and higher ask-prices than the market denominated in the dominant unit of account even if the marginal costs of arbitrage are lowered by technological innovation. Consequently, the market denominated in the dominating unit of account will have a comparative advantage. Complete (economic) compatibility, hence, increases the competitiveness of the market denominated in the alternative unit of account. In the limit, transaction costs between the markets vanish as complete economic and technological compatibility is achieved – the various markets merge to a single one establishing a single market price.

The institutional analysis of the evolution of the structure of new electronic payments systems has to start from the existing structure of the payments system, that is the existence of a dominant unit of account in the relevant market. The discussion of the adoption of alternative units of account in new electronic payments systems is based on the incentive structure of their potential issuers, as well as their potential users. Potential issuers can profit from the economic compatibility of their new electronic payments system with the existing dominant unit of account, that is by fixing the exchange rate of their privately issued electronic money one-to-one against the dominant currency by offering redeemability on demand. Furthermore, this institutional set-up reduces switching costs and sunk costs for potential users. If a new electronic payments system does not engage in price discovery, it has to presuppose (and potentially free-rides on) the existence of markets denominated in the dominant unit of account for both the goods traded and for the alternative unit of account. Even if prices can be calculated, the alternative unit of account would not be accepted as perfect substitute for the dominant currency, such that the alternative unit of account would only be accepted at a spread – thus offering another incentive for users to stick to the dominant unit of account. Assets promising an expected positive return against the dominant currency can be, and indeed sometimes are preferred as stores of value but not as media of exchange. If a new electronic payments system engages in price discovery, then market prices are less accurate, the market is less transparent and the costs of the co-ordination of individual plans based on relative prices increase.

## 3. CONCLUSION

This chapter has analysed the prospects of the emergence of alternative units of account due to technological and institutional innovation in the payments system, that is due to the emergence of electronic money. Since the evolution of the retail payments system is path dependent, the discussion is based on the existence of a dominant unit of account in the respective markets.

An overview of the existing literature shows that the competitive, parallel use of multiple units of account is not desirable. The transaction costs of the co-ordination of individual plans are reduced and the transparency of markets increased by the existence of a uniform unit of account (in the respective market). However, competition between inside monies redeemable in the dominant currency can increase the efficiency of the payments system.

A discussion of the literature on the time inconsistency problem associated with the provision of privately issued fiat-type money points out that users of new electronic payments systems would prefer institutional arrangements that provide redeemability on demand in order to prevent the issuer from inflating infinitely.

Network effects and switching costs, sunk costs and information cost mean that both the issuer and the user of new electronic payments systems face strong incentives to adhere to the dominant unit of account. While the chapter shows that the parallel use of multiple units of account is unlikely, it does not argue against low barriers to entry and currency competition in general. It is not necessary to impose legal restrictions to preserve the unit of account function of the dominating unit of account, at current (moderate) levels of inflation. The imposition of legal barriers to currency competition implies that the respective central bank, however, is uncertain about its own capacity to control the level of future inflation below a threshold at which currency substitution occurs despite the costs involved. Although these costs will be reduced at the margin by technological innovation, the lack of economic compatibility ensures that the costs of currency substitution will remain positive. Consequently, only a central bank that doubts its own ability to (at least) match any expected inflation rate of a potential alternative unit of account has an incentive to impose legal barriers such as Article 3 of the EU eMoney directive.

Finally, it can be concluded that the most likely institutional structure of any new electronic payments system to emerge includes the redeemability of electronic money on demand and its denomination in the dominant unit of account. Therefore, the role of national currencies as units of account is not endangered by the emergence of electronic money. *Ceteris paribus*, public policy intervention in order to preserve the unit of account function of the dominant currency in the respective market is not necessary. Monetary policy will, in principle, be affected only to the extent that the balance sheet of central banks shortens (including a reduction of seignorage) – *ceteris paribus* – and that the relationship between the instruments of monetary policy and the primary objective of price stability might turn out to be less predictable (for example interest elasticities of money demand might change). At current levels of inflation, the irrelevance of monetary policy and the failure of bank issued e-cash to exchange at par due to the displacement of the dominant unit of account by new electronic payments systems based on alternative units of account is unlikely. Whether bank issued e-cash exchanges at par depends on the same determinants that govern the relative prices of other forms of inside money issued by different banks (for example cheques) and the technological interoperability of new electronic payments systems. To uncover the effects of the diffusion of eMoney on the transmission mechanism of monetary policy and on the predictability of the relationship between its instruments and its objectives remains the subject of further research.

## NOTES

*   The author thanks the participants of the workshop 'The Analysis of New Electronic Payments Systems based on Carl Menger's Institutional Theory of the Origin of Money', Vienna, 20–21 October 2000, for helpful comments. The usual disclaimer applies.
1.  See *inter alia* Hayek (1990), Klein (1974), Vaubel (1984, 1985, 1990, 2000) and for a discussion *inter alia* Bomhoff (1990), Hellwig (1985), Issing (2000), Kessler (1990), Selgin and White (1994) and White (1984, 1990, 1999, 2000). Currency competition has to be distinguished from systems that theorize about the consequences of 'pure accounting systems of exchange' and a single unit of account (for example the BFH system proposed by Greenfield and Yeager, 1983) and focus their attention on the stabilization of the latter (for a discussion of the differences between the two approaches see Yeager, 1983). For a discussion of electronic money and the BFH system see Krueger (1999).
2.  See Crede (1995), Matonis (1995), England (1996), Browne and Cronin (1996) and Kobrin (1997), Cohen (2001).
3.  See Issing (2000). For details concerning the legal restrictions in the USA and Canada see Hance and Balz (2000), p. 353.
4.  Concerning a subset of transactions (for example B-2-C eCommerce transactions involving very small amounts) the transaction costs of new electronic payments systems may be lower than the transaction costs of cash. Consequently, the liquidity of the former may even be higher than that of the latter.
5.  See Matonis (1995).
6.  See ECB (2000).
7.  See ECB (1998) and (1999).
8.  Directive 2000/46/EC. The proposed amendment to the original proposal (COM/98/56/EC) led to the inclusion of a right to redeem electronic money and the obligation of the issuer to include the conditions of redemption explicitly in the contract with the user (Article 3).
9.  For different results concerning the Free Banking Area and related policy implications see Selgin and White (1994).
10. The option to switch currency does not, in practice, lead to price stability. According to Dowd and Greenaway (1993) it is a stylized fact that currency substitution only occurs if a currency performs very poorly. Even during periods of hyperinflation, the demand for the traditional currency is significantly above zero. Legal restrictions might currently increase the costs of switching such that their abolition could reduce the level of inflation individuals are willing to accept before currency substitution occurs.

11. See also Bomhoff (1990) and Kessler (1990).
12. In Klein's own model of competitive fiat-type money issue (to be discussed below) the costs of establishing a reputation (the opportunity costs of unanticipated inflation, that is the fall of the rental price of brand-name capital in Klein's terminology) are exactly proportional to the real quantity of money supplied (see also White, 1999, p. 236). Consequently, the natural monopoly argument does not hold in Klein's model.
13. For a similar position see Kessler (1990).
14. See Economides (1996).
15. Examples of network independent benefits of a currency are the value of a unit of the redemption good if the currency is redeemable.
16. Though, one has to bear in mind that legal restrictions usually increase the costs of switching to an alternative currency and may account partly for the 'stylized fact'.
17. See for example Issing (2000).
18. See George et al. (1992), p. 276.
19. See Klein (1974).
20. For a similar argument see Smith (1776) and Wallace (1988).
21. See also Menger. 'Imagine the condition of the monetary system of a country where coins of the same type are valued differently because of inevitable tiny differences in their minting and regularly occurring losses by wear in circulation, [or] a situation in which coins produced from different money materials (particularly fractional coins) function like parallel currencies because of fluctuations in the relative prices of money metals concerned, etc. In this way, obviously, the essential advantages of a uniform national money and coinage system, howsoever economically graduated and implemented, would partly cancel out' (Menger, 1909, p. 24).
22. See for example Calvo (1978), Hellwig (1985), Issing (2000), Klein (1974), Vaubel (1985), White (1999) and Blanchard and Fischer (1990), Ch. 11, as well as the literature cited in these papers.
23. If hyperinflation occurs instantaneously this time interval is zero. Furthermore, if hyperinflation is anticipated instantaneously (e.g. under a variant of rational expectations), too, the demand for real and nominal balances is zero immediately and the (discounted) expected profit from inflating is also zero.
24. Assuming that this interval is relatively short with respect to the time that expected forgone future profits from the provision of outside money are discounted, one can neglect the discount rate as a determinant of the expected profit of inflating. The speed of public learning becomes irrelevant in the extreme case of a hyperinflation occurring instantaneously. Inflating yields a positive expected profit only if individuals do not fully anticipate the hyperinflation.
25. Due to the assumption that consumers and issuer have the same expectations concerning the short-term gain from unanticipated increases in the nominal quantity of money, individuals know about the exact amount they need to raise their demanded nominal interest rate on money holdings in order to offset the issuer's revenue from an unanticipated increase in the nominal quantity of money. This, however, implies that consumers can observe the contemporaneous increase in the quantity of money in order to adjust their demanded nominal interest rate on money holdings accordingly and is contradictory to Klein's implicit assumption that individuals cannot observe the contemporaneous increase in the supply of money. See White (1999).

26. See also Selgin and White (1994).
27. As mentioned above, the issuer of dominant outside money faces a similar time inconsistency problem. A large literature has been devoted to the discussion of institutional arrangements to deal with inconsistency (for example constitutional arrangements, bonds that penalize the issuer for not complying with his initial commitment). For an overview see *inter alia* Blanchard and Fischer (1990).
28. For an overview of the 'free banking' literature see Selgin and White (1994).
29. Currencies have frequently been interpreted as networks (see *inter alia* Hellwig (1985), Selgin (1997), Weinberg (1997), Issing (2000)). Gowrisankaran and Stavins (1999) find empirical evidence of the presence of network effects in the automated clearinghouse electronic payments system.
30. See Economides (1993) and (1995).
31. See Economides (1996).
32. See Katz and Shapiro (1985) and the examples cited therein.
33. See Matonis (1995), Browne and Cronin (1996), England (1996) and Kobrin (1997).
34. See the discussion below for details of the relationship between liquidity, random order arrival rates and the information content of prices.
35. See Hellwig (1985) and Vaubel (1984).
36. See O'Hara (1997) and Goodhart (1989).
37. 'In the age of barter, goods of these and similar kinds offer not only the advantage, to the person who brings them to the market to exchange them for goods he especially needs, that he is far more likely to achieve his purpose than if he goes to market with goods that are not or only to a lesser degree distinguished by their marketability; but he can also with greater probability count on being able to trade them away at a relatively more favorable barter price – since the demand for the goods he brings to market is more extensive, constant, and effective than the demand for other kinds of goods' (Menger, 1909, p. 7). See also White (1984).
38. The same argument applies to new electronic payments systems in which claims are settled by the transfer of securities of fluctuating value in terms of the unit of account (see for example Browne and Cronin, 1996 and the literature cited therein).
39. '... the function of money as a "standard of exchange value" (and "measure of price") evolves by necessity from the original function of money as intermediary on the commodity market ...' (Menger, 1909, p. 55).
40. See White (1984) and Wallace (1988).
41. See Economides (1993) and O'Hara (1997).

# REFERENCES

Blanchard, O. J. and S. Fischer (1990), *Lectures on Macroeconomics*, Cambridge, MA: MIT Press.

Bomhoff, E. J. (1990), 'Comment [on Vaubel (1990)]', in: K. Groenveld, J. A. H. Maks and J. Muyksen (eds) (1990), *Economic Policy and the Market Process: Austrian and Mainstream Economics,* Amsterdam: North-Holland, pp. 287–8.

Browne, F. X. and D. Cronin (1996), 'Payment Technologies, Financial Innovation, and Laissez-Faire Banking: A Further Discussion of the

Issues', in: J. A. Dorn (ed.) (1996), *The Future of Money in the Information Age*, Washington, DC: Cato Institute, http://www.cato.org/pubs/books/money/money18.htm

Brunner, K. and A. H. Meltzer (1971), 'The Uses of Money: Money in the Theory of an Exchange Economy', *American Economic Review,* **61**, pp. 784–805.

Calvo, G. (1978), 'Optimal Seigniorage from Money Creation', *Journal of Monetary Economics,* **4**, pp. 503–17.

Cohen, B. J. (2001), 'Electronic Money. New Day or False Dawn?', *Review of International Political Economy,* **8**, pp. 197–225.

Crede, A. (1995), 'Electronic Commerce and the Banking Industry: The Requirement and Opportunities for New Payment Systems Using the Internet', *Journal of Computer Mediated Communication,* **1** (3), http://www.ascusc.org/jcmc/vol1/issue3/vol1no3.html

Dowd, K. and D. Greenaway (1993), 'Currency Competition, Network Externalities and Switching Costs: Towards an Alternative View of Optimum Currency Areas', *The Economic Journal,* **103**, pp. 1180–9.

Economides, N. (1991), 'Compatibility and the Creation of Shared Networks', Chapter 3 in: M. E. Guerrin-Calvert and S. S. Wildmann (eds), *Electronic Services Networks*, New York: Praeger.

Economides, N. (1993), 'Network Economics with Applications to Finance', *Financial Markets, Institutions & Instruments,* **2**, pp. 89–97.

Economides, N. (1995), 'How to Enhance Market Liquidity', in: R. Schwartz (ed.), *Global Equity Markets*, New York: Irwin Professionals, pp. 60–63.

Economides, N. (1996), 'The Economics of Networks', *Journal of Industrial Economics,* **14**, pp. 673–99.

England, C. (1996), 'The Future of Currency Competition', in: J. A. Dorn (ed.) (1996), *The Future of Money in the Information Age*, Washington, DC: Cato Institute, http://www.cato.org/pubs/books/money/money18.htm.

European Central Bank (1998), *Report on Electronic Money*, Frankfurt/Main.

European Central Bank (1999), *Opinion of the European Central Bank of 18 January 1999 at the request of the Council of the European Union under Article 105 (4) of the Treaty establishing the European Community and Article 4(a) of the Statute of the European Systems of Central Banks and of the European Central Bank on (1) a Commission proposal for a European Parliament and Council Directive on the taking up, the pursuit and the prudential supervision of the business of electronic money institutions, and (2) a Commission proposal for a European Parliament and Council Directive amending Directive 77/780/EEC on the co-ordination of laws, regulations and administrative provisions relating to the taking up and pursuit of the business of banking institutions (COM/98/56),* Frankfurt/Main.

European Central Bank (2000), *Payment Systems in the European Union – Addendum incorporating 1998 Figures*, Frankfurt/Main.

George, K.D. et al. (1992), *Industrial Organisation – Competition, Growth and Structural Change*, London: Routledge.

Goodhart, C. A. E. (1989), *Money, Information, and Uncertainty*, London: Macmillan.

Gowrisankaran, G. and J. Stavins (1999), 'Network Externalities and Technology Adoption: Lessons from Electronic Payments', Manuscript Department of Economics, University of Minnesota, Minneapolis.

Greenfield, R. L. and L. B. Yeager (1983), 'A Laissez-Faire Approach to Monetary Stability', *Journal of Money, Credit, and Banking*, **15**, pp. 302–15, reprinted in: L. B. Yeager (1997), *The Fluttering Veil – Essays on Monetary Disequilibrium*, edited by G. A. Selgin, Liberty Fund, Indianapolis, pp. 363–81.

Hance, O. and S. D. Balz (2000), *The New Virtual Money: Law and Practice*, The Hague: Kluwer Law International.

Hayek, F. A. (1990), *Denationalisation of Money: The Argument Refined*, London: Institute for International Affairs.

Hellwig, M. (1985), 'What do we know about Currency Competition?', *Zeitschrift für Wirtschafts- und Sozialwissenschaften*, **5**, pp. 565–88.

Issing, O. (2000), *Hayek, Currency Competition and European Monetary Union – with Commentaries by Lawrence H. White and Roland Vaubel*, London: Institute for Economic Affairs.

Jordan, J. L. and E. J. Stevens (1996), 'Money in the 21st Century' in: J. A. Dorn (ed.) (1996), *The Future of Money in the Information Age*, Washington, DC: Cato Institute, http://www.cato.org/pubs/books/money/money15.htm.

Katz, M. L. and C. Shapiro (1985), 'Network Externalities, Competition, and Compatibility', *American Economic Review*, **75**, pp. 424–40.

Kessler, G. A. (1990), 'Comments [on Vaubel (1990)]', in: K. Groenveld, J. A. H. Maks and J. Muyksen (eds) (1990), *Economic Policy and the Market Process: Austrian and Mainstream Economics*, Amsterdam: North-Holland, pp. 289–92.

Klein, B. (1974), 'The Competitive Supply of Money', *Journal of Money, Credit, and Banking*, **6**, pp. 423–53.

Kobrin, S. J. (1997), 'Electronic Cash and the End of National Markets', *Foreign Policy*, **107**, pp. 65–77.

Krueger, M. (1999), 'Towards a Moneyless World?', University of Durham, Department of Economics & Finance Working Paper No. 9916, Durham.

Matonis, J. W. (1995), 'Digital Cash and Monetary Freedom', paper presented at INET 95, 26–30 June, Honolulu, Hawaii.

Menger, C. (1909), 'Money', translated by L. B. Yeager with M. Streissler, in this volume; translation of 'Geld', *Handwörterbuch der Staatswissenschaften*, 3rd edn, J. Conrad et al. (eds), IV. Volume, Fischer, Jena, pp. 555–610; reprinted in: Hayek, F. A. (ed.) (1970), *Carl Menger Gesammelte Werke*, Band IV Schriften über Geld und Währungspolitik, Tübingen: J. C. B. Mohr (Siebeck), pp. 1–116.

O'Hara, M. (1997), *Market Microstructure Theory*, Oxford: Blackwell Publishers.

Rolnick, A. J. (1999), 'Panel: Thoughts on the Future of Payments and Central Banking – Maintaining a Uniform (Electronic) Currency', *Journal of Money, Credit, and Banking*, **31**, pp. 674–6.

Selgin, G. A. (1997), 'Network Effects, Adaptive Learning, and the Transition to Fiat Money', Working Paper, Department of Economics, Terry College of Business, University of Georgia, Athens.

Selgin, G. A. and L. H. White (1994), 'How Would the Invisible Hand Handle Money?', *Journal of Economic Literature*, **32**, pp. 1718–49.

Smith, A. (1776), *An Inquiry into the Nature and Causes of the Wealth of Nations*, Verlag Wirtschaft und Finanzen, Düsseldorf (1986) (facsimile edition of the London edition 1776).

Taub, B. (1985), 'Private Fiat Money with Many Suppliers', *Journal of Monetary Economics*, **16**, pp. 195–208.

Vaubel, R. (1984), 'The Government's Money Monopoly: Externalities or Natural Monopoly?', *Kyklos*, **37**, pp. 27–58.

Vaubel, R. (1985), Competing Currencies: The Case for Free Entry', *Zeitschrift für Wirtschafts- und Sozialwissenschaften*, **5**, pp. 547–64.

Vaubel, R. (1990), 'Currency Competition: Free Entry versus Governmental Legal Monopoly', in: K. Groenveld, J. A. H. Maks and J. Muyksen (eds) (1990), *Economic Policy and the Market Process: Austrian and Mainstream Economics*, Amsterdam: North-Holland, pp. 263–86.

Vaubel, R. (2000), 'Commentary [on Issing (2000)]', in: O. Issing (1999), *Hayek, Currency Competition and European Monetary Union – with Commentaries by Lawrence H. White and Roland Vaubel*, Institute of Economic Affairs, Occasional Paper 111, London, pp. 49–53.

Wallace, N. (1988), 'A Suggestion for Oversimplifying the Theory of Money', *Economic Journal*, **98**, pp. 25–36.

Weinberg, J. A. (1997), 'The Organization of Private Payment Networks', *Federal Reserve Bank of Richmond Economic Quarterly*, **83**, pp. 25–43.

White, L. H. (1984), 'Competitive Payments Systems and the Unit of Account', *American Economic Review*, **74**, pp. 699–712.

White, L. H. (1990), 'Competitive Monetary Reform – A Review Essay', *Journal of Monetary Economics*, **26**, pp. 191–202.

White, L. H. (1999), *The Theory of Monetary Institutions*, Oxford: Blackwell Publishers.

White, L. H. (2000) 'Commentary [on Issing (2000)]', in: O. Issing (2000), *Hayek, Currency Competition and European Monetary Union – with Commentaries by Lawrence H. White and Roland Vaubel*, Institute of Economic Affairs, Occasional Paper 111, London, pp. 39–47.

Yeager, L. B. (1983), 'Stable Money and Free-Market Currencies', *Cato Journal*, **3**, pp. 305–26, reprinted in: L. B. Yeager (1997), *The Fluttering Veil – Essays on Monetary Disequilibrium*, edited by G. A. Selgin, Indianapolis: Liberty Fund, pp. 337–61.

# Index